quentin
tarantino

the film geek files

Edited by Paul A. Woods

plexus, london

All rights reserved including the right of
reproduction in whole or in part in any form
This edition revised and updated in 2005
Copyright © 2000, 2005 by Plexus Publishing Limited
Published by Plexus Publishing Limited
25 Mallinson Road
London SW11 1BW
www.plexusbooks.com
First printing 2005

British Library Cataloguing in Publication Data

Quentin Tarantino : the film geek files. - 2nd ed. - (Ultra screen)
    1. Tarantino, Quentin 2. Motion Pictures - Reviews
    I. Woods, Paul
    791.4'375

    ISBN-10: 0859653641

Printed by Bookprint, S.L. Spain
Cover & book design by Phil Gambrill
Cover photograph by Stephane Kossmann/Retna

contents

5. from dusk till dawn

6. tarantinoism

7. the film geek speaks

8. jackie brown

9. Kill Bill

introduction

It seems like a lifetime since, to quote its creator, *Reservoir Dogs* was "so much in the culture". If people had poured out of theatres in his native L.A. a little shocked, then the reactions in this writer's native London were mostly of exhilaration. What kept audiences most audibly entertained, even those who winced at the blood-letting, was that these hoods were somehow *like them*. They fought and they fussed, they cussed and they killed, but they were still good-humoured enough to make smartass cracks as their situation grew increasingly desperate. They may have lived outside the moral confines of polite society, but they could still argue about whether Madonna's 'Like A Virgin' was a hymn to a girl's vaginal capacity like a gaggle of drunken secretaries on a Friday night.

Fast-forward just over eighteen months, and 'Tarantino' had become an international byword for both pop-culture reference and popular post-modern cinema. *True Romance*, Tony Scott's film of an early Tarantino script, layered pop references onto a hackneyed crime plot until they reached self-parodic proportions, but still amused with patches of sharp dialogue. (One thing the boy Tarantino learned from his love of AM radio was the pop musician's ear for rhythm, making his dialogue sing to audiences for whom 'hardboiled' signifies only a three-minute egg.) But the real action took place with the release of *Pulp Fiction*, *Dogs*' epic but still modestly budgeted follow-up. Making a critical and box-office breakthrough at home in the USA, as well as winning the Palme D'Or at Cannes, it brought its garrulous film-geek creator the unlikeliest kind of rock-star status.

Pulp took all the flashy neon references of *Dogs* and wrote them large – two ice-cool hitmen (one a stylistically-cool black dude, the other with emotions turned to ice by smack) went through their murderous motions while eulogising the Fonz and *Kung Fu*, among other trash icons, cheered on by a mostly law-abiding, non-ghetto dwelling audience. While Tarantino's circular-structured portmanteau film cheerfully subverted the hardboiled crime tradition (see Geoffrey O'Brien's piece, 'Quentin Tarantino's Pulp Fantastic'), it was all, as Ian Penman says in his anti-Tarantino diatribe, in the cause of 'A Good Night Out At The Movies'. But, to his admirers, he still had a resonance and significance extending a little way beyond it.

Still, despite being so in tune with his time, the trademark 'geekishness' of Tarantino's subsequent career became wearing. His Robert Rodriguez collaboration, *From Dusk Till Dawn*, was fun for those of us lowbrow enough to love both crime and splatter movies, but best viewed as an accompaniment to pizza and beer. When the man formerly heralded as the saviour of the crime genre gushed about how – at the dawn of the video age – he asked his mother for a tape of *The Great Escape*, when his rewrites for Tony Scott's *Crimson Tide* reputedly contained dialogue on favourite submarine dramas, I, for one, tuned out.

That Tarantino returned to form with his third directorial feature was still no great surprise. What was more remarkable was the low-key manner in which he accomplished it. By the time of promotional interviews for *Jackie Brown* (adapted from Elmore Leonard's *Rum Punch*), the term 'film geek', though it still described his all-encompassing obsession, didn't seem such a fair description of Tarantino. There was a new persona in town – professing to identify with Ordell Robbie, his leading black male character, as a result of his L.A. upbringing, Tarantino seemed to have grown into a more 'authentic' version of himself.

The film plays the same way. When a bail bondsman kills time at a movie in a shopping mall, he chooses a film purely by the length of its playing time. Instead of peppering the movie with pop-references, Tarantino settled for a couple of movie extracts shown on a TV screen and a poignant use of Seventies soul numbers – the Delfonics' 'Didn't I Blow Your Mind This Time' is made to suggest longing and wistful regret, all without hitting a single melancholic note; Bobby Womack's 'Across 110th Street', a song about escaping the Harlem ghetto, is misappropriated as the theme tune Jackie sings as she makes her own escape driving down an L.A. freeway no pedestrian could cross.

And then came near-silence.

Tarantino spent the best of half a decade indulging his film geek reputation to the hilt, releasing Far Eastern epics, Hong Kong monster movies and Italian horror flicks via his Rolling Thunder distribution label. But, as a filmmaker, he had had his moment, so the popular wisdom ran. His once startling slices of pop cinema were now 1990s period pieces.

When he did, eventually, return, Tarantino was insistent that he'd never really been away. He had spent three years writing multiple drafts of *Inglorious Bastards!* – a WWII "guys-on-a-mission" film loosely based on Enzio G. Castellari's similarly titled 1970s spaghetti action flick. It was, says the celebrated Euro-exploitation fan, "some of the best writing I've ever done. But," as he only used the original story as a starting point, "I couldn't come up with an ending."

The screenplay that superseded it, *Kill Bill*, was co-conceived with the woman Tarantino identified as his 'muse', Uma Thurman, on the set of *Pulp Fiction*. By the time it went before the cameras, Miramax seemed to be indulging Tarantino just as the big studios had briefly pandered to the movie brats of the 1970s. *Kill Bill* ran way over schedule and millions of dollars over budget. Rather than demand cuts, however, Harvey Weinstein was impressed enough with the hundreds of feet of footage Tarantino had overshot to inflate its bottom-line 'revenge of the Amazon' shtick into *Volumes 1* and *2*.

His comeback film was to prove significant for Tarantino in one more vital aspect: it was his first *movie* that didn't stop moving. "I've always adored action filmmakers," he testified. "And those are actually what I consider the real cinematic directors." Indeed, *Kill Bill* goes some way toward correcting the view once expressed to me by a film student, who saw Tarantino as a 'literary figure' who wrote genre-subverting dialogue, rather than a cinematic stylist.

Look at the Tarantino Top Ten listed early in this book, and you'll see scant evidence of the grind-house fare that *Kill Bill* would pay tribute to. Maybe it was a case of fessing up to his first loves, but his protracted revenge drama is comprised of elements of Japanese samurai flicks, kung fu movies, spaghetti Westerns (mostly alluded to in the soundtrack of *Volume 1*, stylistically discernible in the slower *Volume 2*) and the latterday yakuza movies of Takashi Miike, which ratchet up the violence to a transgressive level.

Volumes 1 and *2* also saw a definite shift in tone, from frenetic Eastern-influenced action and gore to a brooding, more verbal malevolence (with one nifty piece of pop-culture dialogue from villainous Bill, conflating both Nietzsche's and DC Comics' Superman). That *Kill Bill*'s bargain-basement plot was deemed worthy of two full-length features, however, says less about the material than the fact that Miramax narrowly missed out on the triumph of filming *The Lord of the Rings* as a trilogy, and now saw the chance of producing two Tarantino movies in a year for less than $30 million each.

For now, as ever, Tarantino remains locked into the neon netherworld of pop culture, and the self-referential universe he has created. Repaying best buddy Robert Rodriguez's favour of providing an electric Mex-Western soundtrack for *Volume 2* for only $1, he shot a ten-minute sequence of the hugely anticipated *Sin City* – the *El Mariachi* man's digital realisation of graphic novelist Frank Miller's *noir* comics – for the same princely sum. With a classic *noir* voiceover, Tarantino's scene reputedly brings traditional pulp style to an otherwise high-tech approach.

Recalling the episode of *ER* that featured a casualty with a severed ear, the director has also reinforced his TV geekdom by filming an episode of *CSI: Crime Scene Investigation* – wherein the Nick Stokes character faces a macabre burial alive scenario as redolent of Beatrix's predicament in *Volume 2* as it is of Poe.

As to his own personal projects, the wish to film a semi-faithful version of Ian Fleming's *Casino Royale* has been scuppered by the Bond producers, but he's not short of ambitions. "I'm going to do a war movie [*Inglorious Bastards!*]," he asserts, "I'm going to do a straight-up action movie and I'm going to do my first sequel." The sequel is another long-mooted project, *The Vega Brothers*, resurrecting Vic (aka Mr. Blonde, Michael Madsen) from *Dogs* and Vincent (John Travolta) from *Pulp*. The only drawback being that both characters previously died, which suggests a 'prequel', but neither actor is getting any younger. According to conflicting statements from the man himself, this has either nixed the film or forced him to think outside the envelope. ("I've come up with an idea that won't much matter how much they age," he was recently quoted as saying.)

He has also daydreamed about how "in fifteen years from now, I'll do a third version of [*Kill Bill*]" – one in which Vernita Green's little daughter, from *Volume 1*, has grown into an assassin herself. But this further expansion of the Tarantino universe may possibly be, if his musings reflect his gameplan, the film geek's last. For Tarantino entertains a fantasy of quitting the game after his movie dreams are fulfilled and used up, and running a movie theatre in a small American town.

So ignore him when he says, "the biggest misconception about me is that . . . All I do is watch movies and that's all that I know from life . . ." He may have as much of a 'real' life as many people in our media-saturated Western society, but his heart is in the "movie, movie universe" where his characters live. Asked about the apocalyptic 9/11 attacks, he answered, "It didn't affect me, because there's, like, a Hong Kong action movie . . . called *Purple Storm* and . . . they work in a whole big thing in the plot that they blow up a giant skyscraper." (This, after all, is the man who showed Beatrix's little daughter in *Volume 2* smiling, happy and untraumatised as she drives off with the mommy she never knew, who has now killed her daddy.) It's ballast for Tarantino's detractors who attack him for having "nothing to say" about violence (while rarely possessing the insight that he lacks).

And yet . . .

Out here in the media-dominated 'real' world, Tarantino's films enjoy iconic status. (It's an unsung irony that during the Iraq War, one of the defining moments of recent history, a copy of *Pulp Fiction* was found in the palace of Saddam, the West's former ally.) In this postmodern age, he is the choreographer who merges the cheap evocation of pop imagery with atrocity. For all the flimsiness of *Kill Bill*'s premise, this writer was hooked from the moment he heard Nancy Sinatra intone the words "bang bang, that awful sound" – all the way down the years from his mid-1960s babyhood – over the awful image of a brutalised Uma Thurman. For us media-literate unsophisticates, intense and primitive emotion resonates from juxtapositions like these.

Forget grand opera. Tarantino is Artifice Incarnate.

Paul A. Woods, 2005

1. early
days
and
reservoir
dogs

revenge of the nerd

by Jeff Dawson

A t the beginning of 1992, no one had heard of Quentin Tarantino. By the end of it, he was being hailed as the hip new messiah of filmmaking. In the wake of *Pulp Fiction*, two years on, the media and the film industry had gone into gibbering overdrive. How on earth did a film "geek" from nowhere, with no formal training and with no back catalogue, suddenly become feted as the next big thing?

"I've never seen, in my lifetime, this degree of reaction for a young filmmaker," says Oliver Stone, who directed Tarantino's script *Natural Born Killers*, ironically a parody of media lionisation. "Never have I seen this in my memory. Yeah, there are fads. They go crazy for one film and that film does not generally stand up over time because the fad dies, but I've never seen this. It's unbalanced. It's unnatural."

Unbalanced? Unnatural? Just what is all the fuss about?

Who the hell is Quentin Tarantino and why has a man whose fare is about as politically incorrect as you could possibly get in the touchy-feely Nineties managed to garner such a cult following? Certainly, the Cinderella rise of Tarantino-video-store-clerk-turned-hard-boiled director-has certainly made good copy.

The first rock star director?

Tarantino, unlike any other whose craft has come from behind the camera, now enjoys that kind of status.

Domestically speaking, Tarantino certainly doesn't live like the high priest of hip. His home, where he's been for several years, is in an apartment block buffered against a busy West Hollywood street by a high hedgerow and a small courtyard, an area that's reasonably fashionable but not nearly in the league that he could certainly afford. Maybe he just hasn't got around to it. The place is a mess. Not dirty, just untidy. There are piles of magazines, records and boxes everywhere. On the table is Samuel Jackson's "bad motherfucker" wallet from *Pulp Fiction*. Tarantino now uses it as his own, though, as his friends joke, it doesn't come easily out of his pocket. Dominating the room is an enormous widescreen television, and teetering on top of it is a video marked *Four Rooms*/Finger Chop/Effects.

In a back room there are shelves packed with videos. Rather incongruously, they are diligently filed – you can see where the priorities lie. In the hallway, too, is a cupboard neatly stacked with his well-documented board games, ones based on film and TV shows, including *Welcome Back Kotter*, the show that starred John Travolta. It was the playing of that board game, in this very apartment, by Tarantino and Travolta, that convinced Travolta to take a chance on this film geek and do *Pulp Fiction*.

On the mantelpiece are various dolls – GI Joes, with and without realistic hair and gripping hands, and a model of Boy George in his full Karma Chameleon attire. Huge framed posters dominate the walls – a Japanese *True Romance* publicity sheet and, above the couch, one for Jean-Luc Godard's *Bande A Part* from which he and Lawrence Bender derived the name for their production company, A Band Apart.

It is a shrine to pop, nay, junk culture. That he has not become enveloped by the trappings of fame suggests that success is new to him and Tarantino still enjoys – and plays up – the rags-to-riches story.

He has, though, by his own admission, been more calculating than that, firmly in control not only of his own destiny but also of his public image. His popularity is a direct result of the many hundred man-hours he has spent indulging the media.

The apocryphal story, of course, has it that one minute Tarantino was beavering away behind the counter in a video shop and the next minute directing his very first film, *Reservoir Dogs*. Rarely are stories that simple.

There are numerous accounts, too, of a rough upbringing – a teenage mother, half Cherokee/half hillbilly who grew up in the "swamp of backwater ignorance" of the American South, raising her Huck Finn son in moonshine Appalachia and relocating to Los Angeles in search of work, leaving the high school drop-out to fend for himself on the mean streets of South Central. Rarely are these stories accurate.

Quentin Tarantino is no working-class hero. He was born on March 27, 1963 in Knoxville, Tennessee. His mother, Connie Zastoupil, is indeed a native of that state, but was raised in Cleveland, Ohio before going to high school in Los Angeles, the town she's always considered home.

"I am half Cherokee," she says, "but you wouldn't know it, that's just sensationalism. The only reason I was in Tennessee when Quentin was born was because I was in college there. For some reason I had this romantic notion that I should go to college in the state in which I was born."

Connie was only sixteeen when she became pregnant. A gifted student, she had graduated from high school at fifteen and "only got married to become an emancipated minor. It wasn't a sordid little teenage pregnancy, it was actually more of a liberated thing." The marriage didn't work out. "His father did not even know that Quentin was born. After we separated I found out I was pregnant and never even contacted him."

While she was pregnant and mulling over names, she got hooked on the TV series *Gunsmoke*, and, in particular, the half-breed played by Burt Reynolds – Quint Asper. "But I wanted a more formal name than Quint. Then I was reading a Faulkner book, *The Sound And The Fury*. The heroine's name was Quentin, so I decided that my child was going to be named Quentin whether it was a male or a female. I was also looking for a limited number of nicknames; the shortest would be Quent, which I promptly shortened to Q."

When Tarantino was two, she moved back to Los Angeles where she married Curt Zastoupil, a local musician. Curt adopted Quentin, giving him his surname. It was only when he left school and decided to become an actor that Quentin Zastoupil reverted back to the more stage-friendly moniker of Tarantino, the name of his biological father.

While his mother began to carve out a successful career in the healthcare industry, they made their home in the area of Los Angeles known as the South Bay, first in El Segundo and then Torrance. With Connie out during the day and Curt working nights, the young Tarantino would spend many hours in the company of his adopted father and his artistic friends, the only child among adults.

"We went to the movies all the time, it was one of our favourite means of recreation," says Connie.

Connie remembers, too, the time when she grounded him for a whole summer for having stolen a paperback book from K-Mart (Elmore Leonard's *The Switch*) though this hardly elevates Tarantino to the status of rebellious youth. But with time on his hands, Tarantino began to channel his ambitions.

"I can't remember a time when I didn't want to be an actor. That's why I quit school, to start studying acting."

The British poster for Reservoir Dogs, *with press comment reflecting the effusive reaction to the film in the UK.*

There were big arguments at first, however. Tarantino was already unhappy about being educated at a private fee-paying Christian school and had begun frequently to play truant. And so at the age of sixteen, with his mother's reluctant consent, he dropped out of high school, on the condition that he got a job. His first was as an usher in a porno cinema, the Pussycat Theatre in Torrance.

"Most teenagers would think, 'Cool, I'm in a porno theatre,'" says Tarantino, "but I didn't like porno. I liked movies. And these were not movies. They were very cheesy and very sleazy."

Around this time Tarantino enrolled in the acting classes of James Best, better known as Roscoe P. Coltrane, the sheriff in TV's *Dukes Of Hazzard*. Best's philosophy was simple. In a town where the principal employment for actors was in television, there simply was no need to bother with studying either the craft of theatre or the more detailed Method aspects of film acting. Where landing jobs relied purely on passing fast turnaround auditions, technique relied very much on looking natural before the camera.

The acting, however, didn't appear to be going anywhere and his standard publicity shot as an eighteen-year-old – a gawky gang member with bandanna, leather jacket and earring – certainly did nothing to single him out in a town full of wannabes. As a bold attempt to get himself noticed, he claimed on his CV that he had appeared as a supporting actor in Jean-Luc Godard's *King Lear*, not only because it would look impressive but because no casting director would have had a chance to verify the fact. Even though several notable film guides list him in the credits, Tarantino was most certainly not in that picture, but despite such an audacious move, the parts didn't come his way.

"The only legitimate job I got as an actor was on *The Golden Girls*. I played an Elvis impersonator. I'm one of eight or nine guys, but we got to sing a song. All the other Elvis impersonators wore Vegas-style jump suits. But I wore my own clothes because I was like the Sun Records Elvis."

A friend and associate of Tarantino from the James Best Theatre Centre was screenwriter Craig Hamann who he met in January 1981.

"We hit it off very quickly because we had both seen a lot of movies and also I just thought really he was a great actor, the best, and I couldn't help but respect his talent," remembers Hamann. "We became good friends. He introduced me to Chinese cinema, Italian horror film, and we decided one day that we wanted to make a movie and we came up with this idea and we talked it over, and we wrote a short script and it ended up being a film called *My Best Friend's Birthday*."

"It was a comedy, a Martin and Lewis type of thing," says Tarantino

The 1986 film, starring Hamann and Tarantino was designed to be a means to showcase themselves as actors and was made using every available cent that came their way. And with the pair frequently substituting for other actors who hadn't bothered to turn up, the exercise became a labour of love. It was never finished. "We had a lab accident and we didn't have insurance and we lost a couple of cans of film says Hamann.

"I thought that we were making something really special," Tarantino reflects, "but it was kind of embarrassing when I started really looking at it again."

Back in 1984, however, Hamann introduced Tarantino to Cathryn Jaymes who was to become his manager right up through the filming of *Pulp Fiction*.

"Craig just kept talking about this Quentin character in his acting class who was so interesting and so unusual and so kind of off centre," recalls Jaymes. "Even at that point Quentin was really determined to be an actor. His focus was on acting and it was, 'If people aren't gonna hire me as an actor, then I'm gonna do my own films', and he started thinking about writing his next script, which was *True Romance*. Craig and Quentin were like brothers. Craig was the one who read all the screenplays and handed them back to Quentin and he'd act out all these scenes for us and take them back to the office, all these napkins with hand scratchings on, and revamp them and put everything into context."

One such script was a comedy called *Captain Peachfuzz And The Anchovy Bandit*.

"That was the title of the very first script I tried to write. I wrote 20 pages of it," Tarantino laughs. "You start writing and you think it's the greatest thing in the world and then 20 or 30 pages into it, you come up with another idea, and you keep doing that."

"At one point he was writing a book," recalls Jaymes. "He wasn't, of course, but he would call well-known directors and say that he wanted to spend the afternoon with them and talk about their films because he was writing a book about them. He really just wanted to sit down and talk to them and that was his education. Plus he'd get a free lunch."

John Milius and Joe Dante were just two of the Tarantino meal benefactors.

While all this was going on, Tarantino had found gainful employment at Video Archives on L.A.'s bohemian Manhattan Beach. The original Video Archives has since become Riviera Tuxedo, with the new expanded store having moved a couple of miles to Hermosa Beach. Its owner, as it was in the old days, is the genial Lance Lawson. Lawson remembers the first time the 20-year-old high school dropout walked into the store in 1983, just itching to talk about movies. "He came by as a film buff one day and we started talking about movies and got into a discussion about Brian De Palma. Four hours later we were still talking."

Tarantino came back to the store the next day and talked about Sergio Leone. Eventually, Lawson offered him a job, giving him only four dollars an hour and permission to sign out as many videos as he liked free of charge. According to Lawson, Tarantino dressed mostly in black, drove a silver Honda Civic, stuffed his face with burgers, was a voracious reader of crime novels and comic books, nay, pulp fiction, loved Elvis and the Three Stooges and, as legend has it, was so disorganised in his personal life that he amassed $7,000 worth of traffic tickets. ("I went to jail about three different times just for warrants on me for moving violations," Tarantino confesses.)

His film knowledge was also legendary, even back then. Sometimes the other customers would be treated to Tarantino and fellow video clerk-cum-director Roger Avary's *Top Gun* routine, in which the dynamic duo debated the homoerotic content of that film, a sketch later to be played out by Tarantino in his acting cameo in Rory Kelly's *Sleep With Me.*

One customer impressed with Tarantino was John Langley, creator of the hit TV show *Cops*, who gave him a job on a Dolph Lundgren workout video, where, as a lowly production assistant, he ended up spending most of his time clearing up dog crap from the studio parking lot so that Dolph wouldn't get his trainers dirty.

It was while he was at Video Archives that Tarantino's interest in writing developed. When he wasn't serving behind the counter, he was beavering away on scripts and would shove early drafts under the nose of Lawson. Some of the early references were obvious – Elvis and Sonny Chiba have their moments in *True Romance*, and Clarence Worley's birthday treat in that film, a visit to a Sonny Chiba triple bill, is something that Quentin used to reserve for himself.

"That time is captured perfectly in *True Romance*," recalls Tarantino. "The things that Clarence says are the things that we said."

"You'd recognise so many things," muses Lawson. "Much of it was very personal. For instance, it got to be such an annoyance that I almost stopped going out to eat with Quentin, because Quentin was the Steve Buscemi character in *Dogs*. He wouldn't tip and he had such a problem with it. He just did not understand the concept. These things would pop up, and you knew where they came from. He'd say things like, 'I'm going for a Jimmy Riddle,' and I'd say, 'Quentin, that's a little bit more information than I needed right now.'"

This, of course, ended up being uttered by Uma Thurman to John Travolta in *Pulp Fiction*.

"Back then, Quentin was a bit of a homophobe," Lawson continues. "I'd kid him,

'Would you sleep with Elvis?' And the thought just kind of terrified him, and he'd go, 'No, no, no, no. I'd have to think about that,' and I'd go, 'Come on, this is Elvis . . . The King,' and he'd go, 'Would you?' and I'd go, 'Not necessarily Elvis, but with Bowie maybe,' because I was really into David Bowie at the time. And he'd go, 'You would?' So all those little discussions like that, they end up in the movie."

In this case, the opening scene from *True Romance*. Indeed, Tarantino pays a touching tribute to Lawson in that picture by having Clarence Worley refer to his kindly gaffer, the comic store proprietor, as Lance.

"And then he named the Eric Stoltz character after me in *Pulp Fiction*. I said to Quentin after *Pulp Fiction*, 'If I'd have known you were going to pay so much attention to what I said, I would have tried to have been much wittier.'"

The stand-off that became the emblem of the film: Mr Pink (Steve Buscemi – horizontal) and Mr White (Harvey Keitel – vertical) train their sights on each other.

However, in early 1989, Tarantino decided to call it a day at Video Archives. Hamann, however, thinks that the importance of Video Archives in Tarantino's background has been overblown to suit a better popular mythology.

"Video Archives is a cool place, but before he ever got there Quentin was a film nut. He already was who he was. It's almost like it takes away from him. It's not what Video Archives brought to him, it's what he brought to them. But it makes an interesting story."

Tarantino, in actuality, had been trying to make films for nearly ten years. He is no overnight success. He was driven by a desperate desire to write and direct his own movie. *True Romance* seemed initially the most likely option and Tarantino approached various independent film companies and private parties to invest money in it. However, tired of empty promises as to its viability, after three years he decided to sell it in order to provide the budget for a film he could make himself, a third project he was toying with. *Natural Born Killers*, meanwhile, had been written as a means of raising money to direct *True Romance*. It seemed to be going nowhere, and the rights were naively passed on to his friend Rand Vossler, who had convinced him that he could get a production deal.

(Tarantino eventually sold *True Romance* in 1989 for the Writers Guild minimum of $30,000.)

It was while he was still at Imperial, however, that Tarantino was hired to write a script for $1,500 by the special effects people KNB EFX, the deal being that if he wrote a script for them, they would do the effects on his first film for nothing. The result was the horror film *From Dusk Till Dawn*, "a sort of *Desperate Hours* with vampires."

"I took the $1,500, I quit the job and I never had to get another day job again. Then I got another job for $7,000 to do a dialogue polish and I just kept getting little increments of money."

The dialogue polish was for a script by Frank Norwood called *Past Midnight*, the 1992 romantic thriller starring Rutger Hauer and Natasha Richardson and directed by Jan Eliasberg, the story of an Oregon social worker (Richardson) who becomes obsessed with her killer client (Hauer). Though shot theatrically, it premiered on cable TV in the US.

"They also gave me a credit as associate producer. It was the first credit I ever received in a movie," he gushes. "They hired me to do a dialogue polish and it became like a page one rewrite. By the time they made the movie it became half of my rewrite and half of the original script. Basically, Natasha Richardson did all my stuff and Rutger Hauer did all the other guy's stuff."

So the rags-to-riches bit isn't exactly true?

"It wasn't like I went from the video store to the first day of shooting *Dogs*," explains Tarantino. "It wasn't that different from that, but during that entire time I was trying to put together movies. I had spent a little more than six years trying to direct *True Romance* and *Natural Born Killers*. I tried to raise the money independently, like the Coen brothers did with *Blood Simple* and Sam Raimi did with *Evil Dead*, and it just didn't work. Out of frustration I wrote *Reservoir Dogs*. I was gonna take the script money and a 16mm camera and that was how I was gonna go about it. Then we got Harvey Keitel and it just started picking up steam and it happened. Part of the reason it started happening was because I started making a living in the industry, and I had a script sale to my name. So when they hired me to do the movie, I had never directed anything before, but I was a professional writer, there was some credit to me. The Cinderella story? It's not that different, but there's a little bit more . . . "

There was also the small matter of that *Golden Girls* episode, which had also started to swell the coffers.

"I made a lot of money from that one. It was only one small thing, but *The Golden Girls* is repeated constantly and they took my segment and put it on a *Best Of The Golden Girls* episode so I was getting residual cheques from both ways."

And so Tarantino, still intent on making a movie of his very own, and now with the money to do it, began to hatch a big idea.

"Something literally as simple as the fact that I get a kick out of heist films and I hadn't seen one in a long time," he muses. "So I thought I'd write one . . . "

reservoir dogs

by Todd McCarthy

A show-off piece of filmmaking that will put debut writer-director Quentin Tarantino on the map, *Reservoir Dogs* is an intense, bloody, in-your-face crime drama about a botched robbery and its gruesome aftermath. Colourfully written in vulgar gangster vernacular and well played by a terrific cast, this piece of strong pulp will attract attention but looks like a modest box-office performer.

Clearly influenced by Scorsese's *Mean Streets* and *Goodfellas* and Kubrick's *The Killing*, Tarantino would love to be grouped in such company and employs many bravura effects in making his bid. Undeniably impressive pic grabs the viewer by the lapels and shakes hard, but it also is about nothing other than a bunch of macho guys and how big their guns are.

Strikingly shot and funny opening scene has eight criminals at breakfast arguing about the true meaning of Madonna's 'Like A Virgin'. This vulgar, unlikely discussion, coupled with subsequent shots of them emerging from the restaurant like the Wild Bunch, instantly demonstrates that a smart filmmaker is at work here.

Telling a story much like *The Killing* or *Odds Against Tomorrow*, script fractures very cleverly into an intricate flashback structure that mixes the post-robbery mess with telling character and plot details from the planning stages.

To put it chronologically, crime kingpin Lawrence Tierney and son Chris Penn recruit six pros to whom they assign false, colour-themed names, so that no one will know anything about the others. The diamond heist at an L.A. jewellery store goes awry, however, when it becomes apparent the cops have been tipped off. Two of the robbers and a couple of cops are killed and the gang splits up.

Hotheaded Harvey Keitel takes his injured cohort, Tim Roth, to a hideout where they are soon joined by Steve Buscemi, who is obsessed with remaining "professional". As they ponder who the rat may have been, in comes the psychotic Michael Madsen with a hostage cop. The young officer is brutally tortured in a scene that drove numerous Sundance fest-viewers from the unspooling here, and may make even the brave look away. The worst is left off-camera, but it's still a needlessly sadistic sequence that crosses the line of what audiences want to experience.

This launches the bloodbath for real, and when Tierney and Penn finally show up to identify the fink, Tarantino stages a rather amazing shoot-out that hilariously sends up the climaxes of Sergio Leone's *For A Few Dollars More* and especially *The Good, The Bad And The Ugly*.

Tarantino's complex plot construction works very well, relieving the warehouse setting's claustrophobia and providing lively background on robbery planning, the undercover cop's successful preparations and the gang's crude male bonding.

Dripping with the lowest sexist and racist colloquialisms, dialogue is snappy, imaginative and loaded with threats, and the director, presumably with the help of co-producer Keitel, has assembled a perfect cast. Seemingly relishing the opportunity to pull out all the stops, the actors could all be singled out for their outstanding work, but the same adjectives could be used to describe this terrific ensemble as they yell, confront, joke and strut powerfully and explosively.

The colour-coded hoods who launched a career. L-r: Mr Blonde (Michael Madsen), Mr White (Harvey Keitel), Mr Orange (Tim Roth), Mr Brown (Quentin Tarantino).

With cinematographer Andrzej Sekula's considerable help, Tarantino has put strong visuals on the screen, alternating from ominously moving cameras to recessive long shots to put the action in relief. Sally Menke's extremely impressive cutting keeps scenes tight and the time-jumping plot comprehensible.

As accomplished as all the individual elements are, however, pic feels like the director's audition piece, an occasion for a new filmmaker to flaunt his talents. Undeniably juicy, with its salty talk and gunplay, film is nihilistic but not resonantly so, giving it no meaning outside the immediate story and characters. Pic is impressive, but impossible to love.

reservoir dogs

by Leonard Klady

Reservoir Dogs opens a significant chapter in *film noir*. A seemingly standard yarn of a heist that goes sour (and its brutal aftermath), it demonstrates a fluid style, an ironical undertone and inspired performances.

Only the film's graphic violence and language rein in a mainstream potential, suggesting strong specialised appeal on the order of David Lynch or Joel and Ethan Coen.

From its opening scenes, one immediately recognises that writer/director Quentin Tarantino is a hot new talent. He gives the impression that not much is happening as eight men sit around a diner banquette talking heatedly about the trivial and the mundane. Yet underneath the cant, he's priming us with vital information about his characters.

A moment later, they are filmed in slow motion, off to execute the robbery. However, the bonhomie is rudely shattered as we next see two of the gang driving back to their hideout – one seriously wounded and writhing in pain.

It's a jarring series of contrasting moods, effortlessly flowing from scene to scene and executed with technical and emotional precision. The job has been botched and in its wake the four surviving gang members realise they were set up to take a fall.

The plot is familiar and functional. However, there's nothing ordinary about the characters and the texture of the piece. Anchoring the mayhem is Harvey Keitel as Mr White. His career association with the criminal element makes him a natural for the part, and, assuming the role of apologist for the appalling racial and sexual attitudes of the group, he is at turns mortally amusing.

The remaining cast, without exception, is letter perfect. It's a tribute to the filmmaker and his actors that each comes up as distinct and vivid. Michael Madsen's Mr Blonde is a ticking time bomb with a swagger and Steve Buscemi as Mr Pink is the picture of the 'professional'.

Tarantino obviously knows his movies, dotting *Reservoir Dogs* with homages and flourishes culled from Akira Kurosawa to John Huston.

However, unquestionably his strongest influence is Martin Scorsese, with his fascination and reverence for 'the blood' and the language of the milieu.

But make no mistake, this is not mawkish imitation. The film is a forceful and original vision with a definite niche audience appeal.

mr blood red

by Ella Taylor

A friend calls from the Sundance Film Festival to say that an unspeakably violent movie has taken the festival by storm. I carry on plucking my eyebrows. "So what else is new?" I answer listlessly. "This is the year of slash and burn. Is it any good?" She grins audibly and tells me that in the post-screening discussion *Reservoir Dogs* director Quentin Tarantino, a pipsqueak in his twenties from L.A., brazened out questions about a gratuitous torture scene by declaring that he loved violence. I start tweezing furiously and launch into my rant about how sick I am of black-clad film hacks with geometric haircuts who imagine that one splatter pic garnished with a few slo-mo sequences is going to make them the next Sergio Leone and who think any serious argument about the politics of screen violence is uncool. "That's my girl," crows my friend and hangs up, leaving me to stare moodily at two wildly non-aligned eyebrows.

But the fact is that, torture and all, *Reservoir Dogs*, opening in Los Angeles next week, is one of the most poised, craftily constructed and disturbing movies to come out this year. It's a fond genre movie that's forever chortling up its sleeve at the puerile idiocy of the genre: a heist caper without a heist, an action movie that's hopelessly in love with talk, a poem to the sexiness of storytelling, and a slice of precocious wisdom about life. All this from a first-time filmmaker whose training consists of six years behind the counter of a Manhattan Beach video store, a stint at the Sundance Institute Director's Workshop and a lot of acting classes. Quentin Tarantino is a self-described movie expert who never set foot in film school and who never wanted to do anything but direct movies. "I'm trying to wipe out every movie I ever wanted to make in the first one," he says happily.

For Tarantino, derivation is the sincerest form of flattery. His most obvious homage is to the B-movie, specifically to Stanley Kubrick's 1956 caper, *The Killing*. In *Reservoir Dogs*, six small-time Los Angeles hoods are hired by mastermind Joe Cabot (Lawrence Tierney) and his son Nice Guy Eddie (Chris Penn) for a major diamond robbery. They bond, they josh, they swagger, they kill; the one thing they don't do is confide. They've been chosen because they know nothing about each other; Joe assigns them colour-coded names – Mr White, Mr Blue, Mr Orange. When the heist, which we never see, is interrupted by a waiting phalanx of police, the thieves retreat to a meeting place in a disused warehouse. There, with one dead, one missing, and one seriously wounded, what's left of the group plunges into a morass of paranoid recrimination when it becomes clear that one of their number has set them up and another (Michael Madsen) has shot several bank employees for pressing the alarm.

It sounds odd to say this about a film that has a ten-minute torture scene shot in real time, but *Reservoir Dogs* is a romp: a brave, cocky, enormously self-satisfied adventure in film as manipulation. Tarantino loves to toy with the forms of his beloved action genre: with his favourite themes of professionalism, loyalty and betrayal; but most of all with us, flipping us from laughs to sympathy to horror and back again – he's the maestro of mood swing. Talk about the cinema of excess: from its opening sequence in which Tarantino, in a small part as Mr Brown, entertains his fellow thugs in a cafe with a psycho-literary interpretation of Madonna's "Like A Virgin" ("Dick dick dick dick dick dick dick . . . it hurts . . . The pain is reminding a fuck machine what it once was like to be a virgin"), *Reservoir Dogs* throws down a challenge a minute to the politically correct. Its unheroes are a bunch of career criminals who kill cops without batting an eyelid but show a chivalrous concern for innocent bystanders (so long as they don't get in the way) and spend as much time debating the ethics of tipping waitresses as they do the semiotics of Madonna. Tarantino's dialogue drips with go-for-it racism, sexism and enough undeleted expletives to gladden the heart of David Mamet. And though he insists that he's just letting his characters be who they are, it's clear he relishes the effect they're going to have on audiences and critics shackled by a decade of what he calls a "square dance" mentality in filmmaking.

Quentin Tarantino shows up for lunch at Denny's on Sunset and Gower (his choice) driving the world's smallest rental car. Rumpled in a white T-shirt that says "Tin-Tin in America", badly in need of a shave and any kind of haircut, he apologises cheerfully for being late and applies himself to a meal rich in bad cholesterol. We resume an amiably fractious argument about screen violence that began weeks earlier over the phone from Paris, where Tarantino was attending his film's world premiere. (*Reservoir Dogs* has made its money back three times over in world sales before even opening in the U.S.)

Tarantino would just as soon not have an abstract conversation about movie violence; he would rather talk about his movie's structure. *Reservoir Dogs* is laid out like an exquisitely paced piece of pulp fiction, divided into chapters and moving back and forth in time to explain the characters and the action. "I've always thought that the closer we can hitch movies to books, the better off movies will be," says Tarantino. "There's a complexity to a novel that you don't get in original screenplays. A novel thinks nothing of starting in the middle of its story. And if a novel goes back in time it's not a flashback, it's so you learn something. The flashback is a personal perspective. What I'm doing as the narrator is rearranging the order in the way I want you to get the information."

Tarantino's a show-off, and he has much to show off, smoothly trading off among black comedy, realism and horror as *Reservoir Dogs* swims around in time. After ten minutes of ballsy man-talk around the cafe table, the credits go up, and the hoods in their black suits and shades saunter onto the streets in slow motion, backed by the *Super Sounds Of The Seventies* score that will provide a hilariously inane counterpoint to the action throughout the film. Cut to a blood-soaked Mr Orange (Tim Roth) squealing like a stuck pig in the back of a get-away car while a panicked Mr White (Harvey Keitel), trying to calm him, drives him to the warehouse that will become the centre from which the film's multiple stories fan out.

With the exception of the ridiculously saintly cop he played in *Thelma And Louise*,

Harvey Keitel has never put a foot wrong. He can carry a movie or disappear into an ensemble; in *Reservoir Dogs* he does both as a team-playing professional for whom loyalty and knowing the rules are paramount. He can also shoot three cops at close range and go for a taco. It's largely because of Keitel, who was given the script for *Reservoir Dogs* by a friend of Tarantino's partner that the film got made at all. Tarantino had resigned himself to being a "film geek" living on the fringes of the industry and was prepared to shoot the film guerrilla style. But Keitel was so impressed with the script that he not only agreed to star, but helped raise the money to put the film into production and probably attracted the rest of an all-male ensemble any director, let alone a new one, would kill for.

L-r: Messrs Brown, Blonde, Blue (ex-thief Eddie Bunker) and Pink eat breakfast at Pat and Lorraine's Coffee Shop – all dedicated followers of Madonna's career.

At the Toronto Film Festival, where *Reservoir Dogs* wins the specially created critics' prize for extraordinary achievement by a first-time filmmaker, Tarantino and some of the cast stalk the screenings, dinners and parties in shades and regulation black, backslapping and insulting one another for the benefit of anyone listening. The press conference for *Reservoir Dogs* could pass for a locker-room booster session. A reporter asks Tarantino why there are no women in the film. I choke back a snort; the movie practically wears a placard saying Girls Keep Out. (There *are* two women, onscreen long enough for one to shoot somebody before she's shot herself, while another is pulled through the driver's window of her own car and left sprawling in the road.) "It would be like women turning up on the submarine in *Das Boot*," Tarantino answers sweetly, "There's no place for women in this movie." Thank God, I mutter under my breath.

Like his film, Tarantino zigzags between boyishness and streetwise savvy. He peppers his speech with "cool" and "man" and other speech disorders of the excitable high-schooler. Yet he thinks aloud with the sharp independence of an autodidact (he never went to college) who has read and seen and thought widely without having had to toe the line for a grade-point average.

A boy who was frightened by *Bambi* but saw *Carnal Knowledge* when he was four and understood genre distinctions before he turned ten, Tarantino always chose a movie for his birthday over Disneyland or Magic Mountain. ("And it wasn't like I didn't go all the time.") His mother and the uncle they lived with took him to everything. "The ratings system meant nothing to them. They figured I was smart enough to tell the difference between a movie and real life, and they were right. There was only one movie that my mom wished she hadn't taken me to, and that was *Joe*, with Peter Boyle. I fell asleep. She was really happy because she didn't want her kid to see the cops kill those hippies."

"When I was a little kid, I thought the height of moviemaking was Abbott-and-Costello monster movies. I was just amazed at the genius of the concept of a horror film and a comedy together – two great tastes that taste great together." *Reservoir Dogs* is the work of a man who has lived his life inside movies. Tarantino thinks the death of the mother in *Bambi* would be much more horrifying to kids than the torture scene in *Reservoir Dogs*, which would go straight over their heads. Would he show *Reservoir Dogs* to his (hypothetical) eight-year-old? I ask. He shrugs: "If she [nice choice] reacts harshly and it gives her nightmares, so what? Part of being a kid is having nightmares."

Here's how Tarantino explains the mentality of the hoods in *Reservoir Dogs*: "These guys aren't like the guys in *Goodfellas*. They're not wise guys or gangsters. They're like Dustin Hoffman in *Straight Time*: they do jobs. And a big thing in that line of work is professionalism, which is a way to bullshit themselves into thinking that this is an actual job and profession, not just hooliganism." I ask how he knows this. "It's just the truth. You read a little of this and you see a little of that. And you know the truth when you see it. The truth makes sense."

You probably have to be 29 years old to have that sort of confidence in The Truth. But *Reservoir Dogs* is true to its own imagination, especially when Tarantino stops trying to control our responses, when he lets the genre breathe and allows his characters to expand into life: Steve Buscemi as the opportunist survivor Mr Pink, sounding off about why he doesn't tip; Keitel combing his hair in the mirror and lecturing Buscemi on the difference between a professional and a psychopath; Keitel compromising his loyalty to his father figure, Tierney, when he becomes a father to Roth; Madsen and Penn competing for Tierney's approval and going at each other with homoerotic jock-speak. Toward the end of *Reservoir Dogs*, there's a dazzling chain of scenes that pile one virtuoso piece of storytelling on another for the sheer pleasure of playing one narrative voice off the next. "You're fucking Baretta," an undercover cop tells himself in the mirror. "They believe every word, cuz you're super cool."

Tarantino doesn't so much write his characters as hover over them, protecting their freedom of expression. "I don't play God with my work or clean it up. I don't know what these guys are going to do. I set up the situation and they start talking to each other and they write it. If you had asked me one thing that is powerful about this film, it's that there is no committee saying yes, no, he can't do that because that would make him unsympathetic. I think that while the characters come across insanely brutal, they also come across insanely human."

Yes and no. As an exuberant flirtation with genre, *Reservoir Dogs* is a fabulous accomplishment; but when it pushes to extremes, it becomes an exercise in spurious, sadistic manipulation. At his most self-consciously "cinematic", Tarantino is all callow mastery, and nowhere more so than in his favourite scene in which Madsen, dancing around to the tune of "Stuck in the Middle With You," gets creative with a razor and a fairly crucial part of a cop's anatomy. "I sucker-punched you," says Tarantino, all but jumping up and down with glee. "You're supposed to laugh until I stop you laughing." The torture scene is pure gratuity, without mercy for the viewer. "The cinema isn't intruding in that scene. You are stuck there, and the cinema isn't going to help you out. Every minute for that cop is a minute for you." He's wrong; the cinema is intruding. That scene is pure set piece; it may even be pure art. That's what scares me.

We're really arguing not about violence but about the politics of style. It's partly a question of different sensibilities – Tarantino likes emotional storm trooping, I prefer a slow-building opera – but there are still distinctions to be made between legitimate and gratuitous violence. Tarantino couldn't care less; he's an aesthete. "Violence is a very cinematic thing," says Tarantino, "like dance sequences are cinematic." Though he appears to have seen every movie ever made (his taste runs from Douglas Sirk to Eric Rohmer), for Tarantino the guys who really do it right are the auteurs of excess – Dario Argento, Abel Ferrara, Brian de Palma, Paul Schrader, all of whom, he says, "go beyond gratuity. They are so broad, so stylistic and so loving towards it that it becomes a justification unto itself."

His current hero is Hong Kong *noir*-ist John Woo ("He's re-inventing the action movie"), whom Tarantino considers the most talented action director since Sergio Leone and with whom he's collaborating on a treatment. I remark that even Leone's *Once Upon A Time In America*, an exercise in the theatre of cruelty if ever there was one, used its brutality to say something about the way the world works, but Tarantino believes that filmmakers who work in his genre often use social relevance as a cover. "John Woo's violence has a very insightful view as to how the Hong Kong mind works with 1997 approaching and blah, blah, blah. But I don't think that's why he's doing it. He's doing it because he gets a kick out of it." While Stanley Kubrick used the social commentary in *A Clockwork Orange* to get away with one of the most violent movies Tarantino has ever seen, the social analysis was just an umbrella. "He enjoyed the violence a little too much. I'm all for that."

Tarantino isn't above covering his own ass. "I didn't do that [torture] scene just to say, 'Boy, I'm going to have a boner when this thing comes out,'" he insists. "If you're with the movie, you feel for these people at the end. Does violence put ideas in people's minds? It probably does. You can't make a blanket statement that it does or it doesn't." Nine hundred pages of the Surgeon General's Report on media violence, and countless other studies, agree with him; we haven't a clue how or if people are affected by what they see on the screen. And shot for shot, there is actually less physical violence in *Reservoir Dogs* than in any average action movie. Some of the gunplay is very funny (the hoods are a bunch of little boys playing with water pistols that happen to be loaded) and, aside from Madsen's frolic, you could argue that the brutality in *Reservoir Dogs* is "responsible" because, like Clint Eastwood's *Unforgiven*, it shows violence as it would really be – blood-soaked, panicky, inglorious and slow. But that's not the point. "I'm not going to be handcuffed by what some crazy fuck might do who sees my movie," concludes Tarantino. "The minute you put handcuffs on artists because of stuff like that, it's not an art form anymore."

Tarantino, however, can afford to be the spokesman for art without politics. He's a straight, white male working in a genre that can do no wrong at the box office, and he'll never run afoul of the ratings board, which gets less prissy about violence than sex. (How very Nineties that Tarantino's backers were untroubled by the torture scene but raised their eyebrows at the racism and sexism.) Critics also don't like talking about movie violence anymore, partly because the debate has gotten so mangled between the pieties of the left and the right, and partly because the celebration of style is an easy way out of taking any position at all.

I wasn't having fun in the torture scene; from foreplay to climax I watched it through my fingers, and if this wasn't my job I'd have rushed out of the theatre, much as I did when Bambi's mother died. The torture scene infuriates me because it has no point other than to show off its technique, and to jump-start our adrenaline, which takes some doing these days; we've grown so numb to images of brutality that they have to be jacked up to fever pitch to stir us at all. It's not just *Reservoir Dogs*. Some of our most talented young filmmakers seem to be specialising in designer brutality: Gregg Araki with *The Living End*, Tom Kalin with *Swoon*, Robert Rodriguez with *El Mariachi* (as yet unreleased, but Columbia has snapped it up for a remake) – all highly stylised films that bring to the hot material of random violence a cool, giggly insouciance. (When women work in this mode – Kathryn Bigelow with *Blue Steel*, Katt Shea with *Poison Ivy* – they do it badly.) In the current season only Nick Gomez's *Laws Of Gravity* and Anthony Drazan's *Zebrahead* have the guts and the heart, as did *Unforgiven*, to tell a story quietly and with a genuine feel for tragedy.

Reservoir Dogs is far and away the slickest and cleverest of the bunch. Tarantino brims over with ideas for future movies, including love stories and musicals. He has no doubt that he can continue to make the movies he wants within the studio system. "I'm not coming from the attitude that I want to run as far away from the studios as I can, or the attitude that I want to run up to the studios as much as I can, because there's danger in both. You don't watch out and next minute you're Richard Donner. At the same time, if all you can do is these little art films for ten years for a million or two dollars, you're going to climb up your own ass. When was the last time Nicolas Roeg did a good movie? I'm not ragging on other people, but after I saw *Twin Peaks – Fire Walk With Me* at Cannes, David Lynch has disappeared so far up his own ass that I have no desire to see another David Lynch movie until I hear something different. And you know, I loved him. I *loved* him. I think Gus Van Sant, after *My Own Private Idaho*, has become a parody of himself. A lot of these guys, they become known for their quirky personality, and when they can do whatever they want, they showcase their quirky personality."

Tarantino has made several dazzling movies at once in his first feature – gangster flick, comedy, character study and horror show – and Miramax, an independent distributor, has let him get away with it. Will his future backers (the studios), who are already crawling all over him, give him the room to make more than a standard action picture? His next film, which will be co-produced with Danny DeVito's Jersey Films for six million dollars, has a first-look deal with Tristar. It's an anthology called *Pulp Fiction*, three crime stories for the price of one. After that he joins forces with John Woo – for a musical love story, no doubt.

quentin tarantino's best films of all time

The Timeless Top Three ("not in any order")

Rio Bravo (Howard Hawks): "The most entertaining movie ever made. I've never enjoyed hanging out with anyone more than Dean Martin in that movie. I used to play the part of Dude in acting class."

Taxi Driver (Martin Scorsese): "It's just perfect."

Blow Out (Brian de Palma): "Brian de Palma is the greatest director of his generation. This is his most purely personal and cinematic film."

The Rest ("also not in order, subject to change daily")

One-Eyed Jacks (Marlon Brando): "The personification of the Brando mystique and one of the greatest [directorial] debuts of all time."

Breathless (James McBride): "When I saw this in '83, it was everything I wanted to do in movies."

His Girl Friday (Howard Hawks): "For my money the greatest comedy ever made. Cary Grant gave the greatest comic performance of all time."

Band Of Outsiders (Jean-Luc Godard): "See Pauline Kael's review."

Rolling Thunder (John Flynn): "To me it's the greatest combo of action film and character study ever made. If you like revenge movies, this is the best revenge movie to see."

Badlands (Terence Malick): "A religious experience. Great novelists wish they had written a novel as good as *Badlands* was a movie."

Le Doulos (Jean-Pierre Melville): " My favourite screenplay of all time. You don't have any idea of what's going on in this movie until the last 20 minutes."

The Good, The Bad And The Ugly (Sergio Leone): "Probably the greatest example of re-invention of a genre in film. Horrible brutality, hysterical humour, blood, music, icons. What more could you ask for?"

Casualties Of War (Brian de Palma): "To me, the greatest war movie and the greatest indictment of rape ever captured. The Vietnamese girl's death walk has haunted me ever since."

the men's room

by Amy Taubin

Tim Roth came to the US to act in the kind of films that aren't happening in Britain. The kind of films, he says, that Alan Clarke would be making if he were still alive. Roth made his television film debut in 1983 as the ferocious skinhead in Clarke's *Made In Britain*, then followed with Mike Leigh's *Meantime*, as part of an ensemble that included Gary Oldman and Phil Daniels. "That's what I thought film-making was," he says ruefully.

Currently Roth can be seen on screen in New York and Paris in Quentin Tarantino's *Reservoir Dogs*, coming soon to wherever else the international language of male violence is spoken. The film's structure is pegged to the length of time it takes for a man – Roth's character, Mr Orange – to bleed to death in front of our eyes. How's that for preserving the dramatic unities?

The debut film of director/writer Tarantino, *Reservoir Dogs*, a bungled heist movie, was notorious even before it premiered at the 1992 Sundance Film Festival. It did not win a prize; reportedly, the jury felt that since Tarantino had already catapulted, at age 29, on to the Hollywood A list, he didn't need its help, reducing the status of the competition to a charity agency. Especially as the film that did win was Alexandre Rockwell's *In The Soup*, a more innocuous male-bonding film, which, like *Reservoir Dogs*, soft-shoes around the connection between independent film-making and gangsterism.

Cover-story material for the *LA Weekly*, the *Village Voice*, *Positif,* and a slue of dailies, Tarantino's bio is already common knowledge: how he obsessively watched movies from the age of five; how he never went to film school, but honed his skills by simultaneously working in a video store (where he had unlimited access to the *oeuvres* of his heroes Peckinpah, Leone, Scorsese, Ferrara, Argento, De Palma, Schrader), writing scripts (almost all of which are now in production), and attending acting classes (he had some bit parts on television).

Tarantino originally intended to make *Reservoir Dogs* in 16mm for $30,000. Then a friend got the script to Harvey Keitel. Keitel's commitment attracted several million dollars and the stellar cast. To the *LA Weekly*, Tarantino confessed to being, as a child, "amazed at the genius of the concept of a horror film and a comedy together" in Abbott-and-Costello monster movies. To anyone who suggests a moral queasiness about *Reservoir Dogs' piece de resistance* – a ten-minute real-time torture scene in which a psychopath slices up a cop's face, hacks off his ear, and then asks him, "Was that as good for you as it was for me?" – Tarantino responds: "I love violence in the movies." Such surly moments notwithstanding, Tarantino is universally described as charming, enthusiastic, inspirational – precisely the adjectives that were applied to Ross Perot, although not exactly by the same people.

early days and reservoir dogs

Reservoir Dogs opens with its other *piece de resistance* – a pre-credit sequence in which a bunch of small-time hoods, breakfasting in a Southern California fast-food joint, engage in a close textual analysis of Madonna's 'Like A Virgin'. "Let me tell you what 'Like A Virgin' is about," says Mr Brown (played by Tarantino). "It's all about a girl who digs a guy with a big dick. The entire song, it's a metaphor for big dicks . . . it hurts, it hurts her . . . The pain is reminding a fuck machine what it once was like to be a virgin. Hence, 'Like A Virgin.'

The conversation turns into a debate over the ethics of tipping waitresses. "Jesus Christ, these ladies aren't starving, they make minimum wage," objects Mr Pink (Steve Buscemi) when his buddies try to shame him into leaving his buck on the table just like everybody else. To the nostalgic bubblegum rhythms of K-Billy Radio's *Super Sounds Of The Seventies*, the group swaggers into the street. Dressed in identical sleazy black suits, narrow black ties and white shirts, they look as if they had migrated down from a poster for, if not the actual celluloid of, Aki Kaurismaki's *Calamari Union*, an influence Tarantino has never to my knowledge cited. The credits roll.

Cut to the interior of a car, where Mr Orange is spurting blood from a bullet in the gut (only his red-soaked shirt, already stuck to his skin, keeps his intestines from protruding). Convulsing, he's begging Mr White, who's driving, to take him to a hospital. Mr White insists that they proceed to a prearranged rendezvous point, a cavernous, fluorescent-lit warehouse (the basic location of the film).

With Mr Orange lapsing in and out of consciousness, sprawled on the floor in an ever-deepening pool of his own blood, Mr White and the speedy Mr Pink try to piece together what went wrong. They and the other "professionals" had been hired by bossman Joe Cabot (Lawrence Tierney) and his hulking son Nice Guy Eddie (Chris Penn) to carry out a major diamond heist. The robbers have never met before; their colour-coded pseudonyms are intended to protect their identities. Unfortunately, the cops show up before the heist is completed. The hoods shoot their way out, blowing away cops and "real people". The survivors are left to ponder who among them is the stooly.

Information accumulates a-chronologically The set-up and aftermath of the heist (although never the heist itself) are revealed in flashbacks through the points of view of the participants. Relishing the dramatic irony, Tarantino reveals the identity of the undercover cop half way through the film, implicating the audience in his point of view and the helplessness of his position. In this world, knowledge gets you nowhere. When the icy Blonde (Michael Madsen, who played Susan Sarandon's concerned boyfriend in *Thelma And Louise*) arrives with a young cop he's kidnapped during the getaway, the violence escalates. By the final blackout, the warehouse is as littered with corpses as the halls of Elsinore.

Though the theatricality of the *mise en scène* and the emphasis on play-acting makes the Shakespearean association inevitable, *Reservoir Dogs* is hardly a tragedy. Hyperbolically visceral and self-conscious (it's the combo that gives the film its bigger bang per buck), it's a black comedy of manners that both brags on and derides its genre and its characters.

Tarantino tips his hand in his bravura set pieces. The undercover cop prepares for his "interview" with the boss like a method actor rehearsing an audition piece.

Identity is a fabrication; lies are as convincing as truth, provided they reference a collective cultural experience and are told with an improvisatory abandon. An event that never happened is given equal screen time. And why not? Isn't this a film about film, about fiction. "I love violence *in the movies*," says Tarantino. It's the porno escape value – for him and for us.

Reservoir Dogs conflates masculinity, violence, and the underclass. Tarantino's version of masculinity is deeply regressive, specifically rooted in the seventies mass culture of his own childhood. When the undercover cop checks his costume in the mirror, he's Robert Blake in *Baretta*. Indeed, what makes *Reservoir Dogs* such a Nineties film is that it's about the return of what was repressed in the television version of Seventies masculinity – a paranoid, homophobic fear of the other that explodes in hate speech, in kicks and blows, in bullets and blades. *Reservoir Dogs* is an extremely insular film – women get no more than 30 seconds of screen time, people of colour get zero – yet not a minute goes by without a reference to coons and jungle bunnies, to jailhouse rape (black semen shooting up white asses), to the castration threat of "phallic" women like Madonna or that Seventies icon Pam Grier. (Its insularity also makes *Reservoir Dogs* less interesting, for all its film-making pyrotechnic, than two other recent 'violent arties': Carl Franklin's *One False Move* and Nick Gomez's *Laws Of Gravity*.)

If the unconscious of the film is locked in competition with rap culture, it's also desperate to preserve screen violence as a white male privilege. It's the privilege of white male culture to destroy itself rather than to be destroyed by the other. Violence is the only privilege these underclass men have. It's what allows them to believe that they're the oppressor and not the oppressed (not female, not black. not homosexual).

The problem in *Reservoir Dogs* is that its critique of masculinity is tied up in its money shots: they're one and the same. Mr Blonde carving up the cop and the final bad-joke shootout are guarantees of box-office success. This may have been true of previous films that raised the ante on male violence (*The Wild Bunch*, *Taxi Driver*) but now the field is so littered with corpses that it's hard to make a couple of extra pints of blood seem like a transgression.

What's transgressive in *Reservoir Dogs* is not the level of violence or the terrifying realism of bodies that bleed and bleed, but the way Tarantino lays bare the sado-masochistic dynamic between the film and the spectator. The masochistic (feminised) position of the audience is inscribed in Mr Orange's bleeding body. Mr Orange's pain and Mr White's guilt at not being able to save him bind them together in a sado-masochistic relationship that supercedes Mr White's code of professionalism and leads to his destruction and everyone else's as well. Moreover, the torture scene, far from being gratuitous, as many critics have asserted, is a distillation of the slap/kiss manipulation of the film as a whole. Mr Blonde, dancing around the frozen, fascinated cop (who is literally tied to his seat), changing rhythm mid-step, cracking a joke here, slicing off a bit of flesh there, is a stand-in for the director. And his mocking "Was that as good for you as it was for me?" makes us one with his mutilated victim and leaves no doubt about who's on top.

it's cool to be banned

by Quentin Tarantino

Reservoir Dogs was designed as a really terrific small film, whereas *Pulp Fiction* is designed to be an epic in every shape and form: in size, in feel, in ambition, in intention, in look. *Dogs* is like a wild action painting, whereas *Pulp* is much more of a tapestry, more of a 'sit back and come watch the movie unfold'. If you were to leave during the first hour of *Pulp Fiction*, you can't even begin to say you've seen the movie. You really need to see the last scene before you can say, 'Yes, I've seen the movie.' That's a little unusual, because with most movies, once you've seen the first ten minutes, you can say pretty much that you've seen the movie.

Some people who claim to have seen *Reservoir Dogs* just had a conversation with somebody about the torture scene. The annoying thing is that the torture scene in *Dogs* is my favourite scene; I think it's terrific (so did my mom). I can't think of a movie that came out during the last five years where one scene has been talked about as much as the torture scene in *Reservoir Dogs*. And the problem with that is that the movie has a lot more to offer than that one scene. But it's such a big mountain that people who could have totally handled the movie were scared of it. I was at the *Evening Standard* Awards back in 1992 when the film came out, and I met Emma Thompson. We started having a really nice conversation, chatting away, then she goes, 'I hate to say it, I'm scared of seeing your movie!' I go, 'Really? Oh well, OK.' And then she goes, 'But I saw *GoodFellas* and I loved it!' But *Goodfellas* is four times more violent than my movie! She said she saw *Henry – Portrait Of A Serial Killer*. I go, 'You can totally handle my movie if you can handle those! There's nothing to be scared of, baby!'

I actually kind of get a kick out of the fact that you can't get it on video [the video release of *Reservoir Dogs* in the UK was delayed until June 1995]. It's because it's worked out fantastic for me! It's been playing for two-and-a-half months in a re-release. I didn't believe it when I was in Nottingham when they did the re-release. They all went, 'It's so cool, it's a big re-release, big deal!' I figured it would last about four weeks. I came back and got *Time Out*. 'OH MY GOD! IT'S STILL PLAYING!'

To be truthful, I could care less about the video thing. I think it's cool; I think that's terrific. If they were to cut a frame of the theatrical, I might be banging at the doors of Parliament. But as far as the video is concerned, the easiest way to kill the excitement and cult of something is to make it readily accessible. I always remember back in the days when I was a film geek, hanging out with my friends, how we were always trying to see the sort of film that you couldn't see, like Jodorowsky's *El Topo*: it was completely out of circulation, there was no way you could see it. And the Rolling Stones film, *Sympathy For The Devil*, there was no way you could see that, you couldn't find a print of it anywhere. One of us would get a copy, a horrible, screwed up one – the more screwed up it was the cooler it was – we'd sit around and watch this bad copy, (oh man, so cool, get this ripped, crappy old copy of *El Topo*, look at that, oh boy! you know!).

Spielberg talked about that with *ET*. That's one of the reasons he said he kept *ET* from selling to video for such a long time. Because, he said, 'I worked so hard on *Close Encounters Of The Third Kind* and something just diminished all my hard work when I saw that you could have a video cassette of it just laying on your TV set, ready for you to play at any time. At least if you were going to look at a print of it, you'd have to carry a bunch of cases of heavy film, you'd have to exert some sort of effort in order to view it!'

Mr White and Mr Pink with injured hostage Patrolman Nash (Kirk Baltz), whose torture by Mr Blonde became one of the most controversial scenes of Nineties cinema.

I don't want my films to be disposable. I hope they'll last for hundreds of years. That's the thing that's great about film, that I can make one, and all the critics say, 'It sucks!', but if you've made a good film and nobody got it at the time it came out, history will be the ultimate test and you'll get recognised sometime, five years, ten years, 25 years from now, and it will find its audience if it's good.

It's like pulp fiction: it was garbage fiction, you'd buy it for a dime, read it, and then you gave it to your mate – or threw it away. You read it on the bus to work, you put it in your back pocket and sat on it all day, and that was that. At the time it was completely disposable; and at the time it got no recognition whatsoever. But now all those authors are very well known; now you put it in your library! I don't like being presented with 'Here's this Art.' It's the same with exploitation films: they were presented that way when they came out, but some of them were absolutely fantastic, and they really affected me and my aesthetic.

eastern dogs

by Paul A. Woods

At the 1994 Cannes Film Festival, prior to winning the coveted Palme D'Or award for *Pulp Fiction*, Quentin Tarantino was asked a politely accusatory question by *Film Threat*, the maverick Hollywood movie journal: 'It was reported recently that you borrowed very heavily from the 1987 Hong Kong action movie *City On Fire* to make *Reservoir Dogs*. It seems that both your movie and *City On Fire* are the same, and I was wondering if you'd like to make a comment on that . . . ?'

In their issue (August 1994), an article by David E. Williams had described vital key sequences from both *Dogs* and director Ringo Lam's Hong Kong gangster thriller, noting their uncanny similarity. The buzz had been circulating film fandom for a while: in late 1993, British movie magazine *Empire* had featured a short piece by Jeff Dawson, later one of Tarantino's biographers, giving a similar scene-by-scene breakdown between *Dogs* and *City*.

When invitations for Tarantino to 'discuss Hong Kong action films' were declined due to the marathon promotional schedule for *Pulp Fiction*, *Film Threat* editor Chris Gore took the mountain to Mohammed by sending his reporter to Cannes.

'I was wondering . . . if you ever plan on making any financial restitution to Mr Lam?' asked his emissary. 'None whatsoever,' laughed Tarantino in response. 'I loved *City On Fire*. I got the poster framed in my house, so it's a great movie . . . I steal from every single movie made, all right? I love it. If my work has anything it's because I'm taking this from this and that from that, piecing them together. If people don't like it, tough titty, don't go see it.'

Tarantino had already spoken about the assembly of *Dogs*' component parts: the piecemeal narrative was inspired by Jean-Pierre Melville's underworld thriller *Le Doulos* (1962), in which the plot remains obscure until the last 20 minutes; the theme of men under violent siege from within was taken from John Carpenter's SF-horror remake *The Thing* (1982); even Mr White's (Harvey Keitel's) words when he tries to reassure a fatally wounded Mr Orange (Tim Roth) – part of the dialogue that impressed Keitel so much he thought Tarantino must have grown up around career criminals – were an echo from Brian De Palma's Vietnam drama *Casualties Of War* (1989).

What he hadn't confessed was how much his film's underlying plot and action scenes owed to *City On Fire*. True, he regularly declared his love of the Hong Kong action genre, particularly John Woo's *The Killer* (1989) – which can be read as an unconscious nod toward Ringo Lam's earlier film, given that it re-united hit male leads Chow Yun-Fat and Danny Lee in an operatically-stylised take on hardboiled archetypes. But from Tarantino's apparent furtiveness grew accusations of plagiarism, and pirate videotapes comparing scenes from the two films – prompting his cocky counter-defence that 'great artists steal . . . they don't do *homages.*'

City On Fire is the frantic tale of Hong Kong undercover cop Ko Chow (Chow Yun-Fat), who, like Freddy Newendyke/Mr Orange, infiltrates a gang of hold-up artists while suspended uneasily between the two sides of the law. Plot development is shown from the single point of view of the lawman, providing the audience with more information than the hoodlum characters up until the melodramatic climax.

Central to the film's dramatic tension is the Chinese tradition of *yi,* a code of loyalty and brotherhood. In this aspect, the melodramatics of *City On Fire* are more culturally convincing than the cool plot contrivances of *Reservoir Dogs*. Ko Chow inhabits a twilight world where not even the local police superintendent is aware of his existence. When a young inspector disapproves of his methods, he finds himself on the end of a brutal beating by his own side which would be extreme even for the LAPD. Small wonder he's begun to think of criminals as his friends. Ko's final betrayal of such a friend is intensified by the earlier appearance of a dead gangster named Shing, previously betrayed by him – one of the images from *City* that Tarantino incorporates as a verbal reference in his 'talkfest' *Dogs*, when Orange laments the fate of Long Island Mike.

Ko infiltrates a gang planning a heist from jewellery wholesalers via his underworld contact Fu (Danny Lee). The 'brotherhood' of robbers are assembled by their leader, Zhou Nan, who refers to his young brother hoods by their real names: Brother Fu, Brother Chow (Ko Chow not even using a pseudonym for his undercover work), Brother Joe, et al. Tarantino's Joe Cabot takes this to a further theatrical extreme, christening his footsoldiers Messrs White, Blonde, Orange, etc, and instructing them not to reveal their real names. (Thieving magpie Tarantino copped this from *The Taking Of Pelham One-Two-Three* [1974], in which a gang of subway-train hijackers refer to each other in colour code.)

When the violently disastrous robbery finally takes place, the resemblance to *Dogs* is visible to the eye. Brother Fu – as both a loyal, stand-up guy and a violent psycho – is the prototype for both Messrs White and Blonde. When a female cashier presses an alarm during the robbery, he has no qualms about blowing her all over the wall. Keitel's agonised complaint of 'Jesus Christ, how old do you think that black girl was? Maybe 20, 21' echoes through an ethnic translation of 'Chinese girl . . . maybe 25, 26'.

Outside, the desperate Fu opens up with a Baretta in each hand on a squad car, riddling the two cops inside with bullets. Almost frame-by-frame, this was restaged four years later with Mr White behind the firepower. When Ko Chow opens fire on a cop about to shoot Fu, and is shot in the gut by his victim, his expressionistic shock is compounded by realisation that he's going to die for his sin. With an added cruel twist, Tarantino adapted this scene to legendary effect: as White and Orange hijack an innocent woman's car, the driver pulls a handgun from her glove compartment and shoots Orange in the belly. Impulsively blasting her through the head, his mortified expression acknowledges not only physical pain but that he's joined the bad guys forever.

When Fu helps Ko Chow to their post-heist warehouse rendezvous (staggering, but not as incapacitated as the writhing Orange – testimony to Tarantino's talent for taking a genre scenario closer to real life), an apeshit Brother Nan identifies the 'rat in the house': 'There were so many police around, there must be an undercover here,' he accuses the dying Ko (or, according to later, post-Tarantino English subtitles,

'There was a rat amongst us') – 'And I say it's you!' Not as colourful as Joe Cabot's 'That lump of shit's working for the LAPD – the cocksucker tipped off the cops!', but cornily appropriate for its sense of honour betrayed.

The classic 'Mexican stand-off' ensues when Nan moves to shoot Ko Chow: Brothers Nan and Fu training their handguns on each other, Brother Joe fixing his sights on Brother Fu, helpless Brother Chow looking on. While redolent of spaghetti westerns, *City* was also the progenitor of a classic motif – Hong Kong pro-antagonists going head-to-head with handguns pointed, as featured in *The Killer* and a slew of Eastern gangster pics. By comparison, Mr White's/Joe Cabot's/Nice Guy Eddie's mutually-destructive shoot-out plays like an in-joke to film geeks who recognise the stand-off from *City* taken to its lethal slapstick conclusion.

Back on the Eastern front, the warehouse is surrounded by armed police in a Leone-esque exchange of firepower substituted, in the modestly-budgeted *Dogs*, by the sound of a few sirens and a megaphone. Fu continues to protect Ko Chow, his motivation stemming from the Chinese code of honour – as Ko Chow gunned down the patrolman who was about to open fire on him, his friend is therefore, he believes, incapable of betrayal.

So bound are both by the code of *yi* that the resolution of *City* is markedly different from *Dogs*: the dying Brother Chow confesses that he's a cop, but his sense of honour compels him to command Brother Fu to kill him. Unlike Keitel's agonised histrionics, however, Fu still sentimentally regards Chow as a 'brother'. Waiting for the cops to move in, he even begs the expiring cop to come back from the brink of death so that they can take their girlfriends to Hawaii together.

In the earthier *Dogs*, without the *yi* rationale we're left with the 'honour among thieves' myth that's seen many a Western criminal stabbed in the back – White apparently refusing to believe Orange could be the 'rat' on account of him getting wounded as they escaped the scene together. (This scenario could have applied to any of the rest of the gang, had they been caught in the same time and place.) Tarantino seems to have recognised this plot defect, adding an implicit explanation of the White-Orange relationship: when the profusely bleeding Orange begs White to hold him, the older hood gently whispers something in his ear, unheard by the audience, which momentarily eases his terror of dying. The suggestion of a crush on the younger man, perhaps a hangover from jailhouse experiences, is obvious but unspoken (Tarantino realising the cult value of the odd strand of ambiguity.)

Ultimately, while *Reservoir Dogs* is far from *City On Fire* remade, no one can deny its entire dramatic structure is based upon the climax of *City* – the jewel robbery and blood-soaked aftermath slowed down, fragmented and retold in a non-linear, self-consciously hardboiled literary style – action partly unseen – from the differing perspectives of several gang members, and transported, very convincingly, to L.A.

Almost like the modern artist who slowed Hitchcock's *Psycho* to a running time of 24 hours, Tarantino took the last 20 minutes of *City On Fire*, broke its narrative spine and surgically refashioned it, complete with compulsive pop-culture references and joyfully profane dialogue. The haemorrhaging of Mr Orange is a viscous measure of this – in *City On Fire*, Ko Chow's bullet-wound to the stomach occurs at the film's climax and leads to a suitably agonised expiry in the arms of his betrayed friend.

As a result of a little textbook research, Tarantino knew that such a painful death could be much more prolonged – extending the process so that his protracted death isn't just a nod to authenticity, but the framework for the film's entire narrative.

The fact that Tarantino's hit debut consisted, in part, of scenes from somebody else's movie restaged in a new context proved a double-edged sword. Ironically, it only became a 'dark secret' due to his uncharacteristic coyness about the extent of *Dogs'* debt. Perhaps he assumed every Hong Kong film geek who saw *City On Fire* would regard his parallel scenes as obvious references, while no-one else would care. Or maybe Tarantino saw no great sin in stealing from a genre with such a derivative lineage, synthesizing elements from Hollywood gangster movies and spaghetti westerns – much as he himself was doing, in a dialogue-driven style.

Once everything was out in the open, the controversy didn't detract from either film-maker. Few of those who disliked the Tarantino style of effusive pop-culture reference were aware of Hong Kong cinema, while young Tarantino fans took his plundering as a sign of the genre's inherent coolness. Whatever Ringo Lam's personal feelings, Tarantino's forced admission of the debt didn't do his career any harm – with the 1997 handover of Hong Kong to mainland China looming, Lam made his first move into Hollywood movie-making with the action picture *Maximum Risk*.

Top: facing camera, Mr White opens fire on a squad car. Bottom: back to camera, Brother Fu (Danny Lee) opens fire on a squad car. From City On Fire *(1987).*

It still remains, however, for Tarantino to fulfil the long-stated mutual ambition, dating back to the release of *Reservoir Dogs*, to have a screenplay directed by John Woo, doyen of Hong Kong action directors/mentor of Chow Yun-Fat. Somehow, his plan to move from recycling the influence to working with the genuine article has failed to materialise.

2.
true
romance

natural born killers

by Jeff Dawson

The anally neat 'burb of Westwood, Los Angeles, wedged between the affluent retreats of Beverly Hills and Bel Air, with its designer boutiques and small cluster of exquisite art deco cinemas in the area's central Fox Village, is exactly the kind of place that *Falling Down*'s D-Fens – had he the time – would happily have stopped off at. Just a short walk (though no one does, of course, in the City Of Angels) from the manicured campus of UCLA, this is a safe haven, in an age where pre-empting audience reaction has become Hollywood's all-important marketing tool, for filmmakers to test their product away from the hubbub of the studios.

For tonight's unpublicised preview, however, word is out, and the invited gaggle of hacks have been supplemented by an orderly yet excitable queue of young hopefuls – stretching back a full two blocks from the cinema complex – here on the off chance of filling up the empty seats. Such is the buzz on *True Romance*, Christian Slater and Patricia Arquette burning rubber to this very city with a suitcase full of nose candy and the mob on their tail. A glossy, coruscating tale of lovers on the hoof, it features a top-notch ensemble cast (Oldman, Pitt, Kilmer, Hopper, Walken) and the biggest hail of bullets since Butch and Sundance decided to leg it out of their Bolivian shack.

Those managing to squeeze past the jobsworths on the door are not disappointed, bestowing, as the final credits roll, an enthusiastic standing ovation, the ultimate seal of approval, one would have thought, for British director Tony Scott and local-boy-made-good, screenwriter Quentin Tarantino. But there is something rotten in Denmark. . . .

"It's heartbreaking," grumbles Tony Scott, back at the palatial Westwood Marquis hotel. "Each year the ratings board gets tougher, especially in terms of violence. They don't like movies like this."

Indeed they don't for, even with the radical changes suggested by the Motion Picture Association of America (MPAA), *True Romance* has still been lumbered with an R (Restricted) certificate – not quite the box office poison of an NC-17, but a blow nevertheless.

"The major change for me is that Patricia originally got to shoot Chris Penn [a policeman], which enabled her to be instrumental in terms of their running off with the money," elaborates Scott. "Now it's an incidental character, the Italian lying on the floor, who gets to do the shooting."

Cocaine, guns and – heavens! – even sex are, it seems, acceptable in limited quantities for an American audience, but as for the nailing of a copper by a civilian, especially in this town, that just won't do.

"What made it even worse was it was a woman," complains Scott in an accent still nine parts Teesside. "That's what they said: 'A woman shooting a policeman, that makes it worse . . .'"

true romance

For the 49-year old export from West Hartlepool, dressed in a natty multicoloured waistcoat and matching painted cowboy boots and with a battered baseball cap topping off the regulation jeans and T-shirt, it's been a rocky road to Hollywood A-listdom. After a career as a painter and then as a director of commercials, he had seemed destined to languish in the shadow of big brother Ridley until a chance encounter with uber-producers Don Simpson and Jerry Bruckheimer changed all that.

"After *Top Gun* the movies that I was offered were, for better or for worse, what you call hardware action movies," explains Scott, as the brothers prepare, ironically, to go head to head, each with his own Pancho Villa project. "When I first read *True Romance* I thought, 'Here's another violent movie,' but it wasn't. What I fell in love with were Quentin's characters – it's an actor-based movie, the first time I've had one of those – so I chased it. *Reservoir Dogs* was much more of a head trip, I found it very disturbing, but *True Romance* is like doing speed for two hours . . . I think this is my best work to date."

The script, of course, the ultimate paean to junk culture ("I love movies, I love TV shows, I love breakfast cereal – I grew up with that, it's like one hundred per cent my consciousness") comes from the pen of Quentin Tarantino, the unbound Prometheus who gate-crashed the Hollywood party in spectacular fashion with his writer-director debut *Reservoir Dogs*, a film whose success in Blighty still makes its creator happy.

"It's like Orson Welles, people telling him, 'Oh, you're real big in Europe,' or old vaudevillians saying, 'Oh, I'm real big in Des Moines,'" he babbles at his usual rate of nineteen to the dozen. "It's weird, it's like *Dogs* is so much in the culture of Britain. Even if people haven't seen it, they know what you're talking about – I feel like I'm Ivan Reitman and I just made *Ghostbusters*, it's totally cool."

True Romance was, in fact, Tarantino's first script, written five years ago as a prelude to *Dogs* (the character Alabama – fact fans – being the same lass mentioned by Mr White when interviewed by Joe Cabot). Although he managed to sell it, it remained "in development", so Tarantino was thus forced to make *Reservoir Dogs* independently as a last ditch attempt to get his material to the screen.

"I'd met Tony through a mutual friend and I was a big fan of his," recalls Tarantino. "I'd just gotten *Dogs* off the ground and he had heard who my cast was, so I sent him *True Romance* to read, even though somebody else had it at the time. He said, 'I wish there was something we could do about it.' And I said, 'Take it away from the other guys, I want you to do it.'"

And thus, with the script wrested from the French producers who had been sitting on it, *True Romance* was, as they say, hot to trot, though surely Tarantino would have jumped at the chance to direct it himself?

"No, I'm glad Tony did it," he insists, scratching on a scraggy bit of designer stubble gone wrong. "That goes for *Natural Born Killers* too [currently being filmed by Oliver Stone]. The opportunity was somewhat open for me to direct it because Tony thought about possibly just producing, but you know, I didn't want to. I wrote all three to be my first film and then I made my first film. It's like an old girlfriend, it has a shelf life. And anyway, it was exciting, the idea of seeing my world through Tony's eyes..."

It was also exciting enough a prospect to have Tinseltown's finest falling over each other to be in the damn thing – not least Christian Slater, a man whose currency is surely to head for the stratosphere after his stellar turn as the movie's linchpin Clarence Worley, a sort of comic book movie kid who feeds on junk food, gets messages from an imaginary Elvis and spouts the kind of movie-babble (no violent scene being complete without a reference to Charles Bronson) familiar from *Reservoir Dogs*.

"After I did *Untamed Heart* I wanted to do a film that was outrageous," muses the tanned Slater, his hair now back to its brown medium-length, and with the first signs of a goatee playing about his chin. "I really wanted to do, you know, a *performance*. I don't want to allow my image to rule the choices that I make. It was a daring movie. For me the challenge was to be, in a way, a sympathetic character in all this madness."

Madness, certainly, as you'd expect from a film that's a whirlwind of bullets, sharp one-liners and a cachet of Colombia's uncut finest, but isn't Clarence, well, off his rocker?

"It's difficult to say if he's really crazy or not," he continues in his best Jack Nicholson, sucking on one of a long line of Marlboros. "You know he had to make up a sort of fantasy world for himself and Elvis is sort of the one he chooses to be his guidance counsellor."

The King, it has to be said, would never get a job with the Samaritans, what with urging an innocent to go and blow away the testicles, followed by the remainder, of Gary Oldman's unsavoury pimp Drexl.

"He was just *confused*," apologises Slater, rather unconvincingly. "I thought he was sweet and sensitive. He loved the movies. He always wanted to be a part of them in some way, and Alabama opened the door and it gave him the opportunity to be the hero. Somebody said to me it sorta picks up where *Taxi Driver* left off."

Which is exactly the effect Tarantino intended.

"What I like about what Clarence does is that he makes a choice to go in there and kill this pimp and it's funny because it's kind of psychotic," chips in our Quentin. "That's very erratic behaviour for the lead in a movie. But he's been movie-fed, he's seen a zillion movies about pimps beating up whores and he remembers the scene in *Taxi Driver* when Harvey Keitel is talking about Jodie Foster, describing it in all these real graphic terms. He can imagine this pimp, who he's never even met, talking about his gal, his *lady love*, like that, so he has to go out there and execute him."

Not an entirely convincing argument, of course, but we'll live with it, which is precisely what Clarence didn't do in Tarantino's original draft, expiring from the bullet to the eye rather than recovering to leave a set of tyre marks all the way to Mexico.

"I think it's very nice and sweet that we do end up together," rasps Slater. "And it's a beautiful sunset . . . but yeah, in the original script, that's a rap, which made complete sense because they were living such a fast and spontaneous and chaotic and insane life. But this is the movies . . . and I'm really proud of it."

In a film that has taken its signature from those sort of comic book romances whose final frame is of the hero and heroine sucking face, the *real* lead is actually Patricia Arquette, the narrator of the piece and a character that, Scott claims, Tarantino wrote (confessing all "in a moment of weakness") as his ideal woman: sexy, streetwise and, essential for the ultimate movie junkie, not averse to sitting through a Sonny Chiba triple bill.

"It's like 'Bama isn't like a *dream* girl for me," counters Tarantino, who is about to direct his crime anthology *Pulp Fiction*, starring John Travolta, Uma Thurman, Bruce Willis, Eric Stoltz, Tim Roth, Harvey Keitel, Christopher Walken, Amanda Plummer (and himself) and due to commence work on a screenplay with John Woo. "I had never had a girlfriend before I wrote this, just a bunch of first or second dates. What happened was that she wasn't like my ideal but she was sweet and she fell in love with Clarence, not because he was the coolest looking guy in the world, but because he was good to her."

"You're supposed to believe anything you want, but she's not always telling the truth," waxes the extremely comely Patricia Arquette, impressive in her big breakthrough as the garishly clad but incredibly sweet hooker gone straight. "For starters, as far as I'm concerned, she doesn't really have that Southern accent, that's an affectation. She decided that was sexy and she's gonna be that Southern Belle."

The younger sister of the equally vivacious Rosanna, it is Arquette's participation in one of the film's key scenes, getting belted about the chops by a mafioso killer, that has been a major talking point. Had the MPAA not put their foot down, a battered Arquette would not only have come back from the brink of butchery to have simply shot the killer, but would have repeatedly filled his skull full of lead before battering him to a pulp with the butt of the gun.

"I was thinking particularly about the effect this would have on the audience," explains Tarantino. "Part of the problem with movies recently is that you pretty much know what's gonna happen before it happens. You know when to kind of lean up, you know when to sit back and what I like to do is use that against you psychologically – you turn left and then I turn right – not just for gamesmanship, but to be an interesting storyteller.

"You know I never went to writing school, 'Write A Screenplay In 27 Days', or any of that nonsense. One of the things you get taught as an actor is just get the characters talking to each other. Whatever happens is what happens, what they say is what they say and what they do is what they do. People bring up the torture scene in *Reservoir Dogs*. I didn't set out to write this really bitchin' torture scene. I didn't know Mr Blonde had a razor in his boot until he whipped it out – it's like, 'Oh my God.' The truth of it is that was what Mr Blonde would do when left alone with this cop. To pull back on that because some people might not like it would be lying. One of the things that makes the scene with Alabama work dramatically is that she could die, she was up for grabs."

Definitely up for grabs was Alabama's pimp Drexl Spivey, played as an almost Dickensian villain by Gary Oldman, who we first see involved in a heavy diatribe with Samuel Jackson about the whys and wherefores of "eating pussy" (a scene so pared down on the recommendation of the MPAA as to render the high-billed Jackson's character almost redundant).

"I'd never met Gary before and he said, 'Come on down to the hotel for a drink,'" gushes Scott. "I said, 'You've got to read this,' and he said, 'I don't fucking read scripts. Tell me about my fucking character.' I just said, 'He's a white guy who thinks he's black and he's a pimp,' and he said, '*I'll do it*.' He'd just been working on *Romeo Is Bleeding*, hanging out on the set with a drug dealer. This guy had spent ten years of his life in Jamaica and had a sort of half-Rasta, half-Queens accent. He was his basis for Drexl."

Lovers on the run Clarence (Christian Slater) and Alabama (Patricia Arquette) take a breather on a hotel bed.

If selling a flick with such a fluffy title starring the likes of Slater and Oldman has caused marketing types a spot of bother, the addition of Brad Pitt and Val Kilmer to the cast – as the stoned waster Floyd and the ghost of Elvis respectively – will surely cause confusion among many a moviegoer.

"You know Brad has a mystery and a darkness, I think it comes from the chequered life he had before," smirks Scott, motioning his thumb and forefinger to his lips, puffing on an imaginary spliff. "That's a character that he knew and hung out with at his house, this guy came for a week and stayed for two years – a pothead who never got off the sofa."

"But the bong was my invention," he adds triumphantly, referring to the sweet jar Floyd uses to inhale his weed. "There's a guy I go rock climbing with and he has this bong, a honey bear jar that you can buy across the counter – he calls his Russ. That was a homage to Russ, hahahahaha."

And as for Kilmer's Elvis impression (referred to in the credits simply as "Mentor", so as not to face a hefty legal bill from the Presley estate) . . .

"Val spent eight hours in make-up trying to look like Elvis, and he looked brilliant," continues Scott. "Originally I showed it so I could see his face, but there's only one person who looks like Elvis, and that's Presley and so I redesigned it. But Val is brilliant, he *became* Elvis three months before we did it and he only had two days' work – I'd talk to him on the phone and it's like [affects Elvis voice], 'Hey.' He only plays dead rock and rollers now."

"That's one of the things I should get a big kick out of," guffaws Tarantino loudly. "As opposed to *Play It Again Sam*, with Bogart telling Woody Allen how to get in with the chicks, Elvis is just saying, '*Kill* that guy . . . '"

There is, however, an even tastier caricature in *True Romance*, Saul Rubinek's fictitious action producer Lee Donowitz – the rushes of his latest flick *Bodybag 2* providing the backdrop to the film's climactic shoot-out – who bears an uncanny resemblance to Joel Silver, legendary producer of the *Die Hard* and *Lethal Weapon* series.

"It was Tony who turned him into Joel Silver," adds Tarantino, who at the time of writing *True Romance* didn't move in such esteemed circles.

"Everybody's been saying Joel Silver's gonna kill you," grins Scott, actually a big pal of Silver's. "He was gonna go and see the film tonight. Whether he went I don't know, but I haven't heard from him, so maybe he did, hahaha!"

Drugs, violence and Joel Silver aside, however, the scene that will inevitably cause the most controversy is the exchange between old war-horses Christopher Walken and Dennis Hopper, with Hopper, as Clarence's father, inciting Walken's mafia boss into killing him by taunting him that Sicilians are not the pure-blooded heavyweight champions of lying as suggested by Walken, but, in fact, "spawned by niggers" – an insult, irrespective of anything else that may be deemed offensive in the movie, that will have many a white liberal squirming in his or her seat.

"I actually think 'nigger' may be the most taboo word in the English language," explains Tarantino. "Words should not have that much power, and any time you have a word that does, you should strip the power away. It's nit-picking to be offended just by the use of the word . . . that's a very limited view and it doesn't really affect me, but I love that speech, it's really funny. It was actually a black guy who told me that whole story."

"Yeah. I was more worried about the Sicilians, hahahaha," gurgles Dennis Hopper menacingly, strolling into the room in a rather dapper brown Commes Des Garcons suit. "I figured that it would probably rub a few people the wrong way, but that's okay, and anyway, as a screen actor you don't have speeches in movies any more. *This* is a speech. I'm a great admirer of Tarantino's writing. Actually, I was asked by Harvey Keitel to be in *Reservoir Dogs* but I was doing something else."

Christopher Walken, currently in the throes of filming *Wayne's World II*, is equally unconcerned.

"I don't *ever* confuse movies with real life and I don't think other people should," he says. "It's like when *The Deer Hunter* came out, people were talking about Vietnam. *The Deer Hunter* had *nothing* to do with Vietnam, it had to do with young men going to war thinking that it's adventurous and getting their legs blown off. This film's not about violence, it's about *people*."

And on that, we'll leave the final word to Hopper.

"I did do one thing that had a cause and effect on society. *Easy Rider* did introduce cocaine," he concludes, working himself up into a bit of a lather, "that's one I can't really get out of. In 1969 when they released the film there was no cocaine on the streets and by 1970 it was everywhere, but violence in movies causing violence, I'm not buying that one. It's like Heidi the madame. I mean suddenly Hollywood's gonna get morals and Washington's gonna come and take the violence out of movies. What are we talking about, man? I mean, since when is Hollywood gonna be moral? There aren't gonna be hookers in Hollywood? What, have we gone mad?"

Dennis Hopper has hit his stride.

"Think of Mark Twain," he burbles. "He was dealing with the same things, there's a couple of guys running away on a riverboat going down a river. I mean that's a strange juxtaposition, but we're in the Nineties now and we live in a violent society. How can you write about it and not make some reflection on your culture? Quentin Tarantino, he's the Mark Twain of the Nineties . . ."

walken v. hopper

in *true romance*

by Jonathan Miller

Hollywood has given us many exciting bouts in the boxing ring, but when it comes to a confrontation between two on-screen heavyweights, no one can touch Christopher Walken and Dennis Hopper going mano-a-mano in Quentin Tarantino's classic screenplay *True Romance*. In his use of character and dialogue in the eight short pages of this confrontation, Tarantino proves as ruthless and manipulative as any literary Don King. Pound for pound, this scene is a contender for one of the most powerful and yet unsettling of all time.

True Romance is the story of Clarence, played by Christian Slater, who steals a lot of cocaine from his girlfriend's pimp. Clarence has a brief visit with his father, Cliff (Hopper), before heading out to California to try to unload the drugs.

In his first scene with Clarence, Hopper seems more like the befuddled drunk he played in *Hoosiers* than the character we all know and love from *Speed* and *Blue Velvet*. Both the script and the direction initially make Cliff resemble the unfortunate African boxer Akinwande, who was disqualified for his reluctance to get into the action. Walken, on the other hand, comes out swinging. He plays a Mafia counsel, Coccotti, searching for the stolen drugs. Along with some goons, he follows Clarence's trail to Cliff's apartment. After the goons knock Cliff to his knees and tie him to a chair, Coccotti provides the following introduction:

COCCOTTI

> I am the Anti-Christ. You get me in a vendetta kind of mood, you will tell the angels in heaven that you had never seen evil so singularly personified as you did in the face of the man who killed you.

Walken delivers the lines coolly – as if he's still holding that gold watch up his butt for the last eight years. The early rounds go to Walken. Tarantino doesn't give Hopper much to answer with other than "What are you talkin' about?", and "I don't believe you." Walken, on the other hand, mixes his punches. He floats like a butterfly then stings like a bee as he alternates between insults and empathy. If there was a referee, the fight would have been stopped in the early going. Then Tarantino has Walken slide in for the knockout blow with his infamous "pantomime" speech.

COCCOTTI

> Sicilians are great liars. The best in the world. I'm a Sicilian and my old man was the world heavyweight champion of Sicilian liars. And from growin' up with him

I learned the pantomime. Now there are seventeen different things a guy can do when he lies that gives himself away . . . What we got here is a little game of show and tell . . . You don' wanna show me nuthin'. But you're tellin' me everythin' . . .

This sets up the "purse" for our bout – whether Coccotti can tell if Cliff is lying through his use of the "pantomime". Things look grim – Hopper's Cliff is clearly on the ropes, literally. But after Hopper bums a smoke from Walken, it feels like both writer and actor have played rope-a-dope with us all along.

CLIFF
> . . . So you're a Sicilian, huh?

COCCOTTI (intensely)
> Uh-huh.

CLIFF
> You know, I read a lot. Especially things that have to do with history. I find that shit fascinating. In fact, I don't know if you know this or not, Sicilians were spawned by niggers.

All the men stop what they were doing and look at Cliff.
Coccotti cannot believe what he's hearing.

COCCOTTI
> Come again?

CLIFF
> It's a fact. Sicilians have nigger blood pumping through their hearts. If you don't believe me look it up. You see hundreds and hundreds of years ago the Moors conquered Sicily. And Moors are niggers. Way back then, Sicilians were like the Wops in Northern Italy. Blond hair, blue eyes. But once the Moors moved in there, they changed the whole country. They did so much fucking with the Sicilian women, they changed the bloodline forever from blond hair and blue eyes to black hair and dark skin. I find it absolutely amazing to think that, to this day, hundreds of years later, Sicilians still carry that nigger gene. I'm just quoting history. It's a fact. It's written. Your ancestors were niggers. Your great-great-great-great-grandmother was fucked by a nigger and had a half nigger kid.

Coccotti and the goons don't know how to respond to these low blows. Then Cliff goes in with the coup de grace, and this one goes right to Coccotti's solar plexus, right to his heart.

CLIFF
> Now tell me, am I lying?

Cute little bad girl Alabama is part of the Tarantino universe, name-checked as Mr White's ex-girlfriend and crime partner in Reservoir Dogs.

With his stone cold delivery, the speech ranks up there with "Do not attempt to grow a brain", in *Speed*, and even "He's sane, but his soul is mad", from *Apocalypse Now*, as the most powerful lines Hopper has ever spoken on film.

Coccotti, who owned the ring, has no counter-punch. Cliff has drawn blood and Coccotti is literally speechless. He is unable to get the knockout, to get the necessary information out of Cliff. His only response is to shoot three bullets through Cliff's brain. The stage directions leave little doubt of how hard the blows have staggered Mr Evil Personified.

Clarence argues with his old man. Security guard Cliff (Dennis Hopper) will give his life for his son by provoking mafioso Vincenzo Coccotti into killing him.

Coccotti pauses. Unable to express his feelings and frustrated by the blood on his hands, he simply drops the weapon and turns to his men.

COCCOTTI (to himself)
I haven't killed anybody since 1974 . . . Come back with something that tells me where [Clarence] went, so I can wipe this egg off my face . . .

In roughly 20 years, Coccotti has managed to be a Sugar Ray Leonard – to stay pretty, keeping blood off his hands and the egg off his face. But at the scene's end, he's a Roberto Duran crying "No mas. No mas."

Although both the acting and writing are powerful, there is still something extremely unsettling about the racism in the speech, which is gratuitous. There are no major black characters, and other than a white Gary Oldman's line "This is definitely not white-boy day," there is no other mention of race in the script.

The script gives no other clue that Cliff is a racist, or why Coccotti would be so bothered by the Sicilians' supposed Moorish ancestry. The ancient Moors who conquered Sicily were in fact amazing people. Carthage was the equal of Rome in its day; Hannibal one of the greatest generals in history.

Is Cliff just speaking as a character, or is he speaking for Tarantino? If Tarantino is a racist, and if so, against whom? A decision either way would be far from unanimous.

Shakespeare had a similar taint with his stereotypical portrayal of the Jewish money-lender, Shylock, in *The Merchant of Venice*. Yet Shylock's "Hath not a Jew eyes?" speech is so moving that it could not be written by a total, unredeemable racist. Shakespeare also had the portrayal of a sympathetic Moorish hero in *Othello* under his belt.

Tarantino is no Shakespeare, and a speech that uses "nigger" six times in one paragraph is hardly "To be or not to be." But Tarantino has also redeemed himself with his portrayal of African-Americans in *Pulp Fiction*. Jules, the hit-man played by Samuel L. Jackson, might be one of the most complex African-American characters ever in a screenplay by a Caucasian. His famous "Shepherd speech" in the final scene in the diner, could be a metaphor for a quest for racial identity. A real racist simply could not have created that character or written that speech. Unfortunately, there is no real sense of resolution regarding racism within *True Romance*. The matter is brought up so colourfully by Cliff, and then left hanging.

Perhaps I can add another perspective, an Italian one. "Tarantino" is an Italian name, and Tarantino has some Italian ancestry. The Moors' incursion into the Roman Empire during the Second Punic War began as Hannibal led his army and elephants through the Alps and across all of Italy. According to Leonard Cottrell's book *Hannibal, Enemy of Rome*, a decisive battle was fought at Tarentum, modern day Taranto, in the year 214 B.C. The Moors even had a large garrison in Tarentum for several years. According to Cottrell, the residents of "Tarentum" were called "tarentines", which sounds an awful lot like "Tarantino."

It's a fact. Now tell me, am I lying?

Ultimately, the Sicilian-Moorish connection is beside the point. The speech is about one man trying to break another with his force of will – by his ability to spot the "pantomime". So when Coccotti has to pull out the revolver it's the literary equivalent of biting Cliff's ear off.

Hopper's Cliff might be lying dead at the scene's end, but I'll still give him this one on a TKO. Call Tarantino. Hell, call Don King. I'm still waiting for Walken-Hopper II.

All screenplay quotations from True Romance *by Quentin Tarantino, revised draft: 1 August 1991.*

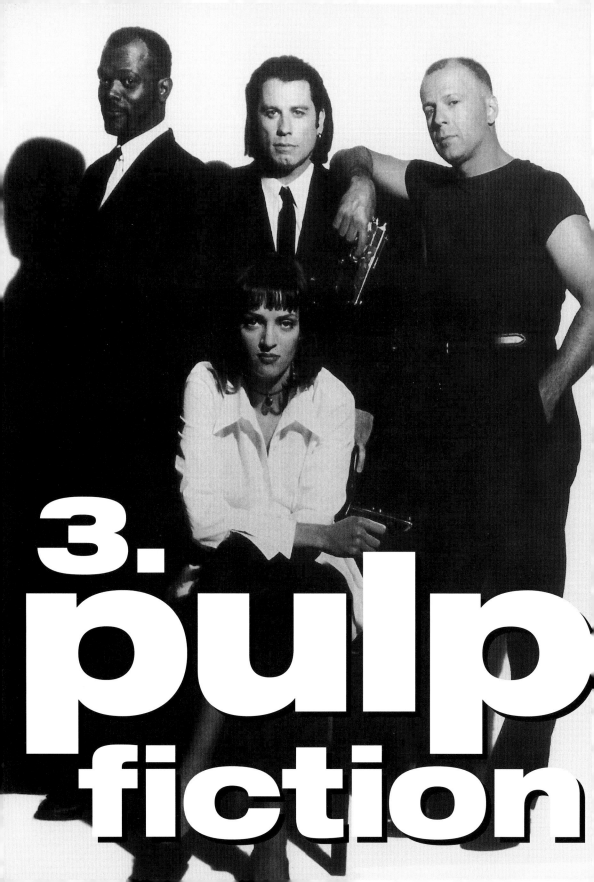

3.
pulp
fiction

pulp action

by Emma Webster

"**W**e're loving it!" Tarantino exclaims. The crew on *Pulp Fiction* are now accustomed to the fact that their director has dispensed with the standard order "Cut!". Brimming with enthusiasm, Tarantino is like a kid with a fabulous new toy. "That was so great, let's do it again just for the sheer joy of it!" The crew segues effortlessly into another take. Tarantino issues more directions from a camera rig outside a grungy motel bedroom and actress Maria De Medieros slinks back into the shadows to take up position.

On this smog-bound winter afternoon the atmosphere on-set is laid-back and humorous, despite a recent car accident in which the Polish cinematographer, Andrzej Sekula, nearly lost his life. Sekula, now laid up in a wheelchair, rests his shattered leg on a box strapped to his chair with gaffer tape. In pain, he stoically comments on lighting adjustments and then gets wheeled off to prepare the next set-up.

The energy level rises noticeably as a taxi pulls up containing the film's biggest star, Bruce Willis. Sporting a blood-drenched T-shirt and puffing on a fat cigar, he strolls around with a demeanour not a million miles away from the bruiser boxer he's portraying. It's time to roll and Tarantino launches into his deep-throat Sam Fuller impersonation, ribbing Willis in a far corner for his attention to detail on make-up. Willis takes up position astride his chopper bike and awaits instruction. The set falls silent in anticipation and Tarantino, relating to the world in the only way he knows how – as one big movie – begins. "This is it! The camera's right on you. You're Robert Mitchum in *Thunder Road*." Actually, he's playing Butch, returning from one of the most violent, harrowing mornings of his life.

Reservoir Dogs may have had an impressive cast for a first movie, but for *Pulp* Tarantino has pushed out the boat. The budget, however, at eight million dollars (less than Willis's single acting fee on *Die Hard 3*), has been kept down to sensible levels, and is much in evidence in sets, camera equipment, and fuelling the logistics of rambling and varied locations. You can bet that what attracted names like Willis, John Travolta and Uma Thurman to the film wasn't fat paycheques – it was the script. That was certainly the case for Samuel Jackson who plays Jules, a regular guy who just happens to make a living out of killing: "I sat down, read the script straight through, which I normally don't do, took a breath, then read it again, which I never do, just to make sure it was *true*. That it was the best script I'd ever read."

Each scene is treated like a story in itself, making the movie a string of set pieces with memorable bravura cameos. On one occasion during filming, the crew burst into spontaneous applause at Jackson's rendition of an apocalyptic passage from the Bible, which he delivers before launching into a multiple assassination. Tarantino seems to have taken to heart the old acting teachers' maxim, "there are no small parts, only small actors", mixing and matching A-list stars with lesser-known talents as he goes, concerned only with strong performances. Maria De Madeiros, a relative unknown in Hollywood who plays Fabienne, Butch's fragile French girlfriend, couldn't believe her luck at being cast opposite one of Hollywood's power elite. "I was very impressed by Bruce. What is extraordinary about the stars like him and John Travolta is that they fell in love with the project and worked on it with the greatest simplicity, as actors, not as stars."

Tarantino's energy is visibly infectious and obviously a main motor to the entire cast and crew. Jackson pays credit to Tarantino's inspirational directing style: "Quentin has an energy about him that's very wild and open, that just has a way of transferring to everyone else. He's so excited about seeing his words come to life, it's contagious. It turns out to be a real productive energy." None of the actors seem to be bursting to change any of their lines, as is increasingly the case these days when big stars collide with written-by-committee scripts. "Having been an actor himself, he's sensitive on how to get performances out of individuals," says Eric Stoltz, who plays a low-life smack dealer in one of the film's key adrenaline sequences. "What he's done here is assemble a strong school of lunatics into his cast. It's like an orchestra and he's the mad conductor."

This is certainly a reasonably accurate description of what can be seen on the extravagant showcase set of Jack Rabbit Slim's. "It's either the best diner you've ever seen, or the worst," Tarantino jokes, "depending on your point of view." His producer Lawrence Bender, clad as an extra in a Zorro outfit, surveys the scene, catching his eye on waitress Marilyn Monroe and Mamie Van Doren lookalikes, difficult to miss for their extremely pneumatic figures. Everyone seems oblivious to the fact that, outside in the real world, large portions of Los Angeles are currently being devastated by the fires that consumed the homes of the rich and famous.

Other waiters dressed as Hollywood icons form part of the diner decor, as do Fifties B-movie posters of films such as *Shock Confessions Of A Sorority Girl* and *Attack Of The 50 Foot Woman*. Steve Buscemi has been ironically transformed from the non-tipping Mr Pink in *Reservoir Dogs* into a suicidally depressed Buddy Holly waiter. "I think Quentin should do a cutaway to show that I don't get a tip," he jokes. Initially it's a shock to see his customers, Uma Thurman with crow-black dyed hair sitting opposite John Travolta in half a sawn-off car, inside the diner, but somehow, crazily, it all comes off in the mix. Any doubts about the casting of Travolta as the gangster Vincent are immediately dismissed.

Stoltz, who shares a major scene with Travolta, giggles at the thought of working with him. "Travolta makes me laugh. He's a blue-eyed movie star with a plane, a mansion, a beautiful wife, but he's a goofball. He just goes around the set making people laugh. What's great about his performance is that it's nothing like him. Vincent's character is cool, subterranean, not bright and violent. John is sharp, loose and funny."

Everyone takes a pause as Harvey Weinstein, the chief of the film's backers Miramax, strolls on to the set to meet with the actors and find out if his eight million bucks are being well spent. It's sobering to see that the hottest directorial talent on the block is still answerable to men in grey suits. But despite the potential pressure, there's a sense of confidence and pleasure on set. From money men to director, crew and ensemble cast, everyone is giving off the same vibe: everything's going to be just fine.

pulp fiction

by Todd McCarthy

A spectacularly entertaining piece of pop culture, *Pulp Fiction* is the *American Graffiti* of violent crime pictures. Following up on his reputation-making debut *Reservoir Dogs*, Quentin Tarantino makes some of the same moves here but on a much larger canvas, ingeniously constructing a series of episodes so that they ultimately knit together, and embedding the always surprising action in a context set by delicious dialogue and several superb performances.

Reviews, cast and heavy anticipation will make this a must-see among buffs and young male viewers, but rough genre, length and bloody mayhem will rep a turnoff for others, creating a real test of Miramax's marketing savvy in turning a niche picture into a crossover item upon late-August release.

Working on a wide screen constantly bulging with boldness, humour and diabolical invention, Tarantino indulges himself with a free hand and a budget several times larger than he had on his first outing.

Some may feel that the film sags in spots due to the director's tendency to try to stretch conceits as far as he can, but Tarantino should be commended for daring to explore the limits of his material, winding up on his feet and beating the sophomore jinx in the process.

As did *Reservoir Dogs*, new pic begins in a coffee shop, with a young couple who call each other Pumpkin and Honey Bunny (Tim Roth and Amanda Plummer) chattering away before deciding to hold up the place.

Next sequence also feels like familiar territory, as two hit men, Vincent and Jules (John Travolta and Samuel L. Jackson), are attired just like the hoods in *Dogs*, in dark suits, white shirts and ties. At once, Tarantino positions himself as the Preston Sturges of crimeland, putting the most incongruous words and thoughts into the mouths of lowdown, amoral characters.

Recently returned from a drug-happy sojourn in Amsterdam, Vincent speaks knowledgeably about the different varieties of fast food available in Europe, while Jules waxes eloquent on the Bible, vengeance and divinity.

After they bump off some kids who didn't play straight with crime lord Marsellus (Ving Rhames), the cool, self-possessed Vincent, as a courtesy, takes his boss' statuesque wife, Mia (a dark-haired Uma Thurman), out for a night on the town.

This "date" occasions the picture's biggest set piece, an amazing outing to a giant 1950s-themed restaurant-club. Even with all the decorous distractions, the plot gets advanced through some tantalising verbal tennis between the two hot lookers, and the evening ends shockingly, with Vincent forced to save Mia's life in a way that will initially have many viewers cringing but will leave them laughing with appalled relief.

Here as before, Tarantino builds up tremendous tension, only to spice it with humorous non sequiturs. When his characters draw guns, as they so frequently do, one never knows if they're going to blow others' heads off, make a funny speech (they often do both), have the tables turned on them or make an honourable, peaceful exit.

pulp fiction

Butch (Bruce Willis) puts new life into the cliché of the boxer who won't take a dive, reminded of family honour by his father's gold watch.

An hour in, pic becomes even more audacious, as Tarantino leads the audience deeper into uncharted territory with new characters whose relationships to those already seen remain unclear for some time.

After a fantastic monologue by Christopher Walken as a soldier giving a prized gold watch to a little boy, a stripped-down Bruce Willis, as a boxer named Butch, is seen jumping out a window and getting in a cab. On instructions from Marsellus, Butch was supposed to take a fall, but he didn't and is on the run for his life.

Butch's existence over the next few hours is agonizingly unpredictable, horrifying and thoroughly zany. Some of the earlier characters begin to drop back into the story, and gradually a grand design starts falling into place.

Overall structure comes clear only after the two-hour mark with launch of the final stretch, which dovetails beautifully back to the beginning but also embraces a new character, the Wolf (Harvey Keitel), an impeccably organized specialist in literally cleaning up other people's dirty work.

Buffs will have a field day with the bold, confident style of the film and with the cinematic points of reference. Tarantino and lenser Andrzej Sekula's striking widescreen compositions often contain objects in extreme close-up as well as vivid contrasts, sometimes bringing to mind the visual strategies of Sergio Leone.

Performances are sensational. Jackson possibly has the showiest opportunities, and he makes the most of them with a smashing turn that commands attention whenever he's present. Travolta, sporting long hair and an earring, is also terrific, especially during his ambiguous outing with Thurman.

With head shaved in a buzz cut Willis is all coiled tension and self-control. Keitel has tasty fun as a criminal efficiency expert, Rhames is as menacing as a person can be as the pic's most powerful figure, and Roth and Plummer are the jumpy couple on the low-rent end of the criminal spectrum.

Most of the coin for David Wasco's production design must have gone into the enormous diner, a delirious creation. Sally Menke's editing reps the definition of precision, and score consists of many judiciously selected rock tunes.

On any number of important levels, *Pulp Fiction* is a startling, massive success.

tarantino on the run

by Jim McLellan

With his usual gangling energy, at his usual mile a minute pace, without notes, without a break, all the while standing up, pacing around in front of a screen, Quentin Tarantino is talking to an audience of film students about working with actors. The directorial masterclass/one-man talkathon got moving at around three o'clock in Nottingham's Broadway Media Centre and has been hurtling along at breakneck speed ever since.

The majority of the audience look vaguely stunned. After about an hour and a half of this high-octane performance one wise guy at the back gets up to ask the jokey question which has probably been on the minds of most of the people in the room. "What is it that makes Quentin run?" Whatever it is seems, at this point, suddenly and temporarily to run out. Looking exhausted, Tarantino retreats to the bar. Perhaps even he needs to sit down and shut up occasionally.

It's something of a surprise to find Tarantino in Nottingham. After all, it's a bit of a step down from Cannes, which is where he was a month ago, picking up the Palme D'Or for his new film *Pulp Fiction*, which weaves three crime scenarios into an epic to follow *Reservoir Dogs*, the most violently inventive and powerful debut feature of recent years. Actually the fact he is here at Nottingham's Shots In The Dark Crime Film Festival is quite heartening. According to festival organiser Adrian Wootton, Tarantino promised he'd come and he actually kept his word, despite his seemingly unstoppable rise and the fame that comes with it.

Tarantino had been at the festival last year to introduce some Hong Kong gangster films by John Woo and Ringo Lam and, according to Wootton, had a great time, deciding that Nottingham was 'really cool'. This year he'd programmed a season of blaxploitation films and planned to come over to introduce them. Wootton admits that after Cannes he was expecting Tarantino to back out gracefully. After all, there are marketing meetings to attend, studio flesh to press and American media to do for *Pulp Fiction*, due out in October on both sides of the Atlantic. But a couple of days ago, Tarantino turned up.

He's now been made the event's 'honorary patron' and, in a way, it's much more his type of event than Cannes. It shows his kind of films, from classic *noir* and existential French *policiers* to Hong Kong action and Japanese *yakuza*. It's a festival for fans rather than for the media or the business, which means it's an event where he can get on with doing what he likes best – watching films. It's also the kind of place where his visceral vision rules unchallenged. The people here aren't the kind who think that *Three Colours*: *Red* should have won the Palme D'Or or that the torture scene in *Reservoir Dogs* goes way too far.

Though it's true that during the sneak premiere of *Pulp Fiction* on the last Saturday of the festival, one person is sick, that seems to have more to do with alcohol than on-screen gore. Otherwise a carnival atmosphere reigns. As the opening credits roll, the audience cheers its favourites – Harvey Keitel, Tim Roth, Christopher Walken. However, it's Tarantino's name that sparks the most noise. "What's happened recently is that the people who work in the crime genre now, the directors, are kind of becoming the stars of the movies," Tarantino observes. "That wasn't necessarily the case before. Horror film directors were like that in the 1970s. If you were a young horror film geek, you went and saw George Romero's movies, John Carpenter's movies, Dario Argento's movies. They were the stars, the heroes. That's not necessarily the case right now for horror films – they don't make that many any more. But in some ways John Woo and Abel Ferrara and Beat Takeshi – they've taken that slot. So it's kind of an exciting time to do those movies."

Certainly, throughout the festival, Tarantino, usually dressed in the kind of film merchandising T-shirts they give away at such events (though he does don a *Reservoir Dogs* style combo of black suit and white shirt for special occasions), is besieged by a steady stream of fans, male and female, who want to get autographs or pictures or hand over their own scripts. The director makes time for them all, perhaps because he knows what it's like. He's been there himself. "I think my biggest appeal amongst young fans is they look at me as a fan boy who made it."

And how. Tarantino is the ultimate fan boy success, the self-styled film geek who grew up to rule Hollywood (at least for the moment). At the age of 31, he not only gets to make films which rework bits and pieces of his favourite movies and star all his favourite actors, he's also become something of a film world tastemaker. He says he likes John Woo's hyperviolent Hong Kong action films and, bingo, Woo gets a Hollywood deal. He says the stark French gangster films of Jean Pierre Melville were an influence and they get reissued. He laughs at this idea. "I don't think that's down to me, but if it is then all the better."

The details of his rapid rise – particularly the fact that he never went to film school but taught himself, fast forwarding through film history while he worked at a video shop – have become so well known they almost constitute a Nineties pop myth. Even now, magazine editors are working on stories about video shops as the new film schools. Journalists are scouring the nation's Blockbuster outlets in search of the British Tarantino.

Actually, he points out, the media myth gets a few things wrong. He already had his film education by the time he got the job at the video store, aged 22, which he held down for five years. In fact, it was why he got the job. He could give people advice on which movies to rent (and telling people what to watch and why is something he clearly enjoys). He could also watch his favourite films over and over, and figure out how they worked.

A hyperactive child (named after a character in *Gunsmoke*), Tarantino grew up in L.A.'s South Bay area. He says that for a portion of his childhood he went to an all-black school, hence his interest in blaxploitation and soul. In general he found school difficult, playing truant to go to see films. His mother encouraged his interest rather more enthusiastically than some parents might have, taking him to see *Carnal Knowledge*, *The Wild Bunch* and *Deliverance* when he was still in short trousers. As he grew up, he tried his hand at scripts, watched TV and read about film, in particular

Pauline Kael (talk to him for any length of time and he'll inevitably end up quoting some review of hers – occasionally word for word).

He also trained as an actor for six years, all the while working on various scripts, the most ambitious being the story of a young comic store assistant, who, while working on a film script of his own about a pair of serial killers on the run, becomes caught up in the criminal world and ends up going on the run for real. Eventually Tarantino split these two ideas up and they became *True Romance*, the story of the comic store assistant, which was filmed by Tony Scott last year, and *Natural Born Killers*, the script the assistant was 'writing', which comes to the screen this summer, courtesy of Oliver Stone. (The script has been rewritten by Stone and Tarantino now only has a story credit on it.)

The Wolf (Harvey Keitel) does business with Monster Joe (Dick Miller). Miller appeared in the Roger Corman films whose posters hang in Jackrabbit Slim's.

But for a long time the two stories were stuck together and he laboured away, amassing a 500-page script. In 1989, feeling desperate, he changed tack and bashed out a script based on an old idea he'd had about reworking the heist movie. Harvey Keitel saw the script for *Reservoir Dogs*, loved it and decided to help produce it. Tarantino was up and running. He hasn't stopped since.

Towards the end of the Tarantino masterclass, another of the students gets up the nerve to ask a question. "Could you tell me – which is the better film, *Reservoir Dogs* or *Pulp Fiction*?" This is not a great thing to ask. After all, Tarantino is hardly likely to say the film he's been labouring away on for the past year or so is not as good as his first effort. When he says he thinks that *Pulp Fiction* is the better film, the student responds with disbelief. "No, but seriously . . ." It's as if he can't imagine something being better than *Reservoir Dogs*. Many younger fans share this reverence for Tarantino's first film. It was as if Tarantino was their film-maker, the first to really reflect the way they felt about the trashy pop cultural landscape they grew up in, and *Reservoir Dogs* was their film, the one that showed them for the first time what cinema could do.

Of course, for Tarantino's critics, *Dogs* is *that* film, the one in which a mobster (played by Michael Madsen) boogies around to an old Stealer's Wheel single then proceeds to torture a cop he has taken prisoner, slicing off his ear and dousing him with gasoline. When the film was released here early last year, the scene provoked walkouts and outrage. It was greeted with articles bemoaning the New Brutalism at loose in contemporary cinema. Since then, in the aftermath of the James Bulger murder trial, the panic about possible links between on-screen violence and off-screen horrors has grown and *Reservoir Dogs*, like Abel Ferrara's similarly full-blooded *The Bad Lieutenant*, has been denied a certificate for video release. This is a situation which is not without its ironies. For all the talk of desensitisation, *Dogs* succeeded in making people *feel* certain images anew and in questioning the pleasure they took from them. Consequently it can seem as if, after years of numbing robotic carnage, Tarantino is actually being punished for making screen violence hurt us again.

However, he seems unwilling to talk about any of this any more. In the past, he would describe, with a gleeful air, how people tended to walk out of the scenes in two waves – the second starting when Madsen began soaking his victim with petrol. Now he prefers to keep quiet. While he doesn't have a problem with violence in films, he does have a problem with talking about violence in films. He's fed up with it. He's said all he has to say.

He does tell me he hasn't read the book at the centre of the moral panic in the US, Michael Medved's *Hollywood Vs America*: "To me, in 20 years' time it'll be viewed like these old panic books where people are going against rock 'n' roll or comics. You know what I mean. It's like: [he puts on a good ol' boy southern twang] that nigger music is turning the white man into an animal. It can turn a woman into a slut, virgins into whores." He sniggers. "Every ten years, there's a book which comes along and says there's violence in the streets, people are starving, anarchy brewing – blame the playmakers. It's their fault."

He reiterates his standard line on the whole subject. "To say that I get a big kick out of violence in movies and can enjoy violence in movies but find it totally abhorrent in real life – I can feel totally justified and totally comfortable with that statement. I do not think that one is a contradiction of the other. Real life violence is real life violence. Movies are movies. I can watch a movie about the Hindenburg disaster and get into it as a movie but still feel it's a horrible real life tragedy. It's not the same thing at all."

As for the *Dogs* torture scene, he remains unrepentant. "I love that scene. I love what it does cinematically, emotionally, performance-wise. To me it's the most cinematic scene in the whole movie." Indeed, those who dismiss the scene as gratuitous have totally missed the point. With its vertiginous shift from bouncy comedy into horrified fascination with the way it exhausts the viewers' guilty laughter then threatens to just keep on going, it's almost like a ten-minute encapsulation of

quentin tarantino: the film geek files

Tarantino's directorial method. As one critic pointed out, it's as if Tarantino is the bopping torturer and the audience the terrified cop, transfixed in his seat, wondering what's coming next.

He returns to this primal scene twice in *Pulp Fiction*, early on, when a hit man delays killing his squirming seated target to ponder which type of burgers are the best and later, when a boxer and a mobster find themselves bound and gagged and being doused with petrol by a pair of hillbilly creeps. There's more than enough in *Pulp Fiction* to suggest that Tarantino will continue to have to talk to journalists about film violence, enough, in fact – from anal rape and drug overdoses (played for zombie movie laughs) to arterial spray and hairdos spattered with brain tissue – to suggest that the censor may have a great deal to say on the subject before the film gets a certificate.

Tarantino argues that the film is much lighter in tone than his previous efforts. *"Pulp Fiction* – while there's wild stuff that happens in it, to be sure – definitely has the most comic tone of any movie I've done so far. All my movies, I definitely stop short of calling them comedies, because there's stuff in them you're not supposed to laugh at. But *Pulp*, more than any, has an overtly comic spirit, pretty much from the beginning to the end."

He goes on to describe it as an epic. Indeed, it's a vast, sprawling effort, with three separate stories jumping back and forth in time. "The idea was to start off with really old pulp ideas – the boxer who's paid to throw a fight but doesn't, the gangster who takes out his boss's girl, knows he shouldn't mess with her, but . . . – and sort of go to the Moon with them, take them to a place you've never seen them taken to before."

The film's script had its origins in the old pulp crime stories published by *Black Mask* magazine. Tarantino says he's drawn to the genre for a whole series of reasons – because of its trashy resonance, its stress on slangy dialogue, its attention to speech and male behaviour, its interest in charting the modern urban landscape. As with blaxploitation films like *The Mack* (which he introduced at the 'Shots' festival) and *Superfly*, which romanticised the pusher and the pimp as hustling heroes, he likes pulp because of the way it sometimes puts bad guys centre stage, courting an amorality which can take an audience into uncharted territories, places where they don't know quite how to feel.

He's less happy with the theory advanced by some critics that *Pulp* (with its violence, profane energy and routine misogyny) is a reaction to political correctness. "That's not really why I'm doing it. I'm interested first and foremost in my characters. But the thing is, once I'm into my characters, I'm not going to have them follow any guidelines of social behaviour other than their own. But it's kind of surprising. At the end of the day, *Pulp Fiction* ends up being quite a moralistic film."

"You could even make the case that *Dogs* ultimately ended up being very moralistic. I never intended it to be this way but in some ways my films go by the old Hays Code. You can do anything you want in the first 88 minutes as long as in the last two minutes there's some retribution for what the characters have done. I never set out to do that. I always thought if I wrote a heist film, I'd do one where they all got away. But it didn't quite work out that way."

pulp fiction

Pulp Fiction uses a similar formula to Reservoir Dogs. Genre expectations gave Tarantino a standard bassline, around which he can work his own jarring riffs. But though it's a second film which manages to justify its ambitious scope, Pulp Fiction is nowhere near as relentless, as tightly focused or as effective. It drifts, and though the Tarantino dialogue is brilliant – shot through with profane poetry, unexpected twists (mobsters find themselves arguing over the definition of a miracle and whether a foot massage could be seen as an adulterous act) and pop cultural in-jokes (about TV shows like Happy Days and Kung Fu), there's also a whiff of self-indulgence about it. While he remains as strong as ever on male manners (the dopey bickering banter that goes on between John Travolta and Samuel Jackson, who play the two hitmen at the centre of the film, is beautifully observed), the female characters never really get the space to develop into anything more than clever assemblages of film references.

*Honey Bunny (Amanda Plummer) is about to lose it during the diner hold-up,
until Jules makes her regain her cool by asking "What is Fonzie?"*

Then again, the film is exhilarating and packed with things to admire. There's a great scene in which Travolta and Uma Thurman (as a drug-addled gangster's moll) do the twist in an impossibly overdone Fifties retro restaurant (and call up the ghost of Anna Karina in Jean Luc Godard's Vivre Sa Vie). Once again, Tarantino makes brilliant use of music (mostly early Sixties surfer guitar tunes, a perfect match for the trashy epic visuals). Once again, he coaxes brilliant performances from his actors. Uma Thurman is good and, as a belligerent boxer, Bruce Willis is more watchable than he's been in a long time. The stand-out performances come from Jackson, who starts out just doing his (criminal) job and winds up pondering verses from the Book of Ezekiel as he tries to figure out where he stands in the moral scheme of things, and

Travolta, as his stoned, clumsy companion.

Tarantino has established himself as an actor's director, perhaps because in an era when all many directors want their cast to do is react to special effects, he actually gives them something to do and something to say. He insists that the six years he spent in acting school, even though it didn't pay off in terms of work, have been invaluable for his career. It helped his writing method, which he describes as a kind of improvisation – he sets up his characters, lets them run off at the mouth and tags along taking notes. And it helped when it came to directing actors, which is, he tells his class of Nottingham film students, the most important thing a director has to do.

As he is giving his audience tips on handling actors and the value of rehearsal, it also becomes clear why actors like Tarantino. Not only does he write their kind of lines; he talks their kind of talk. He's full of chat about "finding your own truth, the thing that works for you", describing rehearsal as "a journey, where the idea is you don't know where you're going, you only know when you get there."

But while spouting this stuff about the actors being his collaborators, he's also supplying the students with a series of useful tips on how to control things on set, so that you get what you want. Manipulative is too harsh a term for what he's talking about but there's a determined side to Tarantino. He knows what he wants and he knows how to get it. Hollywood gossip suggests he is a pushy negotiator.

You get flashes of his calculating side in the jokes he makes about career strategy. A reputation as an actor's director is a good thing to have, he suggests, because then even if your films bomb, you might still get work, because the talent will want to work with you. It's a good idea to start out in a sub-genre as he did with *Reservoir Dogs*: "Making the greatest western is a pretty tall order. But if you set out to make the greatest heist movie, you'll probably get in the top fifteen if you make a good one. Making the greatest ever horror movie is going to be hard. But the greatest ever hunchback movie . . ."

Tarantino explains the origin of this single-mindedness when we're talking about how to handle real-life violence. Oddly enough, he claims that, up until the past five years, fighting was a part of his life. "Used to all the time, though not any more." The way to handle a fight, he says, is to look like you won't back down. "That's always been my point of view when dealing with people. If you look like you won't back down, like you'll go all the way, people start asking themselves questions. You know: "This guy will take it all the way. Do I want to take it all the way?'"

It's one o'clock in the morning. Tarantino spent the morning talking to the press about film. Then he spent the afternoon talking to film students about film. Now he's relaxing with friends, but he's still talking about film. For the most part his companions listen to what he has to say. Arguing with him is a difficult proposition. For one thing he talks louder than everybody else. Plus, he seems to have seen more films than everybody else.

So what does make Quentin run? The answer is obvious. It's his passionate obsession with movies. Most profiles of Tarantino dwell on this, on his loveable film geek status. But he's also brash. He is equally often portrayed as a nutty video junkie, someone who loves everything on film – Roger Corman, sexy nun movies, Jean Luc Godard's New Wave experiments, Italian Horror, *film noir*, bad taste splatter FX comedies, blaxploitation, chop socky – as someone who can't make distinctions. This couldn't be further from the truth, he reckons.

"The thing with film geeks is they're into film. They're passionate about it. They're obsessive about it. They dedicate their lives to it. They don't have much to show for all their hours of obsession. However, one thing they do have to show is a highly developed opinion. They can argue with anybody about their favourite films. When they say Tony Scott's *Revenge* was one of the ten best movies of the Eighties, they fucking mean it and they dare you to question it. If you do, they'll go into a whole long thing – this movie reinvents cinema, you know."

This actually puts them in a strange position of power, he continues. "People who work in the film industry are the exact opposite. They have no opinion. They're afraid to have an opinion. Before I got the Good Housekeeping Seal of Approval, people would read my scripts, which don't read like normal scripts, and even if they did like them, they wouldn't say. They'd want to give it to four other people whose opinion they respected to see what they thought of it, and if those people liked it then they would feel confident to say yes, I liked it. It's absolutely shocking."

But for film geeks like him, who know what they want when it comes to film, this represents something of an opportunity. So does he feel like he's got Hollywood licked? In *True Romance*, Clarence, the Tarantino-style pop culture junkie, goes to Hollywood and comes out on top because he can talk faster and knows more about films than anyone else there. Has that turned out to be the case? "Well, yes, but that's nothing to really brag about. Knowing more about movies than a lot of people in Hollywood isn't a big deal."

Tarantino plans to take a year off after the promotional work is done for *Pulp Fiction*, "because it sounds like fun." He may work on a multi-director movie called *Four Rooms*, with fellow young directors Allison Anders, Alexandre Rockwell and Robert Rodriguez. "It's about four rooms in a hotel and what's going on in them. Steve Buscemi [Mr Pink from *Reservoir Dogs*] might play the bell-hop." But for the most part he wants to hang out with friends, screw around and have fun, "you know, just live a normal life."

This, according to some critics, is precisely what he needs to do if he wants to start making films which are about more than just other films. This kind of criticism is the one thing that irritates Tarantino as much as the violence debate. "Everything I write is extremely personal and has to do with whatever is going on with me at that moment. I was experiencing Europe for the first time when I wrote *Pulp Fiction*, thus John Travolta's character has just come back from Europe and that's all he can talk about."

In the end it all comes back to acting, he concludes. "If I was doing Iago on the stage and I was driving to the theatre and hit a dog, it better find its way into my performance that night. It doesn't mean that all of a sudden Othello becomes about a dead dog, but that is definitely going on with me and to deny that would be false. I would not be there. I would be just saying the lines."

"That's the same thing with writing. If I was writing a swashbuckler and I all of a sudden broke up with a girl I was very much in love with, that would have found its way into that swashbuckler. So thus to me my writing feels very personal. It has to be. Otherwise it wouldn't be true."

x offender

by Sean O'Hagan

Quentin Tarantino is recounting one of the problems he has faced in his meteoric rise to Hollywood super-brat status. "Tristar were originally gonna distribute *Pulp Fiction*," he says, spreading his gangly torso over a plush hotel-room sofa, "but they had big problems with the scene where John Travolta's character shoots up heroin. I'm going, 'Look, guys, relax, it's going to be funny', and they're saying, 'No, Quentin, heroin is not funny. A guy sticking a needle in his arm does not make for big laughs.' In the end I just said, 'You're gonna have to trust me on this one, guys.' They didn't. I guess they just couldn't make the leap."

Tarantino is a film-maker who specialises in 'making the leap.' Scenes like the one described above, where humour and horror coalesce, make for compulsive, if uneasy, viewing, but they have placed Tarantino at the forefront of a new kind of cinema where the staple plots and characters of the *film-noir* thriller are given a distinctly Nineties twist. In his short but dramatic directorial career, Tarantino has stretched the parameters of popular film more than anyone since Sergio Leone, whose 'Spaghetti Western' *oeuvre* he has studied closely. "I like the idea that I'm taking a genre that already exists and reinventing it, like Leone re-invented the whole Western genre," he elaborates, before adding, with his customary self-confidence: "I think I've taken on an established genre like the pulp thriller and made it challenging to myself and to my audience."

To this end, he has already succeeded in creating a contemporary generic hybrid which could crudely be termed the arthouse-action movie. In the process, he has also established himself, at the age of 31, as one of contemporary cinema's supreme stylists as well as the current crown prince of controversy.

If Tarantino specialises in conjuring up a hard, brutal world of the imagination, in the flesh he is charming to a fault. He is also effusive – about films, film-makers and actors, mainly – in a distinctly trainspotterish way. One can see why he had problems at school. He has a gangling, awkward charm and an unselfconscious enthusiasm that is almost nerdish in aspect. Then there's his strange, drawling West Coast diction and the way he bounces forward and gesticulates wildly when he becomes excited about his subject matter.

His first film, *Reservoir Dogs*, was a low-budget, high-profile debut. It was shot entirely – give or take a few flashbacks – in a grim concrete warehouse, in which a bunch of bedraggled and squabbling crooks try to figure out what went wrong after a botched heist. If the basic idea was a simple one, the execution was anything but: the film's intricate structure, surreal dialogue and cast of low-life characters – each called after a colour and decked out in matching black two-piece suits – have made it one of the biggest cult movies of the Nineties. (The late Kurt Cobain even credited Tarantino on the sleeve of Nirvana's *In Utero* album.) The violence helped, too. It is one of the few acclaimed films to have been refused a video licence in Britain. "I like that," says the director. "It's done better in cinemas in Britain than anywhere else in the world, so the ban has been kinda cool in one way."

Reservoir Dogs is probably the first film in which one of the leading characters spends the entire movie slowly and noisily bleeding to death. Then there's the now infamous "ear-slicing scene" in which a suitably chilling Michael Madsen performs some brutal psycho-surgery on a captured cop while miming and dancing along to Stealer's Wheel's once innocuous pop song 'Stuck In The Middle With You'. It has already become one of the key images of Nineties cinema and, more than any other scene, exemplifies Tarantino's talent for surreal, often disturbing, juxtapositions.

If *Reservoir Dogs* signalled the arrival of a formal iconoclast with a warped sense of humour, *Pulp Fiction* announces the presence of a singular, and singularly precocious, major-league talent. Over two-and-a-half hours and three separate but intertwining stories, Tarantino constructs a contemporary *film noir* that is, by turns, hilarious, surreal and shocking. And, like before, the formal and narrative subversion goes hand-in-fist with some resolutely hard-core imagery. The tone is set early on when Vincent and Jules, a pair of murderously funny hired killers, played by Travolta and Samuel Jackson, debate the erotic possibilities of a foot massage before beginning a particularly brutal hit. Later their boss, Marsellus, is bound, gagged and anally assaulted by a redneck cop. (All this in a film released through the Disney offshoot, Buena Vista. Walt is no doubt turning in his grave.)

Then there's the drug-taking. Travolta's shooting-up scene comes early in the film, kick-starting a surreal, chemically laced episode that culminates with Uma Thurman's character, Mia, overdosing on heroin that she mistakes for cocaine. When Tarantino shifts gear from romance to terror, he is in a contemporary class of his own. The scene's denouement is not for the fainthearted, but its evocation of utter panic combined with drug-addled farce make it the most visceral moment in the film.

"That's my very favourite scene in the movie," Tarantino elaborates with an eagerness that suggests he is still utterly enthralled by the myriad possibilities of his chosen form. "One of the things I love most about film-making is that you can make a left turn in the narrative and suddenly you're in a whole new movie. A comedy can turn into a nightmare in one scene and the audience are going, 'Holy shit, man, what's happenin'?' And a lot of the time the characters are feeling the same. That kinda cracks me up."

I ask him if he's ready for the inevitable accusations that he's glamorising hard-drug use. "I don't buy this whole idea that if you show someone shooting up, you're pro-heroin. That's as silly to me as the arguments I had the last time around about glamorising violence. I've said it before: violence in real life is terrible, violence in the movies can be cool. It's just another colour to work with. Now, the whole reason that the OD scene is harrowing and horrific is because I'm showing you what happens after all the thrills and spills. And, yes, there is humour lurking in even the most extreme situations. That's just a fact of life."

Nevertheless, I insist, he is portraying coldblooded killers – one of whom is a connoisseur of heroin – as sympathetic characters. And, his critics would argue, glamorising brutality by the gratuitous use of graphic violence. "I gotta say I can't agree. Surprise, surprise," he laughs. "What knocks me out is when people say to me, 'Oh Travolta is so sweet, so loveable', and I'm thinking to myself 'What?' I mean, he starts off the film by blowing these guys away and not giving a damn."

Perhaps, I suggest, that's the whole point: his films blur the moral focus so much that people leave the cinema sympathising with killers and creeps and remembering the ultra-violence because it's so stylishly delivered. For the first time in the interview, Tarantino looks offended. "I happen to think my films are very moral," he says, after another uncharacteristic pause. "I don't necessarily try to make them as such, but they kinda end up that way. I mean, Samuel Jackson's character, Jules, has that big closing scene where he is altered and decides to give up the gangster life. His whole redemption is set up throughout the film, brick by brick, via a series of close shaves and narrow misses. I mean, *Pulp Fiction* is ultimately a film about forgiveness and mercy, albeit in a hard and brutal world."

Honey Bunny and Pumpkin (Tim Roth) in the diner scene which, frozen in time, both begins and ends Pulp Fiction.

During a discussion of the crime-fiction 'pulp' genre that inspired his latest film, I tell him that T. S. Eliot rated Raymond Chandler as one of America's greatest novelists. "Oh gosh, that's soooo cool," he says, thrilled in a way that only Californians can be. Then, without pause, he's off on a Chandler snippet of his own. "Pauline Kael said Chandler was an illiterate's idea of great writing. I don't agree, but I can see where she's coming from. Chandler could describe a police line-up better than anybody, but, you know, so what?"

Born and raised in the South Bay area of Los Angeles, which he describes as "a wharf community near the airport", Tarantino was steeped in film culture from an early age. As an impressionable prepubescent, he had already seen, with his mother's blessing, films like Sam Peckinpah's *The Wild Bunch* and John Boorman's *Deliverance*, which may go some way to explaining the violence that runs through his own work like a coda. Later, his in-depth knowledge landed him a job in Video Archives on Manhattan Beach, where the staff's preference for the likes of Truffaut, Godard and Pasolini took precedence over the more mainstream tastes of most of their customers.

Tarantino's personal taste is, to say the least, eclectic, an in-depth knowledge of European arthouse cinema co-existing in his over-crowded cranium with all manner of weird minutiae from post-Fifties pop culture. Like John Waters or David Lynch, he is a connoisseur of the trash aesthetic. *Pulp Fiction*, although set in the present day, resounds with references from previous decades, from Dick Dale's Sixties surf music to the Fifties-style diner staffed by Hollywood lookalikes serving Douglas Sirk burgers and Dean Martin milkshakes. Then there's Jules, whose speech is peppered with words like exactimundo (gleaned from his Seventies TV hero the Fonz) and whose dream is to "walk the Earth – like Caine in *Kung Fu*".

This pop-culture worldview and an obsessive's devotion to film history informs Tarantino's work to a degree that has caused problems for some of his critics. *True Romance*, which he wrote and gave to Tony Scott, is self-referential to an absurd degree, while *Pulp Fiction* divided film critics, many of whom thought it was too mannered to deserve this year's Palme D'Or at Cannes. His friend and fellow film-maker Roger Avary – whose debut, *Killing Zoe*, was produced by Tarantino – told *Vanity Fair*: "The one problem people have with Quentin's work is that it speaks of other movies, instead of life. The big trick is to live a life, and then make movies about that life."

I put it to Tarantino that maybe his films have an unreal quality and his characters, particularly the bad guys, an almost cartoonish aspect because he is imagining a world of which he has no first-hand experience. "Well, yes and no" he responds, unruffled. "I mean, Richard Burton didn't have to be a Welsh coal miner in order to play a Welsh coal miner. He drew on various elements: observation, imagination, the books he read and the films he watched. So, personal experience is only one element in a greater whole."

What is interesting here is that he compares himself not to another director, but to an actor. For a long time, while his first script languished in the reject trays of various Hollywood studios, Tarantino persevered with a spectacularly unsuccessful acting career. (He turned up on a recent episode of *The Golden Girls* as a rather unlikely Elvis impersonator.) It is unsurprising, then, that he appears in cameo in both of his films. The experience also informs his working methods, which, given that he has had no formal training as a director, are more instinctive than most of his contemporaries. He is probably the only director working today who refuses to use an on-set video monitor to check takes. This is not just another measure of his seemingly unshakeable self-belief, but an understanding, gleaned from his acting days, that the day-to-day business of film-making has an energy that is diluted when a director spends too much time heeding a monitor rather than his actors. "Because it's the only area I'm formally trained in, I can talk to actors in their language about their sort of problems," he says. "I understand the whole process because I've been through it."

This also explains his painstaking approach to casting. "I talked to damn near every actress in Hollywood about the Mia role, with the idea that when I met Mia, I'd know it. Uma came to dinner and I knew within minutes that she was Mia."

His choice of leading men, too, has been maverick and inspired. *Reservoir Dogs* helped to resuscitate the career of Harvey Keitel, whose profile had declined dramatically after the Seventies. He has since gone on to star in *The Piano* and to appear in *Pulp Fiction*. So, too, does Bruce Willis – who thought Tarantino's script was "like Shakespeare" and whose fee for *Die Hard 2*, according to *Vanity Fair*, "was as much as the whole budget of *Pulp Fiction*." Like almost everyone else, he is upstaged by the chillingly believable Samuel Jackson – and his partner in crime, John Travolta – another overlooked actor whom Tarantino admires.

If any film can exorcise the ghosts of *Grease* and *Saturday Night Fever* for Travolta, it will be this one – although Tarantino does make him dance the twist in one scene (which, the director insists, was written before the part was cast; originally Michael Madsen was offered the role). With hair extensions and a *Reservoir Dogs* suit, Travolta plays Vincent Vega with a sleazy cool that totally vindicates Tarantino's faith in him. "John and Sam Jackson were so electric together," the director says, "that I actually considered making a whole bunch of Vincent and Jules movies, kind of like *The Continuing Adventures of . . .*"

Having hardly stretched himself in his last major role a few years back, in the less than engaging kiddy comedy *Look Who's Talking*, Travolta's career prospects were looking less than promising pre-*Pulp Fiction*. He has since been offered five million dollars to play the lead in Barry "*Addams Family*" Sonnenfeld's imminent Elmore Leonard adaptation *Get Shorty*. "He is," Tarantino states matter-of-factly, "one of the very best American film actors around. He was awesome in De Palma's *Blow Out*. I used to watch that film over and over and wonder why other directors weren't using him."

Blow Out is one of Tarantino's three favourite films, alongside Howard Hawks's *Rio Bravo* and Martin Scorsese's *Taxi Driver*. Of the three, Scorsese's dark urban fable is perhaps the most obvious influence on his own work, a fact that both flatters and annoys him. "I make a point of not talking about Scorsese any more because everyone else does when they talk about me." I ask him if he can see why. "I guess so. I think it's unfair, but I understand it completely. I mean, here's the deal: Scorsese deals in the gangster genre; so do I. Scorsese makes violent films; so do I. Scorsese moves the camera around a lot; so do I. Scorsese uses Harvey Keitel, I use Harvey Keitel. Scorsese is a big film buff, I'm a big film buff. I mean, so what? One guy even said, you use the f-word a lot: did you take that from Scorsese? Occasionally, they'll make a good critical analogy but mostly it's all too pat and easy. What matters is that the end result is so different."

This, of course, is true. It would be difficult to imagine a Tarantino film that touched on Scorsese's psycho-spiritual – read Catholic – terrain. Guilt and sin, thus far at least, are not part of the Tarantino palette. Instead, he has managed to create a celluloid world that is both new and emphatically *now*, but also strangely familiar – mostly from other, older films. We have seen these characters before but not talking like this. (At one point, Jules, whose jheri-curled hairdo places him in the blaxploitation era of films like *Shaft*, says to Vincent: "Let's get in character," just before they interrogate and kill a few petty hoodlums. Here, even the slaughter is laced with irony.)

"I wanted to subvert the Hollywood staples, but with respect, not in a superior pastichey way," Tarantino says. "If you take a film like *The Shining*, I always felt that Kubrick felt he was above the horror genre, above giving the audience a real good scare. Now Godard, I always thought, was at his most engaging when he worked with a genre and ran with it the whole way to the moon. *Breathless* is a good example. Jean Pierre Melville did it with the thriller genre, subverting it but with respect. I mean, a cinephile can watch these films and theorise about them but a regular guy who wants to see a good movie can get into this too. The thing is to tell a good story. My structures might be complex, but I tell very simple stories."

It is, however, the way he tells those stories that has placed Tarantino at the cutting edge of contemporary cinema. His use of dialogue structure make Tarantino one of the most novel directors currently directing in Hollywood. (One of his few heroes from outside film culture is J. D. Salinger.) "When you read a good novel," he says, when I ask him why his films have such intricate and non-linear structures, "and it starts in the middle of story, then jumps back in time, you don't think it's any big deal. It's all part of an unfolding narrative. I'm not against a linear structure, it's just that it's not the only game in town."

From start to finish, too, Tarantino keeps almost total control of his vision, scripting, casting, directing and giving out detailed instructions to everyone from his editor and cinematographer to his costume designer and art directors. Since becoming successful, two of his screenplays have been turned into controversial films by other directors: *True Romance* by Tony Scott and *Natural Born Killers* by Oliver Stone. He thought the first film was "wonderful" but had his screenplay credit removed from the second before the film even went into production. "I've never seen the film. That was just from reading the first half of the script. I mean, I really didn't want anyone to think I'd written some of the stuff that was in there!" He has no interest at present in directing other people's scripts. "That would be kinda scary," he says. "I'd probably want to rewrite it so much that the work I'd invest in it would be better spent on an original script. I have a lot of things that I want to do and I want to do them my way."

And doing things his way, of course, is what has made Quentin Tarantino's name. "I guess I do look at things differently," he says. "I don't think my films are hard to follow. The only thing that's required is that you have to commit to watching them, you have to engage with them totally. I don't make films for the casual viewer." How would he like to be remembered? "As a good storyteller. That's the bottom line. Ultimately, all I'm trying to do is merge sophisticated storytelling with lurid subject matter. I reckon," he says, grinning in the face of posterity, "that makes for an entertaining night at the movies."

quentin tarantino on pulp fiction

as told to Manohla Dargis

I'm going to do a Monte Hellman, do two films back to back, do two three or four-million dollar movies. Shoot one for five weeks, take a week off, and then start the next one, just keep the crew. Then give one to my editor and I'll edit the other one. After *Pulp Fiction* I was going to do a small film and then I was going to try and do a big movie. That was the game plan for my first four movies, but *Pulp Fiction* was such an undertaking it seemed a waste of time to do just one small movie next. I had a lot of fun floating back and forth between the different stories, and felt I could handle more.

I've always been romanced by the idea of Roger Corman going out there and shooting two movies on location, or Monte just pulling it off, as well as anyone has ever done in the history of cinema, with *The Shooting* and *Ride In The Whirlwind*. When I finished *Pulp* I felt my crew and I were so together we could have made another movie if we'd had one ready to go, we were in such a groove.

Pulp Fiction was going to be my goodbye to the crime genre, at least for a while. It's a get-it-out-of-your-system movie, three movies for the price of one. What I wanted to do afterwards is work in other genres, all kinds. I would like to do a musical some time. I'm thinking about doing a movie that would be very personal, about something that happened to me, but again I'd break it down to genre, like a *La Regle Du Jeu-Shampoo* kind of thing. And that's not *The Player* kind of talk, that's just me.

I was going to do other sorts of movies, then revisit the crime genre from time to time. I don't want to be the gun guy. I think I would become really boring if I was just known as the guy who did gangster movies. At the same time, fuck it, if it's what you really want to do . . . It's a little debate I'm having with myself because *Pulp* was designed to be the goodbye.

To me John Cassavetes' movies are a genre, he's a genre in and of himself. Merchant-Ivory are as strict a genre as you're ever going to find, they're stricter than a women-in-prison movie. I love the idea of going into a genre and taking all the familiars we like and giving them back to you in new ways. Say *The Guns of Navarone* had never been made and I read Alistair Maclean's book and wanted to do it. I'd want to deliver all the thrills and the spills, the pleasure and the fun, except that those guys would talk like my guys. They wouldn't be stock characters, they would be human beings with a heartbeat who would talk about things other than just blowing up the cannons. I want to set up a situation you've seen a zillion times before and then throw in real-life kicking and screaming so that it fucks up everybody's plans. Not just come up with a higher mountain these guys have to climb, or throw in a rainstorm or a troop of Nazis, but real-life holes they can fall into.

The Set-Up

Everything in Los Angeles revolves around restaurants. You get together with your friends at restaurants, you have dates at restaurants, business meetings at restaurants. In many other cities you have to be of a certain wealth to go to restaurants, but in Los Angeles we have coffee shops that are open all night long. So you can not have a pot to piss in and still afford to go to a coffee shop and hang out. My friends and I would go to coffee shops late at night and be there for hours, like our version of hanging out in a Parisian café and discussing existentialism, except we were talking about New World Pictures and whether we were ever going to be with a woman.

Costume

When Jean-Pierre Melville was making his crime films, he talked about how it was very important that his characters have a suit of armour. His was the snap-brim fedora and Bogart-like trenchcoat. Leone had the duster, Eastwood the poncho. I've always said the mark of any good action film is that when you get through seeing it, you want to dress like the character. That's totally the case, for instance, with Chow Yun-Fat's wardrobe in the *A Better Tomorrow* movies. The black suits in *Pulp Fiction*, that's my suit of armour. Guys look cool in black suits, but what's interesting is how they get reconstructed during the course of the movie. When you first see Vincent and Jules, their suits are cut and crisp, they look like real bad-asses. But as the movie goes on, their suits get more and more fucked up until they're stripped off and the two are dressed in the exact antithesis – volleyball wear, which is not cool. As to Sam Jackson's jheri-curls, that happened by mistake. I've always like Afros – if I were black, I'd wear an Afro. I talked to Sam about wearing an Afro and he was up for that. The make-up woman went out to get some Afro wigs, but because she didn't know the difference she also showed up with the jheri-curl wig. Sam put it on, and it was great. It was Jules.

Jackrabbit Slim's

Every big city has a couple of them, these Fifties retro restaurants. I don't like them that much, to me they are always trying too hard. In fact, the script even says, "Either the best or the worst of these places, depending on your point of view." This one is a cross between the Fifties restaurants that exist, the nightclub where Elvis Presley and the car racers hang out in *Speedway*, and the bar where all the racecar drivers hang out in Howard Hawks' *Red Line 7000*. The thing that makes it work is the racing-car motif. The dancefloor is done like a speedometer, and I threw in little things, as if I were running a restaurant. Most of the posters are not just from any old Fifties movies, they're directed by Roger Corman. And if I were going to have Fifties icons on the menu, there would be a Douglas Sirk Steak. I wouldn't let them rent out a real Fifties restaurant, I wanted to do it from scratch. But when you have a set that great, you're almost intimidated by it. Oh, my God, how do I make it live? What I tried to do is introduce it through Vincent's eyes as he walks through. But the scene ain't about the restaurant, so after I get through taking it all in, just forget it. Show it off and then, fuck it.

Vincent (John Travolta) gives Mia (Uma Thurman) the time of her life at Jackrabbit Slim's.

Dancing

I always love the musical sequences in movies, and I particularly love them when the movies aren't musicals. My favourite musical sequences have always been in Godard, because they just come out of nowhere. It's so infectious, so friendly. And the fact that it's not a musical, and he's stopping the movie to have a musical sequence, makes it all the more sweet. The last movie I saw that did something like that was Christopher Munch's *The Hours And Times*, where all of a sudden Lennon puts on the Little Richard 45 and starts dancing. Whenever I'd see those scenes in a Godard movie, it made me wish I had a rewind facility in the cinema. Sometimes they almost ruin the movie, because you love them so much, you want to go over it again and again. In *Le Petit Soldat*, when she's doing the interview, taking her pictures, and all of a sudden she puts on some classical music and dances around the room. When she takes the music off, you're like, "Oh, it's over." I learned that for this film, don't let it linger.

The Gold Watch

In Roger Avary's original story, the fact that Butch had a gold watch came out of nowhere. Roger spent all this time trying to sell us on why Butch had to go back into danger, and he did a really good job, but he didn't quite sell it. I thought, well, it's a contrivance, and what you do with a plot contrivance is feature it. At that point in the movie, you're disorientated because the first story has ended. And then you have Christopher Walken doing this whole long thing about the watch, and then there's the title card, 'The Gold Watch', and then there's the boxer, and you're wondering, "What the fuck did that have to do with anything?" And then you get in that motel room and you're there forever. You've forgotten that gold watch and Walken. And then Butch says, "Where's my gold watch?" You can write a three-page monologue and good luck on having someone deliver it perfectly. Chris Walken is one of those actors who can and rarely gets the opportunity to do so. I called him up and said, "Chris, I have a three-page monologue for you and I promise I won't cut a word." We planned to do it on the last day of shooting: when he came in I told him he had all day, we're not going to leave until we get it right. And we did.

As Captain Koons, Christopher Walken delivers his second piece of celebrated Tarantino dialogue, having previously played Coccotti in True Romance.

Drugs

Lance is a totally L.A. type, he's your friendly drug-dealer. Margaret Cho did a hysterical stand-up routine about the problem with going out and buying drugs: you have to feign a relationship with your drug-dealer, like you're not going over to buy pot, you're going on a social visit and drugs are incidental. You have to sit down and talk about things, as opposed to here's the money, give me my shit, let me get out of here.

Mia doesn't do too well by drugs. One journalist told me I could show that whole first scene of her overdose to schoolkids as an anti-drug movie. People ask me where I came up with the story about the overdose: the bottom line is that every junkie, or person who has experimented seriously with heroin, has a version of that story – they almost died, someone else almost died and they brought them back with salt water, or put them in a tub, or jumped them with a car battery. What's interesting is that the scene is very harrowing and very funny at the same time, and that the harrowing aspect and the funny aspect are both coming from the same place, it's the reality of it that is both totally freaky and totally funny.

Lighting

I'm really anal when it comes to the framing, but my cinematographer Andrzej Sekula handles the lighting, that's where he gets to paint. We shoot on 50 ASA film stock, which is the slowest stock they make. The reason we use it is that it creates an almost no-grain image, it's lustrous. It's the closest thing we have to Fifties Technicolor. When I first met Andrzej on *Reservoir Dogs*, I only knew that I wanted it to pop, I wanted the reds to be red and the blacks to be black. It looks great, but it's a pain in the ass to shoot with, you need light coming in from everywhere just to get an image. But because of the way I write my scenes, once you get somewhere, you're there for a while. So we bathe the place in light, create a lot of texture and play around with the depth of field, which is something you normally don't have, particularly when you're shooting with anamorphic lenses. We carry people in the background and foreground as much as I've ever seen in a film with anamorphic lenses. When we looked at dailies, I felt we were pushing the envelope.

Gore

Every time you try and show gore realistically, it looks absurd, operatic. People go on about Tim Roth bleeding to death in *Reservoir Dogs*, but that's the reality. If someone is shot in the stomach, that's how they die. Put them in one spot in a room and they're going to have a pool growing around them. That might look crazy, but it's the truth and it's because you're not used to seeing the truth that it looks pushed. There was a line in *Pulp Fiction* with Jules and Jimmie talking that we didn't shoot. Jimmie asks what the fuck happened to the car and Jules answers: "Jimmie, if you were inside of a car, and you were to shoot a water melon at point-blank range with a nine millimetre, do you know what would happen?" "No, what?" "You'd get water melon all over!" To me, even though it's got a foot in real life, it also has a foot in *Monty Python*. It's funny. It's about appearance: we've got to clean up the car, we've got to clean us up, we've got to get the shit out of his house so Jimmie doesn't appear to be a criminal when his wife comes home. The idea is to take genre characters and put them in real-life situations and make them live by real-life rules. In normal movies, they're too busy telling the plot to have guns go off accidentally and kill someone we don't give a damn about. But it happens, so we go down that track. And it's not just some little hole in the chest, it's a messy wound they've got to deal with, and it's a big problem. The humour to me comes from this realistic situation, and then in waltzes this complete movie creation, the Wolf – Harvey Keitel. This movie star walks in, sprinkles some movie dust, and solves the problem.

quentin tarantino's pulp fantastic

by Geoffrey O'Brien

The two dictionary definitions of "pulp" which Quentin Tarantino posts at the beginning of *Pulp Fiction* both have a direct bearing on what follows. The first, "a soft, moist, shapeless mass of matter", recalling as it does the phrase "beaten to a pulp", invokes from the outset those catastrophes of the flesh which are never far away at any moment in the film's two-and-a-half-hour running time.

Physical risk, the possibility of being damaged severely (perhaps irrevocably) by gun, fist, sword, chain, or hypodermic needle, by falling off a roof or crashing a car: these are not so much plot elements as the medium in which *Pulp Fiction's* inhabitants draw their breath, the background – so omnipresent as to be taken for granted – against which they pursue their endless jags of more or less amiable small talk. This first definition serves almost as a warning of some of the material dangers that await, an appropriate gesture for a movie that ultimately gets comic mileage out of the removal of bits of the brain and bone, remnants of an exploded head, from the back seat of a car.

Through all the blood and injured body parts, Tarantino suggests that everything is going to be all right, even if he says it somewhat in the manner of a hold-up man pointing a gun at someone's head. That trope – the man of violence as the voice of reason urging calm – becomes literal in the final sequence, in which the principle of "nobody move, nobody gets hurt" is carried to its logical extreme in a tableau-like-stand-off, with a gun aimed at every head, that out-Woos John Woo himself. "What is Fonzie?" asks the gunman (Sam Jackson) of Amanda Plummer, who is dangerously close to a lethal tantrum, in order to break her concentration by eliciting the rote response: cool. Fonzie was cool.

They are all cool: Tarantino may set up a demonic universe, but not for him are the demonic emotions that might be expected to suffuse it. There are two states of being, fear when danger threatens, affectless relaxation at other times: more or less the contrast between adrenaline and heroin (both of which play a role in the movie's most indelible sequence, Uma Thurman's overdose and its comic-horrific aftermath). The old-time *noir* passions, the brooding melancholy and operatic death scenes, would be altogether out of place in the crisp and brightly-lit wonderland that Tarantino conjures up. Neither neo-*noir* nor a parody of *noir*, *Pulp Fiction* is more a guided tour of an infernal theme park decorated with cultural detritus, Buddy Holly and Mamie Van Doren, fragments of blaxploitation and Roger Corman and *Shogun Assassin*, music out of a 24-hour oldies station for which all the decades since the Fifties exist simultaneously.

The second definition – "a publication, such as a magazine or book, containing lurid subject matter" – appears to announce some kind of homage or pastiche, and Tarantino has remarked that his original intention was "to do a *Black Mask* movie – like that old detective story magazine". But, as he acknowledges, "it kind of went somewhere else." Each of the movie's curiously linked episodes, in fact, kind of goes somewhere else. If *Reservoir Dogs* could to a certain degree be seen as a reshuffling of previously existing movie bits*, Pulp Fiction* enlists its recognisable elements in a superstructure of considerable originality: the order of difference between the two is roughly that between *Once Upon A Time In The West* and *A Fistful Of Dollars*.

The end result is indeed far from the hardboiled detective stories of Dashiell Hammett, Raymond Chandler, or Paul Cain (the stars of *Black Mask's* line-up). It does however connect rather powerfully to a parallel pulp tradition, the tales of terror and the uncanny practised by such writers as Cornell Woolrich, Frederic Brown, Robert Bloch, Charles Beaumont, and Richard Matheson, with their diabolical tricks of fate and wrenching twist endings, a tradition that led (via Beaumont and Matheson) into the cheap but enduring thrills of *The Twilight Zone* (whose theme music as interpreted by the Marketts is very aptly interpolated into *Pulp Fiction's* time-warp soundtrack alongside Link Wray, Dick Dale, Al Green and Dusty Springfield).

Cornell Woolrich and Frederic Brown were writers who mined the grey zone between supernatural or (in Brown's case) extra-terrestrial horror on the one hand and criminal violence and madness on the other: Woolrich with the humourless intensity of the true paranoid, Brown with a sort of spaced-out whimsy that might have sprung from the brain of an alcoholic reporter steeped in chess and Lewis Carroll. Both dealt heavily in the realm of improbable coincidences and cruel cosmic jokes, a realm which *Pulp Fiction* makes its own.

Just how deeply Woolrich's I-can't-believe-this-is-happening-to-me vision has permeated *noir* mythology is evident from a partial list of films based on his work, including *Rear Window, The Leopard Man*, *The Bride Wore Black*, *Mississippi Mermaid*, *The Night Has A Thousand Eyes*, *Phantom Lady*, *I Married A Shadow*, and Maxwell Shane's poetic quickie, *Fear In The Night* (1947). Brown's work has not been so fortunate – only Gerd Oswald's inimitably sleazy Anita Ekberg vehicle, *Screaming Mimi*, springs to mind – but the diabolically engineered plot twists of his novels *The Far Cry* (1951), *The Wench Is Dead* (1955), *The Murderers* (1961), and his masterpiece, *Knock Three-One-Two* (1951), show a clear affinity with the criss-crossing and recursive narrative lines in *Pulp Fiction*.

Tarantino does not exactly dabble in the supernatural, but he bends space and time in ingenious ways and goes so far as to broach the possibility of divine intervention. Horror movies provide a constant reference point – Uma Thurman's eleventh-hour resurrection might have been lifted from *The Evil Dead*, and the sadists into whose clutches Bruce Willis falls have in their arsenal a chainsaw that would have done Tobe Hooper proud. In any event, we are clued early on that we have entered a fantastic world when – in a visual gimmick worthy of Frank Tashlin – the hand gesture by which Uma Thurman signs the squareness she hopes John Travolta will avoid is transformed momentarily into a glittering rectangle.

Pumpkin trains his gun on the diner chef, before Jules calms him down by showing a mysterious glowing briefcase like the 'Pandora's box' in Kiss Me, Deadly *(1955).*

The twist endings of Woolrich and Brown tended to have the effect of a trap snapping shut: the door slams and there's no way out, the nightmare turns out to be real, the hope of rescue is revealed as an optical illusion. The irony of Tarantino's creation is that its twist endings are all upbeat, in each case re-routing a descent into living hell toward an unexpectedly happy ending. If *Pulp Fiction* is not quite "the feel-good movie of the year", it nonetheless imparts a kind of sweet relief, the relief a hostage might feel at being permitted to live another day.

The comedy – and for most of its length the movie consists of little but comedy – is charged with the sense that "it didn't hurt as much as I thought it would," or alternatively, "we've still got time to joke around before it starts hurting". It's the banter of two hit men killing time between hits with a free-floating dialogue involving Samoans, foot massage, and the French term for "quarterpounder-with-cheese."

Tarantino's vein of chat is steeped in all the speech that came before, in the words of Jim Thompson's schizoid con artists, Charles Willeford's blandly reassuring sociopaths, the laconic schemers in the Parker novels of Richard Stark (aka Donald Westlake), David Mamet's hustlers, in the poker-faced give-and-take of Budd Boetticher's Randolph Scott westerns and Don Siegel movies like *The Line-Up* and *The Killers*, and above all in the free associating riffs in Elmore Leonard's assorted misfits and bandits, the variously wily and demented thieves and assassins who populate *Fifty-Two Pickup*, *Swag*, *The Switch*, or *City Primeval*.

Like Leonard, Tarantino works by ear, letting the narrative shape itself around speech rhythms, as if there were all the time in the world for the circular, repetitive exchanges to play themselves out, as if the flow of talk could by itself keep annihilation at bay. Or, as John Travolta interjects with exquisitely modulated moments, words prove more effective than hardware, from the rapid deal that Bruce Willis cuts with a gangster he has rescued to Sam Jackson's protracted monologue during the final hold-up.

It becomes music, the music of storytelling which was what pulp fiction was always about in the first place. From Hammett to Woolrich, from Frederic Brown to Elmore Leonard, the old hands worked to set lengths and obligatory climaxes, with the plot twists falling into place as emphatically as background music scored by Miklos Rozsa or Alex North. Tarantino has absorbed all that but takes it into a new moment in which different constraints operate, where space feels more wide open and pay-offs are less assured. But it's still just as dangerous: it's always dangerous out there.

the next best thing to a time machine

by Peter N. Chumo II

A lover of movies since childhood and the most famous former videostore clerk in America, Quentin Tarantino has displayed an almost encyclopaedic knowledge of movies and popular culture from a variety of eras and genres. As Richard Corliss points out, Tarantino has led "a movie-mad life . . . He seems to have remembered – and understood – everything he's seen." *Pulp Fiction* (1994), for example, is filled with allusions to popular culture, from references in the dialogue (Fonzie from TV's *Happy Days*, Madonna's 'Lucky Star' video) to the films Tarantino himself draws upon for inspiration (a pre-title sequence that ends in a freeze-frame reminiscent of the opening of Sam Peckinpah's *The Wild Bunch* [1969], a mysterious briefcase out of Robert Aldrich's *Kiss Me Deadly* [1955]).

Tarantino even sees the use of whole plots as a jumping-off point – not a constraint on his creativity – in the very construction of *Pulp Fiction*:

The thing that was cool about it is that what I wanted to do with the three stories was to start with the oldest chestnuts in the world. You've seen them a zillion times. You don't need to be caught up with the story because you already know it. The guy takes out the mob guy's wife – "but don't touch her." And what happens if they touch? You've seen that triangle a zillion times. Or the boxer who's supposed to throw the fight and doesn't – you've seen that a zillion times too ("Quentin Tarantino on *Pulp Fiction*").

Each of the stories, however, takes odd, unexpected turns so that the "oldest chestnuts" are recycled into something new. The date with the mob boss's wife ends with a life-and-death emergency, and the boxer's story is less about the fight itself than the aftermath. Even the film's scrambled chronology gives the old stories a fresh context. Tarantino, then, does not simply copy old plots but changes their elements and form to give them new lives.

While the depth of his filmic knowledge is evident throughout *Pulp Fiction*, Tarantino's use of movie references goes beyond a simple post-modern recycling of old movie bits and generic plot lines to a thoughtful look at how such relics of the filmic past can come alive in the present. In this way, Tarantino is constantly waging a battle with time – while he loves to draw on the past, he nevertheless must strive to make his film live in the present so that it does not become a mere collection of witty filmic allusions.[1]

pulp fiction

Within *Pulp Fiction*'s three narratives, Tarantino's characters enact conflicts that mirror his own. Vincent's revival of Mia, Butch's retrieval of his family wristwatch and later rescue of Marsellus, and especially Vincent and Jules's clean-up of the bloodied car are all essentially battles against time and more specifically emergencies that require the characters to live fully in the present moment. Moreover, just as Tarantino recycles the past to create the present, recycling is thematized within the film itself. Not only does each of the three stories include a place where recycling occurs (Jack Rabbit Slim's, the pawn shop, Monster Joe's Truck and Tow), but, more importantly, those characters who can recycle old genre elements can successfully break out of their one-dimensional roles (Butch as a washed-up boxer, Jules as a hit man). Vincent, on the other hand, lacks the directorial control of the other characters: while he can be recycled by Tarantino for the nostalgic value attached to John Travolta as a celebrity icon, he ultimately finds himself discarded (killed off by a better recycler).

Mia Wallace in the 1950s never-neverland of Jackrabbit Slim's, exuding a fatal mix of sexuality and naivety.

The film's prologue sets up the themes Tarantino will follow throughout the film. Two small-time criminals, Pumpkin (Tim Roth) and Honey Bunny (Amanda Plummer), sit in a coffee shop and talk about their future. They discuss the robbery of banks and liquor stores (really a mini-history of crime in film from old gangster movies to the present) and decide to do something new – rob a restaurant (since no one ever robs restaurants and everyone will be taken by surprise). In microcosm, Tarantino is announcing his plan to us – you have seen the standard crimes many times, he seems to be telling us at the start, but, like the petty crooks who begin their robbery of the diner (and are frozen only to be revisited later), he is going to do something different within an established tradition.

Throughout the scene, moreover, a contrast is set up between the past and the future. When Pumpkin declares he is through robbing liquor stores and Honey Bunny reminds him he always forgets such plans the next day, Pumpkin tells her, "The days of me forgettin' are over, and the days of me rememberin' have just begun" – a fitting epigraph for the film itself, in which Tarantino will remember old movie plots, Hollywood's past, John Travolta's era of super-stardom, and even Tarantino's own rise as a movie director. Most importantly, the freeze-frame that stops the robbery just as it begins is a way for the film director to control time, to stop it and hold the scene in suspension until the film's end. Pumpkin thinks he controls his future, but Tarantino shows us that he, Pumpkin's creator and director, is really controlling him, just as, at the film's end, Jules will take on the role of surrogate director and control Pumpkin's fate.

Nostalgia, Pop Culture, and the Renewal of Celebrity
In the first story, "Vincent Vega and Marsellus Wallace's Wife", small-time hit man Vincent (John Travolta) escorts his boss's wife Mia (Uma Thurman) on a date. Their first meeting takes place through an intercom: Vincent arrives to pick up Mia, but, instead of meeting face-to-face, they talk through an intercom as she watches him over a series of video monitors. The use of a video camera allows Mia to inspect her escort, to see what he is like before meeting him in person. This makes sense in terms of the story, since Mia would want to get the upper hand right away, to inspect her date for the evening, but it also has another level: audiences first became acquainted with John Travolta through his 1970s sitcom, *Welcome Back, Kotter*, and so we are in some sense seeing the history of Travolta himself. As audiences did years ago, Mia acquaints herself with him through television, and so the film suggests that Travolta's status as an icon, as a celebrity to be watched, will be investigated. Even the name "Vincent" is an older, more mature version of "Vinnie", his high-school character from TV.

They go to a grand Fifties diner called Jack Rabbit Slim's, a nostalgia palace/restaurant staffed by employees who dress as dead icons from a bygone era. A sign on the exterior of the building reads, "The Next Best Thing to a Time Machine", which sets the theme for the sequence. (Travolta's most popular film, Randal Kleiser's *Grease* [1978], is a musical set in the 1950s – a time machine all its own – and so Travolta does have a connection to this era.) Ricky Nelson sings on the dance floor, while stars like Marilyn Monroe, Mamie Van Doren, and Buddy Holly wait tables.[2] The scene becomes a meditation on celebrity itself since Travolta, making a comeback in *Pulp Fiction*, is a Seventies icon for whom mainstream success has been elusive for several years. (To match Travolta's situation as one who has been away for a while, his character has just returned from Amsterdam after being away for three years.)

As this man walks through the restaurant with celebrity look-a-likes all around him and B-movie posters on the walls, he is both Vincent Vega, heroin-shooting hit man marvelling at the spectacle so alien to him, and John Travolta, celebrity icon seeing how icons of an earlier era are recycled for their nostalgic value.[3] Movie stars as human beings face the ravages of time, decay and death, in real life, but the restaurant reverses the inevitable by keeping them forever young in new people's bodies, unlike Travolta, whose body has aged since his heyday.

When Mia asks him what he thinks of Jack Rabbit Slim's, he responds that the place is "like a wax museum with a pulse", a phrase eerily reminiscent of the "waxworks" from Billy Wilder's *Sunset Boulevard* (1950), a film that even more explicitly deals with the loss of celebrity (and, like *Pulp Fiction*, employs a circular narrative, albeit one that relies on the device of a flashback). As Leo Braudy points out about that film, Norma Desmond's silent-screen cronies "are embalmed with her in the past, playing an eternal bridge game. Sunset Boulevard thereby documents the way film stars belong to particular eras and disappear, losing their power, when their personalities are no longer relevant to the needs of their audience." Whereas *Sunset Boulevard* suggests actors are frozen into one role and one era and cannot make transitions to another, however, *Pulp Fiction* suggests that film personalities never really die but rather get recycled, living on in the flesh of celebrity look-a-likes and in menu items like Douglas Sirk steaks.

But almost miraculously, the stars themselves can also make a comeback.[4] Travolta can return because Tarantino has written a part that manages to tap into the Travolta persona of self-assurance, toughness, and tenderness while projecting it into the gangster genre.[5] What if *Saturday Night Fever*'s Tony Manero never made it out of his small community? What if, *Pulp Fiction* seems to ask, he became a small-time hood?

Since John Travolta's screen persona as a young man in the 1970s was established in two musicals, John Badham's *Saturday Night Fever* (1977) and *Grease* (both of which feature dance contests), Vincent and Mia's entrance in a twist contest becomes a self-reflexive moment. The song they dance to, Chuck Berry's 'You Never Can Tell', begins with the line, "It was a teenage wedding, and the old folks wished 'em well," which sets up a dichotomy between youth and age and hints at the inevitable passage of time that the song's newlyweds will undergo. John Travolta taking the dance floor again after all these years invokes the memories of his heyday while calling attention to the years that have passed; whereas *Grease's* Danny Zuko and *Saturday Night Fever's* Tony Manero were brash, young men who dominated the whole dance floor with sweeping, expansive gestures (think of Tony Manero's famous gesture of pointing to the sky), in *Pulp Fiction*, the gestures of youth have been toned down by age. As Chuck Berry sings on the soundtrack, "But when the sun went down, the rapid tempo of the music fell." Vincent's moves are precise, not grand or ostentatious – he is, after all, taking out the Big Man's wife, so he has to be careful how he behaves, but, beyond the character's motivations, Travolta's moves suggest a return to the dance floor with caution and humility. He is in fact capturing the "essence of the musical": "the potential of the individual to free himself from inhibition at the same time that he retains a sense of limit and propriety in the very form of the liberating dance" (Braudy).

In *Saturday Night Fever*, the dance floor is seemingly a haven for Tony, the one place where he can truly express himself away from the constraints of work and family. But, as J. P. Telotte points out, when Tony wins a rigged dance contest and is forced to see he really is not the best dancer, he realises that "The disco floor is no haven from the problems of the real world, but simply a gaudy disguise for them." In *Pulp Fiction*, however, the dance floor becomes a real haven for Vincent and Mia. They even win a trophy, as if righting the tainted victory of *Saturday Night Fever*.

More importantly, though, as in many traditional movie musicals, the dance becomes an extension of the relationship. It becomes a testing ground for them as they get to know each other. They do novelty dances like the "Swim" and the "Batman" (pop culture relics from a distant era become a mediating language for them), each trying to keep up with the other. For Vincent, the dance becomes a haven from his gangster life and a chance for him and Mia to connect, and, for Travolta the star, the dance is a return to the days of his former stardom – a little heavier, less cocky, but still able to show his stuff through dance.[6] Nevertheless, it is a limited victory. Travolta is recycled for his nostalgic value and gives the audience familiar with his early work a thrilling cinematic moment, but, as Vincent Vega, he does not break out of the role of the young Travolta.

Whereas John Travolta brings the weight of middle age and a sense of lost youth to the role of Vincent Vega, Uma Thurman brings her own unique quality to the role of Mia – "the tradition of the forbidden woman-child, from Lolita on down" (Kaylin), a persona first seen in Stephen Frears's *Dangerous Liaisons* (1989), in which she played a virgin seduced by a wily aristocrat. Indeed, Thurman's Mia straddles the worlds of childhood and adulthood. She is a tough-talking, cocaine-snorting gun moll with a strong sexuality that supposedly got another man in trouble. At the same time, she is too shy to tell Vincent an old vaudeville joke ("You wouldn't like it, and I'd be embarrassed," she timidly admits), orders a milkshake, and impulsively enters them in the dance contest. Vincent may be her escort, but he is also her baby sitter forced to do whatever the spoiled child wants or else get in trouble. Like a precocious child, Mia knows how to manipulate her sitter: "I do believe Marsellus, my husband, your boss, told you to take me out and do whatever I wanted. Now I want to dance. I want to win. I want that trophy." Mia, then, is a little girl in a woman's body, and so it is fitting that, upon their return home, Mia dances joyfully to the pop song, 'Girl, You'll Be a Woman Soon', a song whose very title suggests a temporal progression and sums up the Thurman persona. Her dance moves range from refined and graceful to wild like a teenager. Moreover, the song itself, originally performed by Neil Diamond in 1967, is performed by the alternative rock band Urge Overkill. Like the 'celebrities' in Jack Rabbit Slim's and other pop culture artifacts, this pop song, even though a product of its own era, can be recycled and given a new life (with a new voice).

Mia's subsequent drug overdose threatens the progression from 'girl' to 'woman' that the song promises and in effect stops time as she becomes a comatose, seemingly lifeless body. By giving her a shot of adrenaline straight to the heart, Vincent starts her up again. On the one hand, time is of the essence in this sequence. Vincent rushes her to his drug dealer's house in complete panic that she could die at any moment. Yet Tarantino stretches out the scene as long as he can – there is the search for the medical book, the argument over who will administer the shot, the close-ups of the participants before the needle is plunged in. Time seems to be moving rapidly ("Hurry up, Lance, I'm losin' her," Vincent yells in panic to the drug dealer) and yet not at all. Jack Rabbit Slim's shows one way time is defeated, and the overdose and shot of adrenaline subsequently show another. Travolta the movie star is resurrected (his character will also make a return from the dead), just as Mia is resurrected – the narrative itself becoming a mirror for pop culture.

Appropriately enough, in the next story, Butch, a boxer played by Bruce Willis, kills Vincent. Just as the 1980s action film superseded Travolta's era of stardom in the late 1970s, it is fitting that an actor known primarily for his action roles (in the *Die Hard* films especially) kills Travolta's Vincent – a metaphor for the march of time in the Hollywood system and the way one movie star supplants another.[7]

The Burden of Time

The main event of Butch's story would normally be the "main event" itself, the fight he is supposed to lose but instead wins, but we do not see the fight (just as in *Reservoir Dogs* we do not see the central jewel heist). Instead, Butch's story, "The Gold Watch", becomes his quest to retrieve this family heirloom and the odd turns his adventure takes.

The story begins with Butch's dream (right before his big fight) of himself as a little boy receiving his dead father's watch from Captain Koons (Christopher Walken), who explains the family history – how the watch was passed down from generation to generation each time an ancestor went to war. Just as Tarantino recycles old plots and conventions, and even John Travolta, history itself may be one big recycling system. When Captain Koons describes Butch's grandfather going to war, he says that, like his father before him, he went overseas to "fight the Germans once again; this time they called it World War II", as if it were the same war as World War I – simply renamed. Just as the henchman taking out the boss's wife or the boxer refusing to throw the fight are old plots with new names, and just as John Travolta is an actor whose name can be changed from Tony Manero to Vincent Vega, perhaps all wars are the same – or just re-numbered, like a sequel to a hit movie.

If anyone in *Pulp Fiction* is obsessed with time, it is Butch; after all, he is the only character with a family history – beholden to a larger time frame, and also bearing the weight of that past. If Mia is a girl in a woman's body, then Butch at an early age may have been a man in a boy's body; Captain Koons says to him, "Little man, I give the watch to you," as if such an artefact required the responsibility of an adult. Butch, after all, did not know his father and so in some sense was always the man of his house. When he wakes from his dream detailing the black comic highlights of how his father and then Captain Koons hid the family watch up their asses to protect it, his trainer enters his dressing room and declares, "It's time, Butch," a fitting epigraph for the episode.

In the film's first story, Butch's boss Marsellus (Ving Rhames) tries to persuade him to throw the fight by emphasising his age:

> Thing is, Butch, right now, you've got ability, but painful as it may be, ability don't last, and your days are just about over . . . See, this business is filled to the brim with unrealistic motherfuckers, motherfuckers who thought their ass would age like wine. If you mean it turns to vinegar, it does. If you mean it gets better with age, it don't . . . Boxers don't have an old-timers' day. You came close, but you never made it, but if you were gonna make it, you would have made it before now.

In double-crossing Marsellus, Butch is also beating time, fighting the decay of his body. In this sense, Butch's victory in the ring is comparable to Vincent's victory on the dance floor. (To enforce this similarity, the Ed Sullivan look-alike's words that introduce the dance contest could just as easily introduce the never-shown fight: "Ladies and gentlemen, now the moment you've all been waiting for.") Butch, however, by becoming a recycler himself, will experience a more far-reaching victory than Vincent does at Jack Rabbit Slim's.

Butch convinces Fabienne (Maria de Medeiros) that everything is going their way from hereon in.

Butch seems always concerned with being precise about time. When his taxi driver wants to know what it felt like to kill his opponent, Butch is careful in pinning down the time frame: "I didn't know he was dead until you told me he was dead, and now that I know he's dead, you want to know how I feel about it?" When he makes a phone call to find out when his bets will come in, he tells the person he is talking to that "Next time I see you it'll be on Tennessee time"; he sees geographical locations in terms of temporality. When his girlfriend Fabienne (Maria de Medeiros) announces she is going to have a piece of pie as part of her breakfast, he asks, "Pie for breakfast?" which suggests that time is a constraint on him, whereas Fabienne's response, "Any time of the day is a good time for pie", shows a freer, more relaxed attitude toward time.

In ironic moments that recall *noir* heroes trying in vain to escape their doom, Butch is drawn closer to the mobsters he wants to avoid. He first encounters Vincent in his apartment and kills him after he retrieves his watch and then literally runs into

Marsellus on the street. Both are injured when Butch hits Marsellus with his car, and then they both stumble into a pawn shop where they are held hostage by two hillbillies. Butch himself is a hostage to time, particularly the grand sweep of historical time, and so it is oddly fitting that, having retrieved his gold watch, he should be imprisoned in a place where history is preserved through a collection of junk and antiques. Moreover, he and Marsellus seem to be reliving his father and Captain Koons's Vietnam experience in a POW camp: "that Hanoi pit of Hell", as Captain Koons calls it in Butch's dream. When Marsellus is being raped in the basement, Butch escapes, but, instead of leaving, returns to save his enemy. Faced with a moral choice, Butch chooses to save the man who moments earlier was trying to kill him. Willis is given the chance to take his action hero persona and stretch the moral parameters of that genre.

His search for a weapon in the pawn shop brings him a series of choices: a hammer, a baseball bat, a chainsaw, and finally a samurai sword, which he uses. The choices are a catalogue of weapons in film, especially the chainsaw of a serial killer and the sword of a samurai warrior. The pawn shop itself is a site of recycling – things no longer useful to people are sold or traded so that others can buy them and make use of them. In this case, of course, Butch is not only making use of a weapon but a whole tradition of samurai films behind it. If his watch represents modern-day wars and the men who fought them, then Butch reaches back further to an ancient tradition of warfare. The samurai sword is yet another 'time machine' that gives Butch a certain moral weight. Instead of being a slave to history, he can use history to fight his own personal war and win. After the episode is over, Butch asks Marsellus, "What now?" Freed of the past, Butch is living in the present. (Incidentally, it is the rapist who must now live the rest of his life in the past; as Marsellus tells him, "I'm gonna get medieval on your ass.") All Butch must do is never tell anyone of the rape, leave that night, and never come back.

When Butch and Fabienne ride away at the end of the episode, they are heading toward Knoxville, Tennessee, where, according to Captain Koons, the gold watch was purchased by Butch's great-grandfather. Butch, then, is travelling toward his future by going back to the family past where time (as represented in the watch) began. Knoxville is also Quentin Tarantino's birthplace. The chronological end of *Pulp Fiction* circles back not just to Butch's beginnings but to the director's actual beginnings so that *Pulp Fiction* becomes a personal time machine for Tarantino himself.

Time and the Director

The third story, "The Bonnie Situation", circles back to the beginning of the film – to Vincent and Jules's (Samuel L. Jackson) retrieval of Marsellus's briefcase and their killing of the small-time criminals who tried to betray them. For the first time, we are conscious of a true shift backward in time, and the audience may be momentarily disoriented. After all, Vincent seems to have returned from the dead (courtesy of the director's godlike power to control time), just as taking the part of Vincent metaphorically resurrects John Travolta's career.[8] Why does Tarantino make this time shift? For one thing, the final stand-off in the diner that concludes the story is more effective at the end of the film as a climactic change in Jules's character than it would be in the first third of the film. As Gavin Smith suggests, "By opting for a structure that scrambles chronology without flashbacks, he [Tarantino] grants centrality to the transformation of the character of killer Jules." Moreover, Jules's two-fold epiphany (that God saved his life by intervening to stop bullets aimed directly at him, and that he must now change his criminal ways) is linked to an acceptance of time and eternity and his metaphoric role as a movie director. While time remains a crucial theme in this section (indeed the pressures of time are most explicit in this story), the theme of filmmaking gradually takes centre stage.

When Vincent accidentally shoots and kills a passenger in their car, Jules drives to the house of his friend Jimmie (played by Quentin Tarantino), who lives near Burbank Studios. Tarantino's appearance in this episode (and especially his friendship with Jules) and the gangsters' location near the filmmaking community signal that film directing is the subtext of this episode. When we first see Jimmie, he is in his kitchen with a clock on the wall behind him. At this moment, the theme of time is fused with the idea of Tarantino making movies; the pressures of time, in essence, are being linked to the role of the director. As Jimmie explains, Vincent and Jules must clean the car and leave before his wife returns home:

> She comes home from work in about an hour and a half, graveyard shift at the hospital. You gonna make some phone calls? You gonna call some people? Well then do it and then get the fuck out of my house before she gets here.

Tarantino directs his actors, and Jimmie directs his guests so that the creation of the film and the narrative itself suddenly meet.

Winston Wolf (Harvey Keitel) is called in to lead the clean-up of the car. He notes that Jimmie's house is "thirty minutes away; I'll be there in ten." As a subtitle on the screen tells us, he arrives "nine minutes thirty seven seconds later . . . " The Wolf, then, is established as a man who can beat time. He then orders the clean-up in a scene that Manohla Dargis calls "cheerfully self-reflexive, since the orchestration of the purge could easily pass for a crash course in spectacle-making" as the Wolf becomes "captain of the clean-up and the scene's producer, negotiating the actors and their actions amid the slaughter ('Give me the principals' names again')." Crime is the quintessential Tarantino subject, and, in this scene depicting crime itself as filmmaking, we see the director's reflection on his own work.

There is a personal tribute at work here as well, which gives this third story a distinctly autobiographical flavour. Harvey Keitel was co-producer of *Reservoir Dogs*, and his love for the script and commitment to act in the film made it possible for Tarantino to get it made and thereby launch his directorial career.[9] Thus, Keitel reprises his real-life role of producer and mentor to Tarantino as he comes in to save Jimmie's marriage. Jimmie cedes his authority to the Wolf, who not only produces but also directs the action. Moreover, in a cute moment of role-reversal, Keitel's Wolf asks Tarantino's Jimmie for a cup of coffee. While Tarantino, the director of *Pulp Fiction*, directs his actor Keitel in the creation of the scene, within the scene itself Tarantino is a kind of gofer on the set fetching coffee for the producer and the other performers. Just as, according to Gavin Smith, Jack Rabbit Slim's "inverts the archetypal waitress-to superstar legend by using lookalikes to reduce dead Fifties idols (Monroe, Dean, etc.) to table staff", so Tarantino inverts his own image as director in this scene. A two-shot of Tarantino and Keitel facing each other in Jimmie's bedroom suggests

Tarantino as Jimmie, the hapless friend gatecrashed by a blood-stained Jules and Vincent, relying on the services of comic underworld figure 'the Wolf'.

a mirror-like multiplication of possibilities: the director of *Pulp Fiction* and his actor, the young director and his mentor, the production assistant and the metaphorical producer, the domesticated husband in his bathrobe and the dapper criminal in his tuxedo.

The whole sequence becomes a race against time, as the Wolf makes clear:

THE WOLF

If I was informed correctly the clock is ticking. Is that right, Jimmie?

JIMMIE

Uh, one hundred percent.

THE WOLF

Your wife, Bonnie, comes home at 9:30 in the A.M., is that correct?

JIMMIE

Uh-uh.

THE WOLF

I was led to believe that if she comes home and finds us here, she wouldn't appreciate it none too much.

JIMMIE

She wouldn't at that.

THE WOLF

That gives us 40 minutes to get the fuck outta Dodge, which if you do what I say when I say it should be plenty.

The Wolf, then, as a movie producer figure, links clichéd Western jargon with the time pressures on their own production. After the car is cleaned, the Wolf and Jimmie proceed to clean Vincent and Jules. The Wolf orders them to strip out of their clothes (the black suits, narrow black ties, and white shirts that Keitel, Tarantino, and the rest of the cast wore in *Reservoir Dogs*), hoses them down, and has them dress in T-shirts and shorts. Shedding the gangster costume and the genre it represents is the first step in Jules's salvation, which will be completed only when he directs his own scene.[10]

To dispose of the car and body, the Wolf tells them, "a few twists and turns aside we'll be goin' up Hollywood Way". Jules's journey is not simply "up Hollywood Way" but figuratively the "Hollywood Way" if he is to survive the last scene (and of course he must since the scrambled chronology has already assured us he does). They take the car, dead body, and bloodsoaked clothes to Monster Joe's Truck and Tow, where the car parts presumably will be recycled. Even Jimmie's linen (a wedding gift) used to camouflage the car's upholstery is essentially recycled into a new oak bedroom set when the Wolf pays him off. Everything else in Hollywood gets recycled – movie stars, plot lines – why not the evidence of a murder? Once everything is taken care of, the Wolf says it is "Like it never happened", which is a clear display of the power to reverse time, a power Tarantino, like his mentor the Wolf/Keitel, exercises through the very structure of his film.

Jules and Vincent then have breakfast at a coffee shop, where Jules makes his decision to leave the gangster life and to "walk the earth":

No longer 'bad asses', Jules (Samuel L. Jackson) and Vincent's absurd predicament is illustrated by dressing them in volleyball wear alongside the dapper Wolf.

VINCENT

And how long do you intend to walk the earth?

JULES

Till God puts me where he wants me to be.

VINCENT

And what if he don't do that?

JULES

If it takes forever, then I'll walk forever.

Jules thus displays an acceptance of eternity – time as a never-ending journey – that no other character achieves. It is a surrender to time but a voluntary surrender that allows him to be patient and see where time will take him. Vincent is dumbfounded but has to stop arguing with Jules to use the restroom. As he leaves, he says, "To be continued", but the conversation never will be continued. Vincent is not a recycler or a director figure – he cannot stop and re-start time at will. When Vincent re-emerges from the bathroom, he finds Jules in a stand-off with Pumpkin and Honey Bunny.

The couple execute the robbery begun in the film's first scene. Tarantino thus circles back to the very beginning of the film, repeats a fragment of what we saw before, and thereby unfreezes what he had originally frozen. Jules is able to disarm Pumpkin but still has Honey Bunny aiming her gun at him. At this point, the theme of the director comes to the forefront. In the midst of the stand-off, Jules's skill as a film director enables everyone to survive a stand-off that could just as easily have led to mutual annihilation (the climax of *Reservoir Dogs* that stems from a similar stand-off). The diner is like a chaotic movie set that Jules must take control of. The once self-assured Honey Bunny (aka Yolanda) is a bundle of nerves once Jules has his gun aimed at Pumpkin, and Vincent is a loose cannon threatening to ruin Jules's direction.

As a good director, Jules first tries to defuse the tension on the set and relax his performers (by recycling the language of pop culture in suggesting they all "be cool" like Fonzie). He then sets up the scene ("Now, here's the situation") and proceeds to use the various techniques at a director's disposal to get the desired performances from his actors. He commands them ("Point the gun at me"), offers praise ("You're doin' great, and I'm proud of you"), reassures ("It's almost over"), and generally encourages ("Come on Yolanda, stay with me baby"). He rejects the gangster genre ("I don't want to kill you"), and, instead of stealing, gives his money to the crooks. Finally, the Biblical passage of vengeance he always recited before killing someone (Ezekiel 25:17) becomes a passage of mercy as he offers several interpretations of it and then comes to the conclusion that "I am the tyranny of evil men, but I'm tryin', Ringo, I'm tryin' real hard to be the shepherd." While the "shepherd" can have many broad religious overtones and can indicate a future path for Jules now that he has been transformed, in the context of the scene, a director is a "shepherd" who guides his actors. Having come to an acceptance of time and having made the pledge to walk "forever" if he must, Jules can stop time during the climactic stand-off and thereby save everyone's life. In ending with Jules's direction of the stand-off (even though it takes place chronologically before both Vincent and Mia's date and Butch's story),

Tarantino not only gives special weight to Jules's spiritual change but also emphasises the linkage of that transformation to the power of the film director. (If it were not abundantly clear that this section is a metaphor for film directing, it should be noted that the producer of *Pulp Fiction*, Lawrence Bender, has a cameo appearance as a hostage in the diner.) If the last section is a tribute to a "movie director" and his ability to recycle his old gangster shtick and Biblical passage of vengeance into a positive direction, then Tarantino's recycling skills have been present all along as he has recycled fragments of Hollywood's pulp tradition into a new direction – one that brings us, of all places, to a surprising spiritual epiphany. As Vincent and Jules put their guns in the waistbands of their shorts and leave the diner together in the film's last shot, they are probably more alike than ever – they even walk in sync. However, one has found redemption and is heading into "forever", and the other has found a different kind of "forever" through death. Jules remains subject to time and yet is able to renew himself by surrendering to it, just as Tarantino is subject to all the movies he has seen, indeed the larger time frame of Hollywood history, and yet is able to breathe new life into the old forms he loves.

Dedication

I would like to dedicate this essay to my beloved Uncle Nick, the late Nicholas P. Chumo. Ever since I was a child, my uncle and I spent many happy hours together at the movies. The last time we went to the show, we saw *Pulp Fiction*. It was one of the many times we enjoyed this movie together.

Notes

I would like to thank Andrew Griffin, Douglas McFarland, and especially Ellen Walkley for their contributions to the final form of this essay.

[1] The pressure of time has intrigued Tarantino since his first directorial effort, *Reservoir Dogs* (1992), in which, he told Gavin Smith, he was fascinated by the idea of taking "genre characters in these genre situations" and making them obey "real-life rules", namely "the fact that the whole movie takes place in real time".

[2] When "Buddy Holly" waits on Vincent and Mia, he playfully calls Mia "Peggy Sue," a reference of course to a Buddy Holly song but also a possible oblique allusion to Francis Ford Coppola's *Peggy Sue Got Married* (1986), in which a woman travels back in time to her high school days of the Fifties.

[3] Travolta himself comments on a dream in which "I was shooting the Jack Rabbit Slim's scene with Uma Thurman, and Quentin yelled cut. They left, the crew left, and I was left with Marilyn Monroe, James Dean, Elvis Presley – all these icons of the Fifties and Sxities. And I thought, 'My goodness, this was a set-up. Am I dead? Is this where we all go? The icon heaven?'" (Quoted in Gordinier – see below.)

[4] In writing about how he chose Travolta for the part, Tarantino uses the language of recycling: "But I've been very sad about how he's been used . . . What is wrong with these directors? Why don't they see what they have – that if they just blew the dust off it. . . ?" ("Quentin Tarantino on *Pulp Fiction*").

[5] Martin Amis illustrates that Tarantino was committed to Travolta from the beginning:
"The day Quentin finished *Pulp Fiction*, he sent it to me," Travolta resumed. "He said, 'Look at Vincent.'" Tarantino had written the part for Travolta; he believed in

Travolta – "but he was the only guy who was thinking that way. Which kind of shows you how my light had died. The studio wanted an actor with . . . a higher temperature. Quentin had much more to lose than I did. Finally, he said, 'You either do it with John Travolta or you don't do it.'"

6 An interesting "time machine" coincidence for John Travolta personally – his first meeting with Tarantino took place in the director's apartment, which happened to be Travolta's old apartment: "The one I rented when I first came to L.A., in 1974" (quoted in Amis). Travolta's return to stardom and respectability, then, began where his Hollywood career began 20 years earlier. The whole process of *Pulp Fiction* was, in essence, one big time machine for him.

7 According to Amis, Travolta has a similar view of his career: "The way he sees it, he was more or less naturally displaced by a new generation of stars: Hanks, Cruise, Costner."

8 At the time of *Pulp Fiction*'s release, much was made of the film as a comeback for Travolta. See, for example, Jeff Gordnier's "The Man In The Plastic Bubble" and Martin Amis's "Travolta's Second Act".

9 To give a sense of Keitel's role in getting *Reservoir Dogs* made, Tarantino stated to Charlie Rose that Keitel "gave us legitimacy. All of a sudden two guys who had never done anything before, well, we had Harvey Keitel, we had a good actor involved . . . and I know the only reason that Richard Gladstein at LIVE who had the power of the pen, all right, that said, uh, 'Yes I'm gonna go with it', the only reason he read the script in the first place was because Harvey Keitel was attached."

10 This may be a metaphor for Tarantino's career as well. He commented to Gavin Smith, "The entire time I was writing *Pulp Fiction* I was thinking, This will be my Get-It-Out-of-Your-System movie. This will be the movie where I say goodbye to the gangster genre for a while, because I don't want to be the next Don Siegel – not that I'm as good."

Works Cited

Amis, Martin. "Travolta's Second Act". *The New Yorker* 20-27 February 1995: 212-16+.
Braudy, Leo. *The World In A Frame: What We See In Films*. 1976. University of Chicago Press, 1984.
Corliss, Richard. "A Blast To The Heart". *Time* 10 October 1994: 76-78.
Dargis, Manohla. "Pulp Instincts". *Sight And Sound* May 1994: 6-9.
Gordinier, Jeff. "The Man In The Plastic Bubble". *Entertainment Weekly* 21 October 1994: 18-21+.
Kaylin, Lucy. "Uma In Bloom". *GQ* February 1995:146-51.
Tarantino, Quentin. Television interview by Charlie Rose. Producer Nick Dolin. Director Bob Morris. Executive Producer Charlie Rose. PBS. 14 October 1994.
Tarantino, Quentin. "Quentin Tarantino On *Pulp Fiction*". *Sight And Sound* May 1994: 10-11.
Tarantino, Quentin. "'When You Know You're In Good Hands': Quentin Tarantino Interviewed" by Gavin Smith. *Film Comment* 30.4 (1994): 32-36+.
Telotte, J. P. "A Sober Celebration: Song And Dance In The 'New' Musical". *Journal Of Popular Film And Television* 8 (1980): 2-14.

true lies

by Jeff Dawson

The Myth: *that the whole movie is actually a religious allegory about redemption in the face of the Devil.*

The evidence for: An idea that gained momentum on the Internet in the States, devotees point to a film positively laden with religious symbolism. Most obviously, of course, there is Jules' (Sam Jackson) recitation of Ezekiel 25:1-7, the "miracle" of the bullets that pass right through he and Vincent (John Travolta) and Jules' ultimate repentance, where he decides to "walk the earth" – especially significant when taken with his professed dislike of "unclean" meat. And, too, the way that those who open the mysterious glowing briefcase seem to be overcome by a Higher Power. As for the presence of Old Nick? The code to the lock on the briefcase that Jules and Vincent are sent to retrieve is – well, wouldn't you know it? – 666, as too is the entry code to Mia Wallace's (Uma Thurman) house. The Devil, who celebrated "tyranny of evil men" as per Jules' recitation, is recognised to have these digits, "the number of the beast", written on his head, perhaps in the very spot that Marsellus Wallace (Ving Rhames) bears a sticking plaster. To cap it all, Butch (Bruce Willis) rides a chopper called Grace.

The evidence against: Surprisingly little. All the stuff that Sam Jackson spouts is there on screen and freely open to interpretation. But as for the 666 stuff? The dialling of such a number was once thought to herald the arrival of three policemen standing on their heads. Anyone anal enough to freeze-frame the movie and make a note of all this *deserves* a spell in purgatory. Grace, by the way, was the name of Quentin Tarantino's then-girlfriend.

The truth: As with the "Who Shot Nice Guy Eddie?" craze from *Reservoir Dogs*, Tarantino loves all the conjecture.

"I heard about it on this radio show," he chuckles. "In the briefcase was 'Hope' and Jules is not just a gangster, he's a serf of the Devil who's turning over. It's a good theory, hahaha."

And as for the contents of the briefcase? Tim Roth (Pumpkin) clears that one up once and for all.

"A lamp and a battery . . ."

4.

four
rooms

four x four

by Peter Biskind

Check into the *Four Rooms* hotel, and you'll discover what happens when four of the hottest independent directors around test their friendship by making a movie together.

Four Rooms is an unusual experiment in collective filmmaking. It was made by Allison Anders, Alexandre Rockwell, Robert Rodriguez, and Quentin Tarantino. Each directed a "room" in a fictional hotel, and all four collaborated on a wraparound story featuring a bellhop, played by Tim Roth, who appears in every room.

Anthology films rarely work. Why did you want to torture yourselves?

QUENTIN TARANTINO: The funniest thing about doing it is to do a movie that, one, doesn't take that long to do, and, two, the weight of the world isn't riding on it. If they like your story, great, and if they don't, too fuckin' bad.

ROBERT RODRIGUEZ: I love short films. *Desperado* is like a series of short films. Most of my room is set-up, until the last five minutes when it builds to a tremendous pace that you can't ever sustain in a feature film.

ALLISON ANDERS: It's exciting when you're just starting to make films, and you first learn about the French New Wave or New German Cinema – those guys all hung out together and they made films together and they were all part of a time. Filmmakers, especially young filmmakers, really want to belong to something. We were all sort of the Sundance Class of '92 and '93.

What are the stories about in **Four Rooms***?*

ANDERS: There were not really any rules, except that all the action had to take place in a hotel room on New Year's Eve, and we had to use the bellhop. We called him Ted. I wanted to put chicks in my room. I was, like, They're in a band – no, they're a bunch of midwives. No, no, no. Finally, it was, like, they're a coven! And what do they need out of Ted? What do I need? Sperm! I found myself writing this story about how they're trying to resurrect this goddess who was turned to stone 40 years earlier because she was cursed on their wedding night, before she could give her virginity. And I had just turned 40. I was raped when I was young and I was never able to give my virginity. So for me, it became this incredibly heavy thing that I hadn't even realised.

ALEXANDRE ROCKWELL: Mine is kind of a weird psychodrama. It's like *Days Of Our Lives* on crack or something. I once heard a story about how Sean Penn tied Madonna up on New Year's Eve, so the idea is a jealous husband with a gun ties up his wife.

RODRIGUEZ: I figured Quentin and Alex would be really dramatic. So I thought I'd go the other way, do a family comedy.

Quentin, your story, about an out-of-control star and his entourage, has personal overtones, doesn't it?

TARANTINO: The character started off being comical, because I thought I could play a character like that really well, and then he ended up shouldering some of my own baggage as – for want of a better word – a celebrity. I am totally teeming with anticipation about how people are gonna react. The media is fucking sick of me. It's never been more evident than in reading the reviews of *Desperado*. Because every review – I think I'm really funny in that movie, I think I kick ass in that scene – is not about me being bad, but "We're sick of this guy. We just don't wanna see his face anymore." They're not gonna give me a break for another couple of years on this. They almost resent the fact that I want to act. Until I keep doing it and doing it and shoving it down their throats, then maybe they'll look at it for what it is. I just got through reading three, count 'em, *three*, biographies of my life. It's a peyote-like experience. They're questioning my character – I'm really a bad person, I've fucked all the Video Archive guys, Roger Avary is the true genius behind all my work. All these questions about what an asshole I've become, what do I do? I come out with a movie where I play an asshole! I play more or less myself in the worst light I could.

What was the most difficult thing about making the movie?
ROCKWELL: In the beginning, it was pretty much Allison and me, because Robert was doing *Desperado* and Quentin was doing publicity for *Pulp Fiction*. But no one wanted to make a decision without Quentin's approval. And here I was, one of the executive producers, and if I wanted to have a toothpick or a coffee cup in the lobby, there would be this "We'd better check with Quentin." I would find myself negotiating with Quentin's third assistant. But when I finally got through to Quentin, it was fine.

Quentin almost dropped out at the very last minute?
ROCKWELL: I had knee surgery, major reconstruction, and I'm lying in bed with a machine moving my knee. I was high as a kite on a morphine derivative, and I get this phone call. It was Allison. She said, "Guess what? Quentin's backing out!" It was one week before she had to start shooting. "Why?" "He's just totally over-stressed. He told me, 'I'm just not excited about it and I don't want to do something I'm not excited about.'" I said, "You know what? He can't back out. That's just not one of the choices. If he checks that box, I'm going to get a gun and shoot him, and then he'll experience violence first-hand. He won't have to watch it in a John Woo movie." Allison appealed to his sense of loyalty. And humiliated and embarrassed him. Very good motivators. So next time I saw him, he was, like, "You know what? I was riding on the airplane and I read it again, and I really started getting excited about it again."

When you saw the rough cut for the first time, what was your reaction?
ROCKWELL: I'm the last guy you want to go to a rough cut with. I wanted to jump out of a window afterward. We all went out to Denny's in L.A., and we're sitting there ordering taco pizzas or sloppy joes and huge RC Colas. I said, "Well, personally, I think the movie really sucked." It was more than two and a half hours long, at least 45 minutes too long. Robert's was the tightest, 24 minutes, but I felt the rest of our stuff was unbearably long. Quentin said, "No way, man, come on. We all just have to go back and rethink this thing." Allison was second-guessing herself, and she's really self-critical. It's a female thing. She's like a human mood ring. With Quentin you know

exactly what he's thinking, but you don't know exactly what he's feeling. Robert is the extreme opposite of Allison. You never know what Robert is thinking or feeling. You can't tell if someone shot his dog. If he tells you anything, it's in a very curt sentence, like "It's too long."

Why didn't you turn over your room to someone else to edit?

RODRIGUEZ: Editing is too subjective. If Alex had turned his picture over to me to cut down, I would've cut it my way, which wouldn't necessarily be right for the film or for his style. In my room, there are 600 cuts in 20 minutes. Quentin's room has three cuts in the first ten minutes. If someone else is telling you to cut something down, you end up with something that's not really yours, and not really all theirs.

What was Miramax's attitude?

ROCKWELL: The biggest challenge to our friendship and the feeling of goodwill about the film was less about ourselves and more about the powers that be. I'm not pointing a finger and saying they tried to divide us. It's just – that's their job. This is a comedy. Put yourself in the shoes of the distributors. You're saying, "A comedy should run about 90 minutes, 100 minutes or something." They're saying, "We want you to cut it." You really couldn't cut Robert's, it's like a comic strip. I don't think Robert has changed a frame since his rough cut. Quentin shot his in long takes so it's hard to cut his. So the pressure was building on me and Allison. Look, I love Quentin's work and Robert's work and Allison's work – but the bottom line is, I have to rally my troops around my film. I said to Bob and Harvey [Weinstein, who run Miramax], "Well, okay, everyone is going to do some cutting right?" And Harvey and Bob crack up and say, "Who's going to tell Quentin he has to cut?" Harvey says, "Well I'll tell him Alex is cutting, but then he's going to think he can add the minutes to his room."

Was it hard to criticise Quentin?

ANDERS: Quentin at one point wanted to direct one last piece, the very last piece in the movie. And I said no. He asked why. I said, "Because I wrote it. It's the end of my story, even though it comes at the end of the end credits." He was, like, "Well, so what?" And I said, "'So what?' What do you mean, 'So what?'" And he said, "You know, you're always saying we're like a band, like the Beatles, where everyone bickers – 'No, I want to sing lead,' 'No, I want to sing lead' – and just makes one record and then splits up." And I said, "Well, there are other kinds of bands that make one hit and disappear like the Buckinghams, where everybody kisses each other's ass." And he said, "Well, I would like a little more of the ass-kissing model right now." And I said, "Yeah, as long as it's your ass being kissed." I won that one.

Will the pressure of "making it" corrupt you all, destroy your friendships?

ROCKWELL: I was sitting there talking to Quentin about how you have to protect your integrity. Look at the Seventies. Hollywood co-opted a lot of those directors. A lot of friends stopped being friends. A lot of people lost their visions. Sean Penn once asked Brian de Palma, "What is it with you guys? What happened?" And Brian said, "Well, after a while people start to second-guess you so much that their voices get inside your head, and you start second-guessing yourself. And once you do that, you can't do anything right." So I said to Quentin, "Believe me, they're going to descend on you like wolves on meat," which, you know, they did. Quentin was looking at me, like, So? I felt like a shmuck. I thought, Oh my God, I'm Mr Paranoid New York. And here's Mr That's a Great Opportunity for Me L.A. – he relishes the challenge of being a pop figure in the middle of the pop cycle.

Was it all worth it? Would you do it again?
ANDERS: Even if we had failed and ended up hating each other's guts, we tried something that had not been done. But, of course, we all feel like the movie works as a film, and that our friendships are actually much better as a result of having gone through this together.

TARANTINO: I don't know. The big problem in making a movie like this is that as far as audiences are concerned, it's a popularity contest: who did the best one, who did the worst. Which is not where we were coming from. I won't do it again right away. I don't want to do anything right away. Anyhow, we're all still friends, better friends than when we started.

four rooms
by Emanuel Levy

Four of America's hottest indie directors – Allison Anders, Alexandre Rockwell, Robert Rodriguez and Quentin Tarantino – get a one-of-a-kind opportunity to display their idiosyncratic talents – and grand follies – in *Four Rooms*, a disappointing, tedious anthology of four short films, set in separate rooms of a once-grand L.A. hotel. Tarantino's cult status and Rodriguez's recent popularity should help initial marketing of this eagerly awaited curio item, but Miramax faces a tough challenge overcoming negative reviews and bad word-of-mouth in guiding this lugubrious extravaganza into the mainstream.

The four stories are set in the same hotel on New Year's Eve (reportedly Rockwell's idea), with a new bellboy, Ted (Tim Roth), the only character who appears in all the segs, on the job. In the rather pointless first story, "Strange Brew", a story about feminine mystery and power, Anders aims to spoof and deconstruct female archetypes.

A coven of witches checks into the honeymoon suite to resurrect their goddess, Diana (Amanda DeCadenet), a 1950s entertainer-stripper. The group includes Athena (Valerie Golino), a gypsy-like high priestess; the glamorous Elspeth (Madonna), who arrives with her g.f. (Alicia Witt), a juvenile delinquent on probation; Raven (Lili Taylor) and Jezebel (Sammi Davis). Each witch brings a body fluid (blood, sweat, tears) to the gathering except for novice Eva (Ione Skye), who accidentally swallowed her contribution – semen. She's commanded to find a replacement specimen for the ritual, and the bellboy is her "victim".

Rockwell's "Two Sides to a Plate", arguably the weakest segment, begins with Ted innocently entering room 404 with a bucket of ice, only to find a man named Siegfried (David Proval) wielding a .357 magnum at his beautiful wife, Angela (Jennifer Beals), who's gagged and tied to a chair. With this supposed psychological adventure, in which hubby tests marital love by accusing the bellboy of having an affair with his wife, pic sinks to an almost irredeemable level of inconsequence.

The movie gets a much-needed energy injection in the third – and undoubtedly most entertaining – sequence, "The Misbehavers", in which Rodriguez again shows his masterly, humorous control of the camera in a story of two kids, Sarah, nine, and Juancho, six, who end up destroying their hotel room while their gangster dad (Antonio Banderas) and mom (Tamlyn Tomita) are having a night on the town.

In the closing chapter, "The Man From Hollywood", Tarantino pays homage to Hitchcock. Chester Rush (Tarantino) – the town's newest comedy star – and his buddies Leo (Bruce Willis) and Norman (Paul Calderon) re-create "The Man From Rio" episode of *Alfred Hitchcock Presents*, in which Peter Lorre bets that Steve McQueen can't light his cigarette lighter ten times in a row, with his pinky finger the price of failure. Bellboy Ted is unwittingly drawn into the fray.

Most disappointing is how pedestrian and unimaginative most of the text is. There's nothing experimental or offbeat about the work, other than the novelty of superstar directors letting their fancy run, though neither wild nor fast enough. As a group, Helmers prove more adept behind the camera than as writers; segments by Anders and Rockwell are particularly meagre. But even Tarantino's notoriously edgy dialogue is missing here.

In a role that was conceived for – and would have been better played by – Steve Buscemi, Roth does a cheap, inconsistent imitation of Jerry Lewis at his most neurotic; Lewis' 1960 *The Bellboy* seems to be the inspiration. But Roth is given no clever lines to deliver, and his work is all mannerisms, resulting in an uncharacteristically weak performance.

Considering the cast's size and calibre, it's shocking that there are no standout performances. The minor pleasures to be had here are detecting the different narrative strategies and visual styles employed by the quartet. Favouring mega-close-ups and furious montage, Rodriguez's segment has the fastest pacing and largest number of cuts. In contrast, Tarantino's elaborate *mise en scène* benefits from extremely long takes, which Andrzej Sekula's astute camera records in a series of pans within the single-set episode.

Animated credit sequence, a tribute of sorts to Frank Tashlin's campy, cartoonish comedies, as well as to *The Pink Panther*, is amusing, and each episode is well shot and edited by consummate craftsmen. But the production's sheen conflicts awkwardly with the thin material, making the movie's lack of wit and quirky playfulness all the more noticeable. Helmers should move into their next projects to put this embarrassment behind them as quickly as possible.

5 .from dusk till dawn

tarantino's pulp horror

by Michael Beeler

Long before he baptised us all in his bloody communion of violence and nonchalant mayhem, Quentin Tarantino was just another nine-to-five working stiff. Back then his writing was just a part-time thing, relinquished to after hours, when the streets were empty and Channel 5 was off the air. Both *True Romance* and *Natural Born Killers* were written during this time in his life when the dreams were big and the pay-checks small.

But, all that changed when he was approached by Robert Kurtzman and Jon Esposito, who had a little story about gangsters, vampires and a south of the border Mexican bar called the Titty Twister that they wanted somebody to flesh out into a screenplay. "Bob Kurtzman's original outline had maybe four paragraphs or about a page and then they get to the Titty Twister and then the next six pages were inside the Titty Twister," said Tarantino. "Well, my tale was, 'Let's put the Titty Twister way, way away! And let's really build up to the point when they get there".

"So, it's just a total suspense film with not even a hint of horror. You don't hear some radio thing saying, 'There have been mysterious disappearances in Mexico!' There's no hint that there's going to be vampires at all. And then when they show up it's like whoosh! And the audience, like the characters in the movie, can't believe what's in their lap and what they have to deal with. The movie really does this kind of about-face."

Tarantino wrote the script in less than a month and with the money he received he was finally able to leave his day job and realise his dream of becoming a writer. "That was the first money I was ever paid for doing my art, for doing what I do," said Tarantino. "I quit my day job on that $1,500. Now, that was not a lot of money to stake yourself on a new life but it worked out all right. I ended up never having to take a day job again because from that job I got $7,000 to do a rewrite on this little film and $10,000 to do a writing job on this little film. I was actually supporting myself. Not beautifully at first but well enough. Actually I was doing better than I had ever done before."

For roughly the next five years, Tarantino's screenplay of *From Dusk Till Dawn* followed the path of many scripts in Hollywood that go into development and then never see the light of day. "The script for *From Dusk Till Dawn* was never really dormant, it was in development hell," said Kurtzman, the K in KNB EFX, who hoped to make the script his directing debut. "I had it set up that we were going to do it as a [*Tales From The*] *Crypt* film. We were in final negotiations to do it as the first film. It would have been *Demon Knight*. And, negotiations just fell through. It was kind of a nightmare."

"After five years of that, I decided to bail out as the director and I became unattached from it for a while. Then once Quentin became big, the project became bigger. People wanted to do it for more money and because I hadn't directed anything they wouldn't let me direct it at a ten million-dollar budget because I was a first-timer. I struggled with that for a while and then decided it was time to move on and just get the movie off the ground. I took the producing credit and story credit and did the effects."

It was about this time that Robert Rodriguez (*El Mariachi*, *Desperado*) was brought into the project as the director and Tarantino agreed to do a rewrite of his first screenplay. "Robert was actually the real reason why the project got going," said Kurtzman. "I optioned the script to some producers and they hooked up Robert, whom I had never met before. Robert took it back to Quentin and said, 'I think I want to do this.' And, Quentin said, 'Great, then I'll be involved!'"

Noted Kurtzman, "The script really hasn't changed very much. When Quentin came on to do a rewrite, he just really polished up a lot of dialogue and stuff that he wanted to play with, but it's the same movie."

Most of Tarantino's rewriting of the script concentrated on taking what he described as two-dimensional exploitation characters and giving them a more three-dimensional feel. "I'd written the script a long time ago," admitted Tarantino. "I wrote it to be an exploitation movie and that's exactly what it was supposed to be. It wasn't some lofty concept film."

"So, I looked at the script again that I originally wrote with no money and in three weeks. And I felt like I could improve on it because now I had a little bit more time and I'd become a better writer. I kept the structure almost exactly the same. In fact, every time I tried to add a scene I realised how good the structure was because all of a sudden things didn't make sense, things didn't work as good as they did. But what I could really do was really invest a lot into the characters."

The teenage Kate Fuller character was improved upon when Tarantino found out that Juliette Lewis would be playing the part. "I'm friends with Juliette, and she called me on the phone," said Tarantino. "She said she had read the original script and was interested in doing it. She's one of the coolest young actresses in America and I thought I better make this part worthy of her. I expanded her part a little, just to make it worth doing."

But Tarantino's investment in the characters did not include painting the vampires of the movie as brooding, sensitive outsiders dealing with the guilt and horror of their undead state. "I find it really kind of misleading to call this a vampire movie," said Tarantino. "And that's just because of the way that vampire movies are done these days. They're revisionist. Everything is revisionist. Vampire movies now get into the psyche of the vampire's pain from killing all those people and the torture of having to live for thousands of years."

"This isn't about any of that! These vampires are a bunch of fucking beast monsters! They don't have a soul! They don't give a fuck! They're vampires because they exist off of blood and if they bite you, you'll turn into a vampire. They're bat, rat, filthy, odorous creatures, just disgusting monsters. We never identify with or respect them and have no remorse in killing all of them."

Tarantino confessed that there is deeper meaning to the script than just a bloody Mexican gore fest. The subtext, he feels, may not be for everyone. "There's subtext in all my work," said Tarantino. "There's definitely a second drama going on underneath. That's what makes it special. It's there for you if you want to get into discussions about the loss of faith. It's treated seriously, but it's subtext. That's what makes it worth doing. I don't like to highlight it. I'm not making a message movie."

In retrospect the script and the process of finally bringing it to the screen had a very dramatic impact on Tarantino's life. It was the project that finally allowed him to bring his highly electric form of storytelling to the doorstep of the world. "Even more than directing my first movie, writing *From Dusk Till Dawn* was like the most exciting time in my life," said Tarantino. "When your life changes over from your writing in your spare time and working your day job to where you can actually support yourself doing what you do, that was so terrific. I'm getting goose bumps just thinking about it. There was no other jump that I have had in my life that was as big a jump as that."

Seth and Richie Gecko (George Clooney) and (Tarantino) open From Dusk Till Dawn *with a liquor store heist.*

tarantino rewrites tarantino

by Cynthia Baughman

Late in 1990 Robert Kurtzman, a makeup and special effects artist and partner in the special effects company, KNB EFX Group, was looking for a screenwriter to flesh out a script from a story he had written with John Esposito and wanted to direct. On the basis of two unproduced scripts sent to him as writing samples, *True Romance* and *Natural Born Killers*, Kurtzman hired a writer for $1,500, thus becoming the first person to actually pay a then unknown Quentin Tarantino to write. At one point slated for *Tales From The Crypt*, the script was kicked around for years while Kurtzman tried, as an untested director, to get financing and Tarantino became famous. After the success of *Pulp Fiction*, Tarantino was offered the chance to direct his old script, but he declined, instead agreeing to rewrite the 88-page *From Dusk Till Dawn* for Robert Rodriguez (*El Mariachi*) to direct.[1] Tarantino stuck with the original characters, story, structure, and much of the original dialogue, but added about 25 pages which develop the characters and increase the suspense. Comparing the two versions of the script, written some five years apart, reveals aspects of Tarantino's process of revision which can be instructive for any screenwriter, as well as contributing to an understanding of Tarantino's developing *oeuvre* and its themes, including exploration of fantasies of violence, and particularly sexual violence.

From Dusk Till Dawn begins as a Tarantino action movie/thriller with two blacksuited bad guys, brothers this time, in a tense situation. Seth and Richard Gecko have just robbed a bank in Abilene, and in the script's opening scene psychopathic Richard turns a trip to a convenience store into a bloodbath. "What did I tell you? What did I tell you? Buy the road map and leave," fumes the more controlled Seth as they leave the liquor store in flames with two bodies, including a Texas Ranger, on the floor.[2] Now they have to hotfoot it to Mexico where a contact, Carlos, will shelter them. At a seedy motel along the way, they cross paths with a widowed former preacher, Jacob Fuller, and his teenaged son Scott and daughter Kate, and force the terrified family to smuggle them across the border in their Winnebago, to an all-night biker-and-trucker bar where Carlos will join them sometime around dawn. After a bar-room fight at dusk, almost two thirds of the way through the script, the thriller suddenly changes genre, metamorphosing into a horror movie, when the denizens of the bar, literally smelling blood, transform into vampires and bolt the door. The bad guys and the hostages bond, as they try to keep the vampires at bay until daylight when Carlos will show up and, more crucially, sunlight will vanquish the undead. At the end of a long night, only

Seth and Kate, who seems to have found her calling as a vampire killer, remain, to ride off in the Winnebago with the Abilene loot; they could be re-born as Mickey and Mallory (*Natural Born Killers*), or Clarence and Alabama (*True Romance*), or Butch and Fabienne (*Pulp Fiction*).

Tarantino's most extensive revisions of his earlier draft involve the development of bad brother Richard from simply a vicious kidnapper/thief into a sexual predator. In both scripts, the two brothers take dad Jacob and son Scott hostage in their motel room, and when sister Kate returns from a swim in the motel pool, dripping in her swimsuit, Richard begins to ogle her threateningly. In the revised 1995 version, in a creepily effective moment, Richard hallucinates Kate inviting him to "do me a favor and eat my pussy" (1995; p. 35), and the script makes clear that he truly believes that he heard this voice: later, as he guards Kate and Scott in the back of the Winnebago, he asks her softly, and to her complete befuddlement, "Did you mean what you said back there? . . . Were you serious, or were you just foolin' around? I'm just bringing it up, 'cause if you really want me to do that for you I will." (1995; p. 45)[3] While Richard is in the back of the Winnebago experiencing these delusions, Seth sits up front with Jacob, driving towards Mexico, and making him a deal. The following exchange comes from the 1991 version of the script, but the terms of the deal are the same in both versions:

SETH
[. . .] You get us into Mexico and you don't try to escape, I'll keep my brother off your daughter and let you all loose in the morning.

JACOB
You won't let him touch her?

SETH
I can handle Richie, don't worry. (1991; p.29)

The 1995 version adds the following to Seth's claim that he can handle Richie.

SETH
[. . .] I give you my word.

Seth can't help but think about the last time he gave his word. (1995; p.42)

The tension of the 1995 version of the script is considerably heightened by the addition of the sequence comprised of the events Seth recalls here, "the last time he gave his word". In the 1995 version of the script, when the Gecko brothers arrive at the motel, in a moment reminiscent of Mr. Blonde's arrival at the warehouse in *Reservoir Dogs*, they open their car trunk to reveal that "a woman in her late forties is lying scrunched up in the trunk. She is the HOSTAGE BANK TELLER from Abilene. She's stiff, scared and looks an absolute mess." (1995; pp.14-15.) In the motel room, "Seth turns to the hostage, grabs a chair and slides it up in front of her."

SETH

    Now, we need to have a talk. What's your name?

HOSTAGE

    Gloria.

He shakes her hand.

SETH

    Hello, Gloria, I'm Seth and that's my brother Richie. Let's cut to the chase. I'm gonna ask you a question and all I want is a yes or no answer. Do you want to live through this?

GLORIA

    Yes.

SETH

    Good. Then let me explain the house rules. Follow the rules, we'll get along like a house on fire. Rule number one: No noise, no questions. You make a noise . . .(he holds up his .45)
    . . . Mr. 45 makes a noise. You ask a question, Mr. 45 answers it. Now, are you absolutely, positively clear about rule number one?

Seth goes on to explain the remaining rules, and then promises,

SETH

    Gloria, you hang in there, follow the rules, and don't fuck with us, you'll get out of this alive. I give you my word. Okay?

She nods her head yes. (1995; pp.17-18)

Seth leaves the motel room, and after he is gone, Richard looks to the TV, then looks to Gloria sitting across the room in the chair.

RICHARD

    Wanna come up here on the bed and watch TV with me?

You can tell she doesn't want to.

He pats the empty space next to him.

RICHARD

    Come on.

She gets out of her chair, walks across to the bed and sits down next to him. (1995; pp.18-19)

The scene ends and this is the last time we see Gloria alive. Seth conducts his business outside the motel, and we cut back to the motel room where Richard is smoking pot and watching TV news reports of the Gecko brothers' criminal histories and recent spree. We learn from a television reporter that Richard has just sprung Seth from prison where he was serving time for armed robbery and that Richard is "a known armed robber and sex offender" (1995; p. 20).

Eventually Seth returns with a six pack and two bags of Big Kahuna burgers (*Pulp Fiction*'s menacing omen). Seth and Richard start in on their dinner, and chat about their plans until, Seth stops talking and looks around.

SETH
Where's the woman?

RICHARD
What?

Seth's out of his chair.

SETH
What'd ya mean, what? The fuckin' woman, the hostage. Where the fuck is she, Richard!?

RICHARD
She's in the other room.

SETH
What the fuck is she doin' in there?!

He goes to the door of the adjoining room.

RICHARD
Seth, before you open the door, let me explain what happened.

Seth stops and looks at his younger brother. He knows what he means. He can't say anything, only point at his younger sibling. Then he BURSTS open the door.

The dead, naked body of Gloria Hill lies on the bed. It's obvious Richard raped her and killed her.

Seth covers his eyes with his hands. He slowly enters the room with the dead body.

SETH (to himself)
Oh, Richard, what's wrong with you? (1995; pp 26-27)

Richard tries to convince Seth that Gloria tried to escape, and that he had no choice but to kill her, but Seth does not buy this excuse.

SETH (slowly approaching)
> Is it me? Is it my fault?

RICHARD
> It's not your fault, it's her fault!

Seth grabs Richard and THROWS him in the corner of the room, holding tightly to his wrist.

SETH
> Is this my fault? Do you think this is what I am?

SETH
> This is not me! I am a professional fucking thief. I steal money. You try to stop me, god help you. But I don't kill people I don't have to, and I don't rape women. What you doin' ain't how it's done. Do you understand?

RICHARD
> Seth, if you were me -

SETH
> Just say yes! Nothing else, just say yes.

RICHARD
> Yes.

SETH
> Yes. Seth I understand.

RICHARD
> Yes, Seth, I understand.

Seth hugs his little brother. Tight.

SETH (whispers in Richie's ear)
> We get into Mexico, it's gonna be sweet Rosemary, 100 proof liquor, and rice and beans. None of this shit's gonna matter. (1995; pp.25-29)

And with these words Seth makes the second of his promises that will be broken in the course of this script.

The gruesome facts of Gloria's death hover over the scene in which Seth makes the same bargain with Jacob that he made with Gloria, of protection in exchange for co-operation. By developing Richard into a psychopathic sexual offender, and by graphically showing us that Seth's promise to protect Kate may therefore mean nothing, Tarantino considerably intensifies the suspense level of the script. One might also argue that with this development, Tarantino gives some kind of psychic logic to the abrupt change in genre which marks this script. Just as Marian Crane's miserable fate in the horror half of *Psycho* reads as a kind of retribution for her transgressions in the drama/thriller first half of the film, or Melanie's dalliance with lovebirds in the romantic comedy opening act seems to unleash the subsequent fury of *The Birds*, perhaps it is Richard Gecko's gratuitous bloodletting in the convenience store, and more importantly his sexual predation on the hostage Gloria Hill (whose name, a vulgarisation of *mons veneris*, suggests that she represents female sexuality in general), which unleashes the vengeance of the vampires. And thus the entire script might be read as a fantasy of female vengeance for male sexual predation.

The bar where the Gecko brothers expect to meet up with their protector is called "The Titty Twister", and stage direction tells us that,

Underneath the joint's proud name on the sign, and on top of "Biker/Trucker bar, Dusk till Dawn" is a well-endowed woman, whose breast is being twisted by a neon hand. (1995; p.56)

Thus the sign announces the joint as a palace of the sexual harassment of women. A barker out front advertises women for sale with repugnant proprietorship: "All pussy must go [. . .] we're slashing pussy in half! This is a pussy blow out! Make us an offer on our vast selection [. . .]" (1995; p. 57)

Inside the bar, waitresses, prostitutes, and entertainers are pawed voraciously, but the dancer Santanico Pandemonium introduces a new spirit of female aggression. An announcer proclaims,

RAZOR CHARLIE
And now for your viewing pleasure. The Mistress of the Macabre. The Epitome of Evil. The most sinister woman to dance on the face of the earth. Lowly dogs, get on your knees, bow your heads and worship at the feet of SANTANICO PANDEMONIUM! (1995; p. 70)

Stage direction tells us that "this Mexican goddess" has "the beauty of the siren who lures men to their doom", and when she spots the Fuller/Gecko table, she "zero[es] in on our boy Richard" (1995; p. 70-71). Santanico dances around Richard, pours whiskey down her leg, and lets him suck it from her toes; Richard is mesmerized, and "Kate, oddly enough, is turned on by the controlling power this woman has over a man she's deathly feared" – Santanico does seem to be achieving a kind of vengeance for Kate. The song ends and Santanico grabs Richard's hair, yanks his head back painfully, and dribbles whiskey from her mouth to his. At Seth's prompting, Richard invites her to sit with them, and she does, until a fight between the brothers and the bar owners opens the wound on Richard's shoulder and Santanico smells blood. "A special aroma fills her nostrils. Her eyes lock on Richard. The look on her face could easily be read as intense sexual desire." Then Santanico leaps at Richard, and in what could be a metaphor of rape,

[. . .] LANDS on his BACK and SINKS her FANGS into Richie's wounded SHOULDER.

Richard lets loose with an agonizing SCREAM.

Seth turns to his brother's cry.

He sees SANTANICO PANDEMONIUM, like a mongoose attached to a cobra, legs wrapped around Richard's waist, fangs buried deep in his shoulder, and Richard screaming and slamming about, trying to knock her off. (1995; pp.75-76)

Richard dies and,

The bikers and truckers who have been transfixed, watching the impossible, realise that the waitresses, naked dancers and whores who they were pawing just five minutes ago, have turned into yellow-eyed, razor-fanged, drool-dripping vampires. (1995; p.76)

Certainly Santanico does not know about Richard's history of sexual crimes against women, but her attack on him does seem to arise as retribution in horror films frequently does: the crime is not overtly indicted, but the forces of dark nature seem to respond and punish it nevertheless.[4] But to argue that the vampire segment of *From Dusk Till Dawn* is partly a fantasy of female revenge on male sexual aggression is not to argue that this is a script with a feminist animus.

The fantasy strikes me as a male fantasy of female revenge, in which anger turns women into monsters, or in which enraged women reveal themselves to have been monsters in disguise all along, and in the face of this anger, men become the innocent victims of evil bitches. It is a fearful fantasy of what might happen if abused women took revenge, but it is also a comforting fantasy in which ultimately the avenging women are vanquished. The only woman who remains standing at the end of the script is Kate, for whom the experience with the Gecko brothers seems to be a passage from innocent cross-wearing adolescence into bonded heterosexual adult womanhood.[5]

The development of Kate's character is another addition to the 1995 script, and it occurs primarily through another new sequence which enhances the film's suspense. In the 1991 script, as the Winnebago approaches the Mexican border, Seth order Scott to sit up front with his father, and packs himself, Richard, and Kate into the bathroom. As the camper stops at the border, Richard whispers that he is sure Jacob is asking the border patrol for help; Seth shushes him; Kate silently weeps, and after a tense moment the camper starts moving again and Scott comes to the door to give the all-clear. In the 1995 version, the border crossing sequence is much more complex and suspenseful. Not only does the precedent of Richard's treatment of Gloria make us fear for his treatment of Kate in the close quarters of the bathroom, in this version, Richard's suspicion that Jacob will inform is much stronger, and he and Seth argue the point intensely while Scott, up front, quietly insists that his father indeed inform: "Dad, I watch those reality shows . . . Anybody will tell you, in a situation like this, you get a chance, you go for it . . . If you don't tell the cops, I will." (1995; p. 49) As the camper stops at the border, we do not know if Scott will obey his father and keep his mouth shut, but in fact he does, as Jacob calmly tells the border guard that he has only his son aboard. At that moment, to shut Richard up, Seth slugs him, and the guard hears a thump from the bathroom. Jacob attributes the noise to his daughter in the bathroom, whom he had simply neglected to mention earlier, and the guard, now suspicious, says he is coming aboard. The script cuts to the bathroom where we see only Kate's frightened face. The guard knocks; Kate tells him she is in the bathroom, and the guard opens the door to see only Kate, sitting on the toilet. "Do you mind?" she says. "Shut the fucking door." The guard apologises and leaves, and we discover that Seth is hiding in the shower, with the knocked-out Richard slumped on its floor. The camper successfully crosses the border, and Seth and Kate emerge from the bathroom.

This sequence not only is more suspenseful than the relatively smooth border crossing in the earlier script, it also gives new shading to Kate's and Seth's characters and sets them up for their coming partnership in vampire liquidation. After the border patrol cops leave the Winnebago, Seth emerges:

SETH (to Kate)
> You were magnificent! You told him to shut the fucking door. I'm hiding in the shower, and I'm thinking to myself, "Did I just fuckin' hear what I just fuckin' heard?" And what does he do he shuts the fucking door!

Kate kind of half smiles.

SETH
> If I was a bit younger, baby, I'd fuckin' marry you!

Seth goes up front and slaps Jacob on the back.

SETH
> I gotta hand it to you, Pops, you raised a fuckin' woman. (1995; pp.52-53)

And what kind of woman is this? A woman who is bold and resourceful, but who uses those qualities in the service of the men who hold her hostage. Just before Santanico Pandemonium jumps on Richard, Kate warns him to look out; she joins with a squadron of men to vanquish these apparitions of female vengeance, and the script ends with her bonded to Seth. "You're my family now," (1991; p.88) she says.

Elsewhere I have argued that Tarantino is capable of profound and revealing exploration of fantasies of violence and rape.[6] But Tarantino does not surround the sexual violence in *From Dusk Till Dawn* with the layers of material which comprise *Pulp Fiction*'s revealing explorations of psychic territory. While I argue here that *From Dusk Till Dawn* does explore fantasies of rape and violence, this script suggests to me that violence between men is the subject that Tarantino really warms to, and which brings out the best in him.

From Dusk Till Dawn yields many of the familiar pleasures of a Tarantino script: inventive uses of genre; hilariously obsessive conversation about trivial points, or pop culture references, in the midst of a crisis; brilliant timing; and, for those familiar with the Tarantino *oeuvre*, the recurrence of names and topoi. Just as, in *Pulp Fiction*, Jules's brush with death brings him to a spiritual renewal and a new appreciation of his favourite Bible verse, so Jacob Fuller's confrontation with the vampires restores his lost faith. Early in the script we learn that Jacob is an ex-preacher, who lost his faith after the death of his wife, and resigned his pastorship. In the confrontation with the vampires, it becomes clear that crosses indeed work, and that faith is a useful weapon.[7] In the 1991 version of the script, Jacob Fuller walks through the bar as it swarms with vampires, trying to get to his children, huddled in a back room.

Then they hear Jacob's voice in the barroom, booming out.

JACOB (OS)
> The path of the righteous man and defender is beset on all sides by the iniquities of the selfish and the tyranny of evil men.

INT. BARROOM - NIGHT
Jacob holding a cross made out of two sticks and reciting appropriate verse from the Bible is keeping the vampires at bay. But as Seth predicted, it is the shining power of his restored faith that is his mightiest weapon [. . .] Jacob recites the verse from the Bible in a threatening, mean, motherfucking, servant of god tone. As he speaks with authority and strength, he sees Frost lying on the ground, bat things on him like ants on a candy bar. But Jacob is too much in control to let even this repugnant sight trip him up.

JACOB
> Blessed is he who in the name of charity and good will shepherds the weak through the valley of darkness. For he is truly his brother's keeper, and the father of lost children. And I will execute great vengeance upon them, with furious anger, who poison and destroy my brothers. And they shall know I am the lord when I raise my vengeance upon them.

Jacob has backed himself up by the door.

JACOB
> Open the door.

The door FLIES open. Jacob jumps inside.
The door SLAMS shut.

INT. STOREROOM - NIGHT
Kate and Scott hug their father. Jacob's eyes
look up at Seth.

JACOB
> Ezekiel 25:17. (1991; pp.65-66)

The 1995 version of the script does not include *Pulp Fiction's* touchstone Bible verse;

rather the stage direction simply tells us that Jacob recites "verse from the Bible [sic] in a threatening, mean, motherfucking, servant of god [sic] tone" – the tone of a "Bad Motherfucker"? With or without the verse from Ezekiel, however, Jacob Fuller's restoration of faith is not as profound and thoughtful as is Jules's in *Pulp Fiction*. From *Dusk Till Dawn* has neither the structural or emotional complexity of *Reservoir Dogs* or *Pulp Fiction*. The narrative marches ahead in chronological order, covering a period of about 20 hours, and the emotional development of the characters is limited; faced with vampires, Jacob Fuller recovers some of the faith he lost when his wife died, and Kate surprises us with her capacities for vampire killing. In Tarantino's best work, at least a few of the deaths are dwelt upon – we count the moments as Mr Orange bleeds, and suffer with the torture victims of *Reservoir Dogs* and *Pulp Fiction*. But Seth says to Kate when her father dies, "Fight now, cry later" – and that moment of mourning never comes (1995; p.105). *From Dusk Till Dawn* does not aspire to the complexity of *Reservoir Dogs* or *Pulp Fiction*. It aspires to be an effective horror script, and it succeeds at that, while playing with genre and exploring horror's psychic structure. Tarantino has good taste combined with good luck in his own scripts, keeping the richest ones for himself to direct, and letting other people take the joyrides.

Thanks to Jane Parry, Jill Schuman, Michel Theriot and Deborah Fort and the Department of Moving Image Arts, College of Santa Fe, for assistance in the development and preparation of this essay. Thanks also to Richard Moran for our continuing conversation about Tarantino.

Notes
[1] Jami Bernard, *Quentin Tarantino: The Man And His Movies*. New York: HarperCollins, 1995, pp. 105-113, and Anthony C. Ferrante, "The Bad Boys of Horror", *Fangoria*, Number 149, January 1996, pp.32-37; 76).
[2] Quentin Tarantino, *From Dusk Till Dawn*, 1995, p.9. In this essay I quote from two versions of the script. The title page of the 1991 version reads: "FROM DUSK TILL DAWN by Quentin Tarantino; story by Robert Kurtzman", and the title page of the 1995 version reads: "FROM DUSK TILL DAWN; Screenplay by Quentin Tarantino; Story by Robert Kurtzman; Directed by Robert Rodriguez." Subsequent references will appear in parentheses in the text, with the script date followed by the page number, i.e., "1995; p.9". As this essay goes to press, the Miramax film has not yet been released, and thus was unavailable for review.
[3] Much later in the script, when bitten humans transform into vampires, the transformation is heralded by a voice as they hallucinate the call, "Thirst, thirst." Thus the script suggests some equation between the grip of the sexual predator's fantasies and the grip of the vampire's thirst for blood.
[4] In his fine and comprehensive book on the poetics of the horror genre, *The Philosophy of Horror*, Noel Carroll discusses a psychoanalytic interpretation of the vampire myth which argues that the belief in the return of bloodsucking dead masks a wish for the incestuous sexual visits of ancestors/relatives, and for a blameless

passivity in the face of their molestations (New York: Routledge, 1990), pp. 168-170.

[5] In the last relaxed moments before Santanico jumps on Richard, Seth tells a joke which encapsulates another ultimately comforting fantasy of female revenge for male violence:

SETH

> Which reminds me of a joke. Little Red Riding Hood is walking through the forest and she comes across Little Bo Peep, and Little Bo Peep says: "Little Red Riding Hood, are you crazy? Don't you know the Big Bad Wolf is walking these woods and if he finds you he's gonna pull down your dress and squeeze your titties?" Then Little Red Riding Hood hitches up her skirt and taps a .357 Magnum she has holstered on her thigh and says: "No he won't." [. . .] So finally she comes across the Big Bad Wolf and the Big Bad Wolf's laughing and says: "Little Red Riding Hood, you know better than to be walking around these woods alone. You know I'm just gonna have to pull down your dress and squeeze your titties." Then Little Red Riding Hood whips out her .357, cocks it, sticks it in the Big Bad Wolf's face and says: "No you won't. You're gonna eat my pussy, just like the story says." (1995; pp.72-73)

In Seth's version of the fairy tale, a girl threatened with the vaunted activity of the "Titty Twister" itself, reveals herself to be an aggressive phallic woman, but what does she do with the gun holstered on her thigh? She does not vanquish the wolf, but rather asks just the question Richard fantasised Kate asking earlier in the script.

[6] Richard Moran and I argued, in an earlier essay, that the rape/torture of Marsellus occurred within a context of thoughtful exploration of masculine bonding, fantasies about the masculine/paternal body, and about the suffering of American POW's. See "'A Moment of Clarity': Retrieval, Redemption, Resurrection, and Narrative Time in *Pulp Fiction*", *Creative Screenwriting*, vol. 1, no. 4, Winter 1994, special issue on Quentin Tarantino, pp. 108-118.

[7] Tarantino wittily acknowledges that familiarity with vampire lore comes primarily from other vampire movies – while *From Dusk Till Dawn* does not abound in pop culture references as do Tarantino's other scripts, the following exchange acknowledges its place in the movie genre:

JACOB

> Has anybody here read a real book about vampires, or are we just remembering what a movie said? I mean a real book.

SEX MACHINE

> You mean like a Time-Life book? (1995; p.90)

tarantino and juliette

by Mim Udovitch

Quentin Tarantino has a cold, and since it's his, it's one motherfucking badass cold; he is unshaven, wearing jeans and a T-shirt and, even in a weakened state, capable of projecting an upbeat egotism so enormous that it almost amounts to generosity, a sort of open house of the self. Juliette Lewis is tired, slender, and chic in a tailored black jacket with a nipped-in waist, a synthetic blue shirt, and an air of cosmic smouldering. Together, at the Hamburger Hamlet, they have, as they point out, a funky vibe. Tarantino is expansive, reflexive, and hyper, in his work and in his person, while Lewis is internal, instinctive, and serenely sensual. The two bonded on the set of *From Dusk Till Dawn* (opening next month), which was written by Tarantino and directed by Robert Rodriguez, and in which they co-star – in a stunning reversal of the old caricature, Tarantino is a director who *really wants to act*.

However different their routes, Lewis and Tarantino are both living at the heart of Mondo Hollywood: They are successful on their own terms within the framework of the Industry; the work of each is inimitable in its individuality; and in a way that has less to do with their work than with the weird psychic demands America places upon celebrity, both have been known to get on people's nerves. (Especially Tarantino, whose image has gone from demigod to despot in near record time; recently, critics have begun attacking him for movies – *The Usual Suspects*, *Things To Do In Denver When You're Dead* – with which he had absolutely nothing to do. "It's natural, it's gonna happen," says Tarantino of the wave of backlash headed his way. "If you don't read it, it can't hurt you. And if people think I'm an egotistical loudmouth asshole, then yes, they're wrong.")

Nevertheless, in an age of grumpy celebrity, both love their jobs. "I mean every independent filmmaker you talk to will just rag on and on about how fucked everything is," says Tarantino. "And it's like: Well, if it's so fucked why are you doing it? If life is so tough for you, stop making movies!" "Acting for me is a release sometimes," says Lewis. "I almost get giddy and light, and it's just amazing because I'm stepping out and creating this whole other, nonexistent world in front of a little camera. And other times," she adds, pragmatically, "it's just work."

All right. Are you ready?
JULIETTE LEWIS: Oh God, we're playing truth or dare.

Why are movies so bad?
LEWIS: I think it's the big war between the money people and artists. And that money people have this idea that it's either independent-artsy or it's commercial-bad. But movies can be both.

from dusk till dawn

So why do they cling to the idea that they can't?

QUENTIN TARANTINO: Well, I don't think they do anymore. The rules that they've been playing by don't quite work anymore and everyone's kind of like realising it right now. It's because basically that whole Touchstone formula that was existing in the Eighties, that couldn't miss, is missing now. It doesn't work.

LEWIS: Yeah! Like *Home Alone* was a huge hit and no one predicted that. No one can predict *Congo*.

TARANTINO: Yeah, the formulas of the last ten years don't work anymore. The movies that are like sequels to the real big ones work because the audience has an investment in that franchise. But either the movies that used to be making $100 million are barely making $20 million or they're not even making that. I think right now is the most exciting time in Hollywood since 1971. Because Hollywood is never more exciting than when you don't know.

It's like alternative rock, which is an alternative to what, really?

TARANTINO: Exactly. I did that Kennedy show on MTV, *Alternative Nation*, all week long when *Pulp Fiction* opened and I said that: "Alternative to what?" It's the biggest-selling shit out there.

You have to let Juliette talk more.

TARANTINO: She was the one doing most of the talking!

Okay, let's plug From Dusk Till Dawn. *What do you play?*

LEWIS: I play a preacher's daughter, Harvey Keitel's daughter. He takes the kids on a vacation, in their little camper, and he's questioning his faith because his wife died, so he's a little bit mad at God, and then through this, we meet up with these two little thugs – and that's Quentin and George Clooney – and they kidnap our little family. Of course the two thugs get in a fight and then it's vampire hell.

TARANTINO: One of the cool things about the vampires in the movie is they're just a bunch of carnivorous banshee beasts, they're like rats, they're these horrible things. There's none of that soul-searching or the angst of living forever and having to suck other people's blood, all that revisionist vampire stuff. They're just a bunch of monsters, and you should kill as many of them as you possibly can, because they're trying to kill you.

LEWIS: And then my character turns into a real badass and it's cool. She has to turn into a warrior to kill these monsters.

So basically she gets in touch with the inner badass. An underrated aspect of the character.

LEWIS: Yeah! Well, you don't get it challenged much in life.

Well, you seem to be in touch with your inner badass. What's George Clooney like? He's a fox-and-a-half, in my view.

LEWIS: I guess. He's cool, and a lot of people, if they're cool they're foxy. I remember finding Scorsese sexy from being around him.

quentin tarantino: the film geek files

You know, from a distance that doesn't come through for me, but I'm willing to take your word for it. Do you get crushes on directors?
LEWIS: Not directors. I get these five-minute crushes on like room-service guys, valets, grips, actors – but not truly, just for five minutes.

The room-service waiter thing I can totally get with.
LEWIS: Actually what's a little more of a challenge is the bellhop, because he's a little more of the silent type. I don't act on it, because I can't really, I'm so guarded. And guys don't really come on to me.

Preacher's daughter Kate Fuller (Juliette Lewis), a born-again 'bad-ass' vampire killer.

LEWIS: Oh, here's the big observation! I like this one.
TARANTINO: Juliette is a true chameleon. If she was walking around the Redwood Forest she would all of a sudden look like a lizard on a tree. And so we go walking around this outlet mall and we all realise our demographic like that. I walk into kind of like a hip place, and the counter girl will be: "Oh my God, it's Quentin Tarantino!" And when we walk into a K-mart kind of thing, all of these ladies, the fat ladies in the stretch pants are like: "George Clooney! Dr. Ross!" But Juliette is rarely approached, and not because she's not famous.
LEWIS: Because I was wearing red shorts and a red-and-white tube top and sandals . . .
TARANTINO: And she looked like a native. People didn't even remotely turn their heads. If they recognised her, they thought they went to school with her.
LEWIS: Yeah, but if I wore something like this, then . . .
TARANTINO: Then you'd stand out. You are a fucking badass. And I'm just here, from being sick all day, wearing a T-shirt.
LEWIS: But Quentin has cool outfits.
TARANTINO: But you look *bad*. Badass. But anyway . . .

LEWIS: The waitress has to come, Quentin, because we have to get our hamburgers.

And I have talking points.

TARANTINO: Okay, well, hold on, hold on, I'm not finished with my story yet. So all the young wannabe hip people, they knew who I was, the white-trash people knew who George was . . .

LEWIS: Oh boy.

TARANTINO: . . . and Juliette just *looked* like trash . . .

LEWIS: Yeah, yeah, yeah.

TARANTINO: . . . *but*, we all looked like Bobby Sherman compared to Cheech Marin. Cheech is the most famous fucking guy on the planet fucking Earth. I mean it's like he walks through there, people would stomp us to death to get to Cheech. We go into the Dairy Queen and Cheech is in business, man. There's like a line. Truck drivers . . .

LEWIS: Yeah, and little kids because of *The Lion King*.

TARANTINO: Yeah, yeah, exactly! And it's like: "*Heeey*, Cheech, smoke a bowl! Cheech! Mr Marin, can I get your autograph? Cheech, where's Chong?" He's the most famous guy in America!

What do you think are people's fantasies about Hollywood? What is the Hollywood myth?

TARANTINO: I don't know. To me that's the problem with marketing research and executives – it's everyone assuming that they know what the public's thinking. I know what *I'm* thinking.

LEWIS: The public would have to be asked.

TARANTINO: I know what I'm thinking. When I do a movie, I know what I want to see and I'm going to bet there are other people out there like me. I don't know if there's much of a myth of Hollywood anymore. But what I find interesting is something like the E! channel. The whole idea is to demystify celebrities and make the people that watch the E! channel think they're friends with the celebrities, because you're just constantly seeing a barrage the entire time you're watching.

But don't you think that's the same as the old-time stars doing homey things – like when Joan Crawford would be with her kids reading **The Night Before Christmas** *over the radio the night before Christmas? It's like this highly mediated reality.*

LEWIS: I do. I think with the media . . .

TARANTINO: No, can I interrupt you, just for two seconds? I think it's the exact opposite. Because it's like you're taking all the celebrities on the planet and you're trying to make them like they're your neighbours. Where in the old days they wanted the stars to be gods. They didn't *identify* with Joan Crawford or Clark Gable, they *worshipped* them. Where that totally exists now is Hong Kong, the Hong Kong film industry. The stars in Hong Kong are like movie stars in the Thirties and the Forties, man. I mean, they are *gods*. In a weird way, just like the old movie stars, they're almost not real people, they exist on the screen.

LEWIS: I do think E! is the Nineties version of sensationalising movie stars. The *normalcy* is sensationalised, like: "Look, she eats French fries with her hands!" And like in articles: "And she crosses her legs and looks up to the ceiling and sighs and rests her head on her fucking hand." You just draw such attention to such normal behaviour that it does sensationalise it. All people have their own little mannerisms, so I don't see why movie-star mannerisms are more interesting.

TARANTINO: It's funny, because the thing that I find really bizarre when I read interviews with myself is I start getting ridiculously self-conscious about just being me. 20 articles talk about how fast I talk and that I talk with my hands and all of a sudden I'm like: "Oh, maybe I shouldn't talk so fast. Maybe I should comb my hair. Maybe I shouldn't talk with my hands so much." I'm a geek. I'm a freak.

Don't go changing.

TARANTINO: But no one can deal with that kind of self-consciousness, and all of a sudden you're afraid to be who you are. Normally I go into photo shoots and I'm so defensive, like I go in there like I'm gonna get into a fight with the guy or the girl who's doing the thing. I'm like: "No, no, no, I'm not gonna lay in a bucket of blood and I'm not going to put my face against a brick and you're not going to shoot me with a razor blade in my mouth or pins in my face. You're going to shoot me like I'm Sharon Stone. I want to be handsome in this photo, all right?"

LEWIS: (*crosses her legs and looks up to the ceiling and sighs and rests her head on her fucking hand*) Even I've been guilty of this. You can't understand how someone can do an intense part and not have some kind of neuroses. That's the only thing that sucks sometimes, is you can be talking to someone and you're just being normal, but they think at any time your head's gonna spin, like in *The Exorcist*.

TARANTINO: Everyone makes all these jokes or observations about how I'm mentoring John Travolta as far as his career choices in other movies. Well, he's mentoring *me* in photo shoots.

Okay. The next question is, Joe Eszterhas: Why?

LEWIS: Who's Joe Eszterhas?

TARANTINO: He's a screenwriter. He's actually bad-mouthed me quite a few times. I don't know about quite a few times, but . . .

LEWIS: I'll go break his shins for you.

TARANTINO: . . . he did this profile on TV and I never saw it, but apparently he spent ten minutes of the 20 talking about how he writes real screenplays and he's a real screenwriter, and I'm just jerking off.

But he wrote Jade *and* Basic Instinct *and* Showgirls. *Those aren't jerking off?*

LEWIS: Oh my God! And he said that about you? You can't even respond to something like that!

TARANTINO: To tell you the truth, I thought *Showgirls* was fucking great. I'm thinking about writing an article in *Film Comment* in complete and utter defence of *Showgirls*.

What did you like about it?

TARANTINO: I'll tell you exactly what I liked about it. Joe Eszterhas's script was the least of it. I think Sharon Stone made him a star, she's really enjoyable in *Basic Instinct*. But the thing that's great about *Showgirls*, and I mean great with a capital G, is that only one other time in the last 20 years has a major studio made a full-on, gigantic, big-budget exploitation movie.

And that was?
TARANTINO: *Mandingo*, which is one of my favourite movies. *Showgirls* is the *Mandingo* of the Nineties.
LEWIS: Quentin has these thoughts.
TARANTINO: And the thing is, what's so great about it is that no one else but Paul Verhoeven would have the balls to shoot that the way it should be shot. He knew he was making an exploitation movie. Roger Corman started this whole sub-genre in exploitation films on video – *Stripped To Kill* is the first one – and they're always about like a bunch of topless dancers and there's usually some killer wiping them out, the best one being a film called *Naked Obsession* with William Katt. And *Showgirls* is a $40 million version of that. The thing that was also great is the sex in *Showgirls* was dirty. There was nothing pretty. The only scene that didn't work for me at all was where Elizabeth Berkley and Kyle MacLachlan have sex in this pool. But the scene where she lap-dances on him and dry-humps him, that was a good scene, man!
LEWIS: I just think all that shit's boring.
TARANTINO: But in *Showgirls*, just as the sex started to get boring in the last fifteen minutes, they played the violence into it. And Elizabeth Berkley turns into Pam Grier and fucks up this bad guy and she does a great job. And you leave the movie on a high note.
LEWIS: How does she kill him?
TARANTINO: She doesn't kill him, she just beats the shit out of him.
LEWIS: With her hands?
TARANTINO: Well, she's tall, she's like a redwood, and she's got these big boots and he's raped her best friend. I mean horribly. So she takes out a switchblade . . .
LEWIS: Cool, knives are good.
TARANTINO: Unfortunately, she doesn't carve him up with the knife. . .
LEWIS: . . . Oooooh, why doesn't she use the knife?
TARANTINO: . . . but the guy's really big and she beats him to death, damn near!
LEWIS: Did he get the knife away from her?
TARANTINO: No. She gets him down so he won't say anything and then she proceeds to do these like intense roundhouse kicks with these big boots on.
LEWIS: Kick boxing. Knew it.
TARANTINO: And she fucks him up, man! It's really cool.
LEWIS: Wow. You know what I'd like to know? I'd like to know all the rumours on me.

I don't think I've heard any. I think you satisfied the need for rumours by coincidentally living with Brad Pitt, another famous person, at the height of your fame. That just filled the hole.
LEWIS: And the rumours after that, about being with other famous people? I've never been with any other famous people. Just because I'm in the same age bracket as Johnny Depp and Leo DiCaprio doesn't mean we all screw together.

And you do tend to hear gay rumours about almost everybody.

LEWIS: Yes, the gay rumour goes wild. For everyone. Like with Leo, he was like: "Is Brad gay?" And I said, "Leo, *you're* gay, don't you know? Haven't you heard?"

TARANTINO: I always thought it was really cool when Jami Bernard interviewed me for her book on me, she goes: "How do you feel about (1) the rumours that you're gay, and (2) the fact that the gay community has embraced your movies and claimed you as one of their own?"

LEWIS: Whoa! Quentin has a gay rumour too!

TARANTINO: And I go: "Really? That's cool, man. I totally dig it."

LEWIS: Because they're the underdogs or whatever. I have kind of the underdog connection too.

TARANTINO: You kind of look like Underdog.

Okay. The last question is, what are you looking forward to?

LEWIS: Just the future. The future at large.

TARANTINO: I'd like to be in a situation where I can direct a movie, then act in a movie, direct a movie, then act in a movie. Because one of the big problems with directing is it takes so fucking long. It was great to give my heart and soul to something and then when shooting was over, it was done. And I liked being another person, and thinking another person's thoughts.

LEWIS: And he's really menacing and threatening and perverted, it's really gross.

TARANTINO: Other than that, I guess I'm too self-obsessed to think of anything that isn't personal. I used to have directors where I was counting the days until their movie came out, but I don't think that way anymore. I'm looking forward to sleeping late.

LEWIS: I'm looking forward to seeing who becomes the love of my life.

I'm looking forward to seeing that too. I mean, not who becomes the love of your life, although, of course, I'd like to know that as well.

TARANTINO: All of America is looking forward to that.

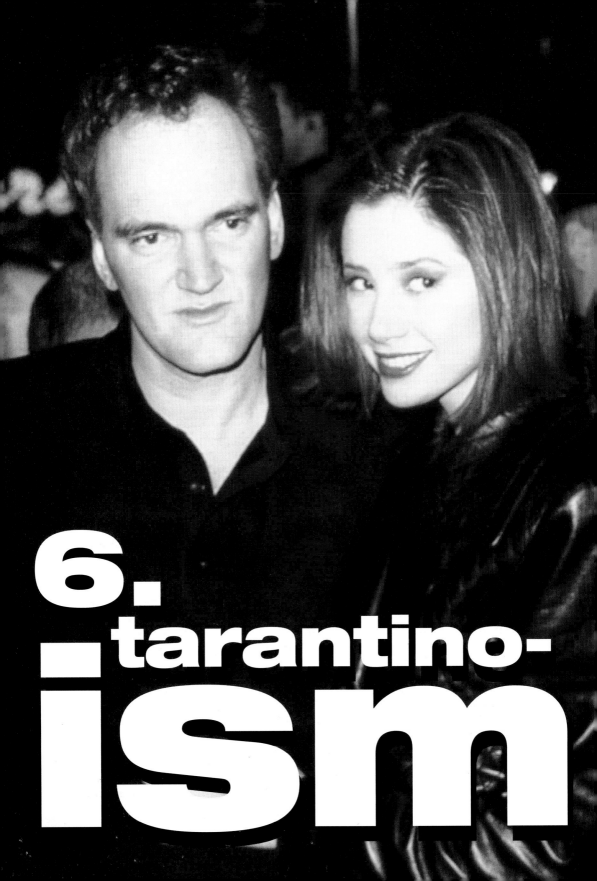

6.
tarantino-
ism

the price of fame

by Michael Beeler

Fame is a tough snake to charm and right now no one knows that better than Quentin Tarantino. A former video store clerk in Southern California, he rocketed to critical as well as commercial success with the release of *Pulp Fiction*, only the second film he directed. Since that time, Tarantino has begun the process of learning to live under the heavy scrutiny of the self-appointed dogs of Hollywood. It hasn't been easy.

Critics were quick to laud Tarantino's directing talents in *Reservoir Dogs* and *Pulp Fiction* and many of them praised his screenwriting abilities on *True Romance* and *Natural Born Killers*. But when it comes to his acting skills, movie reviewers have not been kind. Tarantino was probably slammed the hardest for his stint in *Destiny Turns On The Radio*, a knock Tarantino feels may be justified. "I couldn't have been more distracted at the time than when I did [*Destiny Turns On The Radio*] and I think it shows," admitted Tarantino. "I don't think I was as bad as some critics said I was, but I was mediocre."

"Some critics wrote that I was shit. And you could make the analogy that mediocre is shit. I'll buy that. All right. But I don't want to be mediocre. So, yeah, I was the worst form of shit, as far as I was concerned. But part of it was just because I was distracted. I started shooting that movie the week before *Pulp Fiction* opened. I couldn't have been so not there."

"But the cool thing about it was when I looked at myself in the movie, it was like, 'Okay, I can't do that ever again!' If I'm going to do it, I've got to commit 100%. This isn't the celebrity show. I'm not Charro. I'm an actor. In a way, the lessons I learned from that movie are hopefully going to be bearing fruit."

Regardless of how the critics may perceive him, Tarantino is loved by audiences. He has become a well-established member of the MTV generation, the new, young, smart Hollywood that is quickly taking over the sacred landscape of filmdom. In Europe, *Pulp Fiction* posters displayed more pictures of Tarantino than the movie's extraordinary ensemble cast.

"It's pretty cool," said Tarantino. "You hear old vaudevillians say, 'I kill 'em in Omaha! A big marquee and lines around the block.' I'm that way in England. It's great. How could you not love it?"

Tarantino does admit that fame does have a cost and there are some real mental drawbacks to being so popular and well-known. He noted, "One of the bummers is, I like to walk. I'm one of the few people in Los Angeles who likes to walk. And the neighbourhood that I live in – West Hollywood – is one of the few areas that is sort of village like, you can actually walk. And I find that I make less eye contact with people on the street. Basically everyone turns into a homeless person. You make eye contact with a homeless person and they start going toward you. That's kind of how everybody is now."

"It's also kind of a bummer when I'm with my girlfriend and we're out having dinner or just trying to have an evening by ourselves and people just keep coming up. I never lose it, but that's the only time when I say, 'You have eyes. If I were you I would see that I'm with my lady and know how to respect that.'"

The other problem Tarantino is learning to deal with is the fact that it is becoming increasingly more difficult for him to frequent the places he used to love to go to and hang out. "The days of going into a used record store and just zoning out, looking through records for three hours, are gone," lamented Tarantino. "Going into a video store and going through the videos, looking at every title they have, trying to find some old spaghetti western, that's gone. [Goes into a sort of hippie cool dude voice] 'Could you like sign this poster, dude?'"

"I still do that, but it's not like the way I used to do it. I've got to deal with people. Either I'm signing or sometimes I'll just say, 'It's my day off.' And they respect that. I'll shake their hand because I don't want to make anyone feel bad about anything. It's just that I want to live my life, too. I'm not going to give up my life, but I'm not going to give up my courtesy either. So, it's just about finding that balance."

tourantino!
by Jayne Jain Kennedy

Los Angeles. The City of Angels. The Movie Capital Of The World. The plastic surgery centre of the universe. A city of a million contradictions. To better appreciate the tainted glamour of L.A., a city Quentin Tarantino loves as only a townie can, forget the regular tours of the stars' homes or the countless other day trips on offer and take a Tourantino of the diners, vacant lots, lodging sites and killing zones of *True Romance*, *Reservoir Dogs* and *Pulp Fiction*.

Start with a hearty breakfast and several refills of coffee at Pat and Lorraine's, 4720 Eagle Rock Boulevard, the diner where most of the colour-coded *Reservoir Dogs* ate what turned out to be their last meal.

"There are customers who come in because they've seen the film and they like the food and the service is good," says waitress Leslie Harwood, who says she hasn't seen *Dogs*, but insists that tips have always been forthcoming despite Mr Pink's impassioned refusal. Nor has she ever seen a group of black-suited, black-tied men arrive early one morning bickering about the lyrical content of Madonna songs. But if they did?

"I'd think I was on *Candid Camera*," she coos.

While in the neighbourhood, be sure to check out many of the blood-drenched sites that figure prominently in *Dogs*. After filming was completed, the disused mortuary that stood in for the warehouse where the Dogs reconvened after the bungled diamond heist was considered as a site for an after-school arts programme. Inner city youths would have fashioned crafts in the same place Mr Blonde worked his own cut-and-baste magic. When that plan fell through, though, the building was demolished.

You can still enjoy the alleyway, however, where the bullet Mr Brown caught finally takes effect and Mr White unloads into a squad car and kills two cops: it's between Avenue 55 and Avenue 56. Just a random bullet shot away is the stretch of road where Mr Orange guns downs the woman in the white Mustang who shoots him by 5518 Marmion Way.

Now it's time to settle in to Los Angeles properly, so head west down Figueroa, past the shops Mr Pink runs by while fleeing from the police with the loot, to Riverside Avenue. Follow that to just beyond Glendale, site of the River Glen Motel, where Butch and Fabienne hole up in *Pulp Fiction*. Only rugged travellers or those on a severely tight budget will opt to stay here since it has been blighted by gang graffiti, quake damage, floods and the myriad of Biblical disasters that Los Angeles is prone to instead of weather. A good opportunity for actual crime presents itself here, as relic seekers tend to hop the fence and tear up a piece of carpeting from Butch and Fabienne's room.

For more gracious digs, try the Safari Inn, 1911 Olive Boulevard by Buena Vista, in Burbank where young lovers Christian Slater and Patricia Arquette stayed in *True Romance*, and the decor is cheesier than a Big Kahuna Burger. Prices range between $60 and $120 a night with views of the pool or the smog-kissed mountains to choose from.

"People come and stay because they've seen the video," admits the Safari's operations manager Johnny De Lesley Jnr. "There were even a couple of thirteen-year-olds that came by. They said they wanted to be where *True Romance* was filmed. They wanted to sit up on the sun deck."

According to De Lesley Jnr. the inn has been a very popular location for film crews down the years and has been used in everything from *The Patridge Family* and *Project X* to, rather ironically, *T. J. Hooker*. But why the Safari?

"It has a clean look. You take something basic and then build it up. They brought in different palm trees and gave it a more Hollywood look, even though it's in Burbank. It's going to be in *Apollo 13* as well," he continues, "it's going to play like it's in Florida in 1970. We have ocean view rooms even though we're 35 minutes away."

De Lesley Jnr. says the *True Romance* crew spent an entire day at the inn, filming in the office, lobby, parking lot, by the pool and on the stairway. The room that Slater and Arquette stay in does not actually belong to the inn. "We do *not* have leopard-skin rooms, you know," he insists.

Hungry? Lunch can be partaken at Johnie's Coffee Shop, 6101 Wiltshire Boulevard at Fairfax, where Tim Roth's Mr Orange meets with his cop mentor in *Reservoir Dogs*.

tarantinoism

Used in many films – Lily Tomlin worked here in *Short Cuts* – the owners renovated the place recently and their new patio area is affectionately called the Altman Annex. During a one-night shoot, the *Dogs* crew spent twelve hours at Johnie's, the movie magic enhanced by owner George Medenas who snapped on the rarely-used pulsating lights that line the rooftop of the diner which normally closes in the late afternoon.

"Many films have been made here," says Medenas. "*Miracle Mile*, *Mistress*, *Short Cuts* . . . They like it because it's old. It was built in 1950."

Waitress and manager Barbara Castro has worked at the coffee shop for 24 years.

"A lot of people come in and ask about the films that have been made here," she says, "I've seen a lot of them."

So did she see the Quentmeister at work?

"That one I was on vacation. Sorry."

Hey, no problem.

From Johnie's it's a quick trip down Beverly Boulevard, veering right down to the vacant lot on Second Street at Toluca, where Mr Orange rehearses his cover story in *Reservoir Dogs*. Long a meeting ground for L.A.'s dispossessed, this site is best viewed during daylight hours to appreciate the popped colours of the graffiti – and, it must be said, to better avoid getting yourself popped.

While most Hollywood afflicted *auteurs* make Hollywood a fantasy land of neons, salmon stucco and lime green palm trees, hardcore home town boy Tarantino lovingly records the mushroom browns, dingy beiges, and burnt oranges of most of Los Angeles. With a little hunting, you can find the apartment building where Jules and Vince ice the young criminals who've betrayed Marsellus Wallace in *Pulp Fiction*, on Van Ness, above Sunset Boulevard. You'll know you're in the right spot when you can taste the fumes of the 101 Freeway.

The delirious decor of Jack Rabbit Slim's restaurant, scene of John Travolta and Uma Thurman's hip-twisting interlude in *Pulp Fiction*, was a set built especially for the film by production designer David Wasco – but you can visit its very obvious inspiration, Ed Devebic's, 134 North La Cienega. The pricey burgers are served up by waiters dressed as cottage industry icons such as James Dean and Marilyn Monroe while Donny Weaver, a member of Ed's super perky staff, answers the phone with a boisterous carnival barker cry of: "Not good lookin', just good cookin'! The hardest workin' man in food, Ed Devebic!" Donny says that while his staff enjoyed the film, "Deep down inside, we knew they were ripping us off."

Or you could eat at the Hawthorne Grill, on Hawthorne Boulevard off El Segundo Avenue, where Honey Bunny and Pumpkin laid siege in *Pulp Fiction* until Jules and Vince taught them a lesson in criminal etiquette.

On your way back to the airport, make the extra effort and take a detour trip to pay homage to the birthplace of all things Tarantino – the former site of the original and now legendary Video Archives. A strip mall on Pacific Coast Highway, by Manhattan Beach Boulevard, in Manhattan Beach, it's where Quent learned his moves watching the videos he was meant to be renting out. Now an Asian bakery, you can pay tribute to the Prince of Homage with a tasty red bean curd cake as you polish off your whirlwind Tourantino of Pulpy L.A . . .

Clarence and Alabama in True Romance,
with the Elvis-style pink Cadillac in which they hit the road to LA.

don't try this at home

by Ian Penman

Quentin Tarantino says that the frisson fission fiction of his pulp gulp films comes from one basic conceit: "I want to take these genre characters and put them in a real-life situation." Which, when you think about it (which you're not supposed to), is really only a pseudo-adult kind of *Roger Rabbit* with guns.

So, you see – unreal people in real situations – that's the reason that despite their spitty hissy tom-cat woozy-Uzi male-violence, these are real 'feel-good' movies. (Or only half-real: half-real and half-reel as it were.) A real feel-good deal for People Like Us. People who can spot pop-trash references the way people used to spot wildflowers and lap-wings. People too sassy smart to get a feel-good fillip out of *Forrest Gump* but yet too squishy-brained to make the effort to get haunted by some Kieslowski meditation on the fracturing of late twentieth-century identity. Because these (last) days People Like Us want our fractured identities signed sealed and delivered inside a fast-food pop-cult package – you see, we don't want to be haunted; we don't want to wake up later in the night with strange visions shifting around the bare room of our conscience, or tears of trepidation asking to be cried; we don't want to ask too closely about the failure of love in our lives and the fever of disappointment that stalks us daily. No, we're far safer in San Quentin, the adult Theme Park where everything is just a mild wild half-teen half-toon update of old nasty *noir* references; where pasty-faced men in black suits are our version of giant Mickeys and Goofys who pat us on our nodding heads on the way to the exit as they say: It's OK little children, go home safe in your fan-fan-fantasies . . .

(So you see, I'm not a big Tarantino fan.)

(But you see, it's more than that: because I was fatally seduced at an early age by the serious tragedy and sensuous vortex of the cinema screen, I stumble and tremble like a lapsed Catholic whisky priest through a Greene-land desert of a soul: I think the cinema stinks of decadence these days, but I'm still tied to it with the blasted ugly fervour of a fallen acolyte, and I can't stand to see the soft-suck pabulum version of it people now comfort themselves with. So, you see . . . it's not that simple.)

So, what do you see when you don't see through Tarantino?

What it is, you see, is that despite these films being populated by the scum of the earth, people who have nothing in common with nobody you know and everything in common with a Nothing you personally have never known, you still come out of Tarantino feeling as if you've – hey! – at least and at last finally had A Good Night Out At the Movies: like, this is what the movies are supposed to be about (as so many people tell me when I endlessly and over-passionately rehash these heated arguments over too many cold drinks), this is why you gave the movies your time and money in the first place. Because if cutey-pie QT is one thing, he's a damned good salesman;

a huckster narcissist from a long American tradition, from a long line of guys who may not have any looks or any grace or any grand vision but they have the eye for the main chance and the gall and sometimes the balls and they alchemise their very gracelessness and guilelessness and gawkiness – alchemise all this into what it is that they ultimately sell: themselves. These films are in fact – if you look just a teensy bit closer – violently affectionate hymns . . . to Quentin Tarantino.

Now, see this, the Boy Wonder sells confidence: confidence in himself and in movies as a minor debased form of redemption; and in his audience's projected ability to dig the same stuff as him, to groove on the same in-joke riffing and pop-cult rifling – which is, let's face it, a pretty attractive proposition after a decade in the doldrums which is pretty much (in relative terms) what the Eighties was for movies. There may have been isolated movie freak scenes (e.g., *Blue Velvet*) but nothing like the collective Whomp delivered by the whole Altman-Scorsese-Schrader-etc. nexus in the Seventies.

And see, here's the rub: if those Seventies films were about alienation – an entire nation now alien to itself after Watergate and Vietnam – and about a nation of men now strangers to a formerly sure certain legacy of US Frontier manliness and masculinity – then QT is somewhere else altogether: his is a cinema of pretend togetherness. These supposedly so-so-so-hep flashily sick fluently slick sharkskin-ballet no-ethics no-feelings hardboiled reel-world spiels are actually groovy little group therapy feel good sessions for an audience cut off from its own emotions but that still wants (needs?) to congratulate itself on having one basic response left: laughing in rhythm. An audience that sees the – their, any – cultural past as a sweet shop to be picked and mixed – and so on and so forth until we all complacently slum together in the strangely one-dimensional glow cast by these movies because all they ultimately do is they tell us so sweetly surely sagely how People Like Us, we dig the same things.

When you buy into the Tarantino aesthetic it's not like some movies which darkly nudge you into areas you've never been before (or sharply nudge you back into areas you shouldn't have gone, but did). QT's QED pictures are a celebration of the fact that we're all the same, that – don't worry, it's OK – we get it – and that's OK! (No disturbing after-shock or after-effect that lingers for days and nights and weeks and months.) QT is the ultimate director-as-dweeb – Quentin: ha! what a dweeb's name to start with! – because his success speaks to us like this: if I can be cool, so can you just by enjoying my film and repeating the lines afterwards with your friends in the pub where they have the *Pulp Fiction* CD on an endless loop on the CD-jukebox . . .

(Cue that dreadful surf instrumental that no one in their right mind ever wants to hear again; or 'Stuck In The Bloody Middle Of The Road With You' for that matter.)

He doesn't take us anywhere dark or uncanny, or to the real cruel places of the lamentable American or late-twentieth century soul; instead, he gives us cartoon versions of the spectres that haunt our cities. (*Reservoir Dogs* is at times like *Mean Streets* re-made by the *Top Cat* Team.) A bit like Oliver Stone (albeit not on the same mockalyptic scale), really, and the more you ponder this pair the more Tarantino begins to look like Stone's grotesque polar/younger twin. Stone at least has the excuse that he has lived through a lot of this stuff, and that his cinema is like an obsessive psycho-therapeutic raking over of certain personal and collective dark clouds. QT is, of course, just dependably and defensibly 'postmodern', whatever the meaningless hell or meaningful shell that means these days. These two natural born thrillers are gargantuan hacks who both have learned the trick of turning what is a flaw – their compulsive chatter, their inability to shape and sublimate and economise – into a supposed virtue. It's like a great scriptwriter God in the sky gave them everything except the edit facility. You could say: Stone is all subtext and Tarantino is none. Stone's voracious apocalyptic flash is just an excuse to proselytise at us. QT's supposed 'subversion of genre' is just an excuse to flashily dazzle us.

QT seems to be reaching out to tackle scenes way outside his own limited, limited-life experience. (If his experience of life is limited, his experience of soul seems to be less than microscopic: even though his films are action films Tarantino is in reality anti-Existentialist man.) In reducing his range of (love) objects down to the degraded level of pulp and video and late-night TV repeat and small talk, he makes it easy on himself . . . nothing ever develops here, everything remains at the one stalled stilted level of discourse.

(At times I think I have sussed him as a one-trick pony: all he has done is transfer films that should take place in the squared-off Mondrian confines of New York and relocated them in the wide bright boulevard of L.A.)

You see, you see him interviewed and you notice that he can't seem to answer any question – serious or trivial – without reaching for an aid, a pop cultural yo-yo or pogo stick or pet rock . . . it's like wow see this Jean-Luc Godard film it's like SO cool and I took the colour red from this scene and see this Fifties car it's SO cool and that's where I got the idea for this hamburger heaven and see this Sam Fuller poster it's like SO cool and . . . it's like . . . it's like he makes his film the same way: just tossing in bits and set pieces like the directorial equivalent of one of Oliver Sacks' casebook studies: *The Man Who Mistook His Life For A Map*; or: *The Man Who Mistook A Video Collection For His Life*.

Because the real truth is that QT's career is about taking a supposedly 'real' character (i.e. himself) and putting him in all these far far far out situations – that he's never been near in real life and never will. (The only film he could convincingly make would be about the Film Festival circuit.) That's why I suspect they represent a gigantic evasion – what used to be called 'bad faith'. Because if you check out all the B-movies by the likes of Sam Fuller that QT so adores you'll find real darkness and doubt and bad dreams and debts – sex, madness, guilt, the great themes. (With Quentin, we get 'celebrated' dialogue about what hamburgers are called in Europe.) Tarantino's *mise-en-scène* seems to take place in no particular era or every particular era: take any given scene and without prior clues you could accurately guess that it was 'meant' to be set in the Forties or the Fifties or the Eighties or, in other words, entirely in QT's playground mind: it doesn't matter: it's all just Letraset to the Lippy Hipster Kid.

OK, so we can hardly demand of every film maker that they have previously lived out what they portray – this would render, *inter alia*, *RoboCop*, *Jurassic Park* and *Mary Poppins* pretty unfeasible projects. But I think there's a deeply ingrained way in which QT's lack of interest(s) outside his own gee-whiz aesthetic casts a very specific shadow over his films. To begin with, I couldn't put my finger on why his films made me feel so queasy and unsatisfied rather than exhilarated like all those around me. I felt like I'd been fed from one end of a week to the other on nothing but cheeseburger and milkshake and cheap speed: an unrelieved diet of something simultaneously

Tarantino as married man Jimmie, with Samuel L. Jackson as his hitman friend Jules. Jackson claimed the script for Pulp Fiction *was the best he had ever read.*

over-rich and under-nourishing. And maybe the reason – or a great symbol for the underlying reason – is this: if you detach yourself for a moment you may notice that every single one of QT's characters talks with the same voice: his. He can write, boy, can he write and write and write – but it's all just straight from his burbling swamp place mind straight to the page straight to the screen. Thus in *Pulp Fiction*, we get a six-foot-plus hypercool black assassin who . . . talks with the voice of a nerdy white video-rental-store manager. This ice-blooded Isaac Hayes of the hinterlands talks about things like *The Brady Bunch* and *The Partridge Family* and A Flock of Seagulls and stuff that nobody talks about – black or white – unless they're a QT kinda pop cult bore; unless they're QT in OD.

And so, unlike anyone from Travis Bickle to the Bad Lieutenant, or anyone in any book in a lineage that stretches from Jim Thompson to James Ellroy – who mine the same vein of relentless street nihilism as Tarantino – QT's bad guys are just one-dimensional parodies of badness: boy-men facing unreal pulp dilemmas. On some level – like a lot of society – QT is both dazzled by the glare of 'bad' men and frightened of the real evil that lurks in all our tense hearts.

OK, OK, OK. The problem with Quentin is that there seems to be no sensible middle-ground: people either rave relentlessly and uncritically on about his gory glory or (like me) just Don't Get It. In my weaker moments I might have to concur that what is wrong with QT is not so much wrong with QT as it is the cultural scene. In any decent movie-going era QT would not be centre stage – he'd just be gearing up to do something better, being helped along by criticism rather than adulation. A minor player; a marginal entertainment. And so yes it may be that poor little unquesting unquestioning Quentin is just taking the wrathful rap for all my monumental ire, and that the poor baby is guilty – or desperately abjectly innocent – of nothing more than being the wrong guy in the wrong place at the wrong time.

Just like one of his – real gone, unreal goon – characters.

7.
the film
geek
speaks

a rare sorrow

by Quentin Tarantino

If I had to pick the five greatest Western directors of all time, the problem wouldn't be to pick five, but to figure out how many Westerns a director had to make to be considered a Western director. Does one film do it? Can I make a case for Marlon Brando, since *One-Eyed Jacks* is one of my five favourite Westerns? How about Philip Kaufman? Can I with good conscience put him on the list above King Vidor, Henry Hathaway and Sam Peckinpah, on the strength of *The Great Northfield Minnesota Raid* (the best of the Jesse James movies with Robert Duvall, the scariest and most psychotic Jesse on film), and writing the script (and directing about a week) of *The Outlaw Josey Wales*?

This dilemma solved itself when I came to Monte Hellman. There's no way in hell Monte ain't going on the list. I don't care if he's only done three, but two of them – *Ride in the Whirlwind* and *The Shooting* – demand that honour. Monte also made me come to grips with the whole Marlon Brando/*One-Eyed Jacks* problem, because much as I like *The Shooting*, had he never made it, just doing *Ride* would have been enough for me.

Producer Fred Roos, who would later produce *Apocalypse Now*, had a deal to do two films in the Philippines to be shot concurrently. He had seen Roger Corman's *The Terror*, starring Boris Karloff and Jack Nicholson, and had heard that two young directors had shot the majority of it. Their names were Monte Hellman and Francis Ford Coppola. Roos' response was "send me either one". Monte got the job.

The deal was simple. Roos had to make two cheap action-adventure films set in the Philippines. He had the script for one, a war film called *Back Door To Hell*, but the second one was open. Monte suggested that they use the young actor from *The Terror*, Jack Nicholson, who he knew was also a screenwriter. The idea was that Jack would act in *Back Door To Hell*, write the script for the second film, and act in that one as well. The script Nicholson wrote was *Flight To Fury*.

Monte's first film, *Beast From The Haunted Cave*, written by the great Charles Griffith, was a lot of fun. *Back Door To Hell* is pretty good, but *Flight To Fury* was the first of the great Monte Hellman pictures, and *Little Shop Of Horrors* aside, the first film in which Jack Nicholson came into his own as an actor. Nicholson, in a part he wrote for himself, finally had the assurance, the experience, the words and the director to deliver the performance that had eluded him up to this point.

The film's other lead was Howard Hawks' regular Dewey Martin (*The Big Sky*, *The Thing*), an underrated actor who should have done better in the Fifties than he did. Nicholson's feral, hip, cerebral, Sixties style of acting plays well with Martin's hardboiled, tough Fifties cool-guy style. (On a personal note, I get a special kick from watching them because Martin resembles Michael Madsen in my movie *Reservoir Dogs*, and Nicholson resembles actor Steve Buscemi.)

The teaming of Hellman and Nicholson played well too. As can be seen from the film I made – *Reservoir Dogs*, I like what I call "kitchen-sink movies" which means "there's everything in it but . . .", and there are about four movies crammed into *Flight To Fury*. The first fifteen minutes are an action adventure murder mystery full of exotic locations (the Philippines), a rugged hero (Martin), a sexy Oriental *femme fatale* (who will be dead by the fourth scene), and shifty characters who are not what they appear (Nicholson at first appears to be a likeable nerdy guy, but then is quickly revealed to be an ice-cold killer with a hidden agenda). Then Martin and Nicholson hop on an aeroplane, where we're introduced to a whole new batch of interesting and suspicious characters. After flying the friendly skies with them for about 20 minutes, as they sniff each other out and philosophise (Nicholson's conversation about death with a fellow passenger, the late Jacqueline Hellman, seems to come straight out of a Hal Hartley movie), in what plays like the oddest and greatest *Airport* movie ever made, the plane crashes. Which turns the film into a skewed version of Max Frisch's novel *Homo Faber*, as the survivors stranded in the jungle fight to stay alive, fight bands of marauding pirates and fight and kill one another.

Hellman and Nicholson made a terrific little film and a terrific team, so a partnership between the two was struck. Nicholson wrote a script for a Western that the two could do cheap, and they took that script, *Ride In The Whirlwind*, to Roger Corman. Corman liked Nicholson's script very much and agreed to do it. Then added, in that way that has made the man a legend, "Since you'll be out there on location, why don't you do two movies?" So the two partners repeated the duties they had just done with Fred Roos in the Philippines: shooting the two movies concurrently with the same crew, Nicholson writing and starring in one, acting in the other and Hellman directing both. However, this time Nicholson would produce both films as well.

The other film was *The Shooting*, starring Warren Oates, Millie Perkins, Will Hutchins (then star of the television show *Sugarfoot*) and Nicholson as a Jack Palance-inspired gunfighter named Billy Spear. The script was written by a friend of Nicholson's from Jeff Corey's acting class, Carole Eastman, who would go on to write for Nicholson *Five Easy Pieces*, *The Fortune* and *Man Trouble*. Her script, written under the pseudonym Adrian Joyce, is like a metaphysical version of Budd Boetticher's *Ride Lonesome*. Corman apparently hated it, but proceeded anyway because it was the only one ready to go, and at that price he couldn't lose.

Today *The Shooting* is widely considered the masterpiece of the two. Kevin Thomas, film critic for the *Los Angeles Times*, wrote: "The difference between the two [*Ride In The Whirlwind* and *The Shooting*] is the difference between the definitely good and the arguably great." Most critics in France and the US agree (with Michel Ciment an important exception), and Monte himself prefers *The Shooting*. But for me, it's the simplicity, the naturalistic tone, the awkward-sounding (because it's so authentic) cowboy vernacular, the feeling of sadness that's between every line, the burst of ridiculous comic moments, the beautiful underplaying of Nicholson and Cameron Mitchell, all wrapped up in a wing-ding plot, that make *Ride In The Whirlwind* one of the most authentic and brilliant Westerns ever made.

Monte made Westerns unlike any before or since. He slowed down all the action so the scenes play at a real-time pace unheard of in a Western. The effect is almost as if Monte were in the projection booth, grabbing a fistful of film as it passes in front of the bulb and yanking it down, so each frame is illuminated longer for better examination. The film opens with a stagecoach hold-up that produces giggles due to the lazy, laconic manner of the robbers. It's the exact opposite of the snappy action scene we've become accustomed to (a robber gets a laugh from me every time for the way he unhurriedly moves a log out of the stagecoach's way). In direct contrast with Monte's tone is Nicholson's plot, which is far from existential. In fact, it could easily be a great rip-snorting episode of *Bonanza*.

Three cowhands riding together, Wes (Nicholson), Vern (Mitchell), and Otis (Tom Filer), come across a gang of desperadoes holed up in a shack. The desperados have just robbed the local stage and are hiding out. The outlaws figure these saddle tramps want nothing more than to bed down (they're right), so they oblige them. The cowhands put two and two together real fast and figure out these are bad men and "look forward to partin' company with them fellas" in the morning; however, morning brings a posse hell-bent on shootin' and hangin' everybody. Filer is shot, and Nicholson and Mitchell escape with the posse hot on their trail. The two men, scared and sorrowful (because of the death of their friend, beautifully conveyed by the way Nicholson just folds up in grief after dismounting from his horse) must now make their way out of the territory on foot, all the while trying to keep two steps ahead of the ever-approaching posse. "If we get some horses we're out of it," Nicholson says.

So to that end they commandeer a ranch tended by an old man (George Mitchell) and his wife (Katherine Squire), and their nineteen-year-old daughter (Millie Perkins). Holding the family hostage and stealing their stock turns the two innocents into the outlaws the posse believes them to be. One of the truly brilliant things about the movie is Nicholson's sparse and authentic Western dialogue, taken from letters and journals of that time. These are inarticulate people living in simple times using a spare vocabulary. Sometimes this language is funny, as when the three cowhands come across a hanged man and, after looking at him a good long while, Nicholson responds. "Man gets hanged." At other times, it's moving, as when instead of going on and on about how they're innocent and it ain't fair, or how scared they are, Nicholson says to Mitchell on the run, with just the right touch of emotion, "No one's gonna put a name to me and that's it."

Attempts to explain their innocence to the family fall on deaf ears. This family's existence seems to be a hand-to-mouth one: they live on an ugly, barren piece of dirt away from any other people (when anyone approaches their world, they become threatened). The old man doesn't work a farm, he just chops monotonously all day at a tree stump with an axe. The women just seem to cook grub.

These people have nothing and then these two dangerous outlaws (as they're told earlier by the posse) take what little they have . . . the old man's dignity (he runs the small shack like a king, but now must let two other men dominate him in his kingdom and rule over his women), and what little they own of value, their stock (horses). It is in the attempts of these two non-verbal men to articulate their innocence and desperation to their innocent and desperate hostages that the film achieves a rare sorrow. As Mitchell and Nicholson sit at their table after eating their food, and play checkers, as the old man whacks away outside at the formidable stump, Mitchell says, "We borrow their checkers, we steal their horses, there just don't seem to be no end to it." "No use to that," Nicholson replies.

The acting has a strangely eccentric quality. Harry Dean Stanton as the outlaw leader Blind Dick, and Squire and George Mitchell as the old folks are right as rain. When I met Harry Dean Stanton I told him how much I loved *Ride*. He said, "That's the best Western I was ever in, and one of the best I ever saw." But Peter Cannon as a hot-headed outlaw and Millie Perkins give some eccentric line readings. Cannon's voice has a strangely effeminate quality, "I shoulda picked them off original." Perkins' performance is an oddball classic. Her "Yes, we do" when they ask if she has any checkers has affected the way I say "Yes, I do." But Hellman built the film around the performances of Cameron Mitchell and Jack Nicholson, and it's easy to see why . . . these two men are terrific.

To see Mitchell, who has since unfortunately gone the way of Aldo Ray (another talented actor of the Fifties), appearing in anything, including porno movies, that will pay his price, do the subtle, unmannered, personal work he does here is to shed a tear for all the wonderful actors in film who never had the opportunity to fly where their talent could have taken them. When a fine actor, who has managed to keep his instincts even after appearing in junk for a long time, gets a real role with something to play, a special light goes on in his eyes. You can see it in Martin Landau's performance in *Tucker*, Joe Don Baker's scene-stealing turn in *The Natural*, and Richard Crenna's menacing dinner table conversation in *Body Heat* – all performances in big pictures that stopped or saved those actors from plunging into an exploitation movie hell. That same light shines brightly in Mitchell's eyes throughout *Ride In The Whirlwind*, and it's that light that accounts for what must be the finest performance of his long career.

Jack Nicholson, on the other hand, went on to become one of the biggest stars in the history of movies. Both a great star and a great actor, but more than that, Nicholson has passed over into cultural-icon status like Bogart, John Wayne, James Dean, Marilyn Monroe and Madonna (witness the references to him in Disney's *Aladdin*, and Christian Slater's homage in *Heathers*). Anybody who tunes into *Ride In The Whirlwind* as a curiosity to see the work of a star-in-the-making will be shocked.

Nicholson's work in *Ride* ranks as one of his finest performances, as Robert De Niro's work in *Mean Streets* is one of his finest performances. Not only is Nicholson wonderful as Wes, but he does the kind of no-nonsense meat-and-potatoes work I'd love to see him do again (the closest he's come recently is his work in the much-maligned *The Two Jakes*, which I, for one, loved). Seeing Nicholson play small, after a decade of playing large, reminds us that Nicholson became the icon he is not just by being a great Nicholson, but by being a great actor.

If ever a director was due for critical rediscovery, it would be Monte Hellman. With his naturalistic style and pace, his invisibly punchy editing rhythms, and the journeys his characters inevitably set sail on, his influence can be found in the work of such directors as Hartley, Wim Wenders, Jim Jarmusch, and Terrence Malick (as Pauline Kael noted, though unfavourably, in her review of *Badlands*). This year Monte starts a new film, *Dark Passion*, based on the Lionel White novel *Obsession* which Godard used as his jumping-off point for *Pierrot Le Fou*. Movie theatres would be much happier places with a new Monte Hellman movie playing in them.

to the dawn and beyond

by Anthony Timpone

Quentin Tarantino has been making his dreams come true for some time now. He has written and directed three critically praised films (Reservoir Dogs, Pulp Fiction and Jackie Brown); worked with many of his favourite actors and re-launched their careers (Harvey Keitel, John Travolta, Pam Grier, Robert Forster, etc.); dusted off his first script and starred in the subsequent film (From Dusk Till Dawn) and even tackled Broadway in his stage debut (Wait Until Dark). So what's left?

Like many fans of Eighties splatter flicks, the 35-year-old Tarantino wants to relive the old days when you could see an Italian gore film on the big screen – and like all the other goals he has set for himself, he has made it happen. Thanks to Tarantino's speciality company Rolling Thunder, in conjunction with Grindhouse Releasing and Cowboy Booking International, Lucio Fulci's 1981 classic The Beyond began a new assault on theatres this summer [1998]. In this exclusive interview, Tarantino speaks of his fascination with Fulci, the fun he's had menacing Marisa Tomei in Wait Until Dark and the scoop on two new From Dusk Till Dawn films.

Have you always been a fan of Lucio Fulci's work?
QUENTIN TARANTINO: The first thing he did where I actually remembered his name was *Zombie*. I went to a drive-in a couple of times in the Eighties and saw it. I've been a fan of his for a while now, actually. *Gates of Hell* was always my favourite of his flicks. Then I saw *The Beyond* and liked it, but I only saw that crappy bootleg version off a Japanese laserdisc. I've seen a lot of his spaghetti Westerns and Mafia movies. I was a big fan of *The Psychic* [aka *Seven Notes In Black*], and I tried to release it in America. We worked six months trying to do that; we wanted to release it in Italian with English subtitles, because I've seen it in Italian and it plays well that way. But it is really hard to get the rights to these Italian things because people over there just don't care. We tried to get the rights to *Blood And Black Lace*, the Mario Bava film, and release it in Italian with English subtitles. We couldn't do that. It's not even about money; they don't care, they don't want to go through the trouble.

What made you select The Beyond *out of Fulci's horror films to re-release?*
TARANTINO: The thing that made me select *The Beyond* was that it fits really well because of the interest in Fulci. *The Beyond* has a big cult status. It has a major following among horror fans, gore fans and Italian film fans. [Distributors] Bob Murawski and Sage Stallone went to Italy and got the rights. Not only that, but they struck a brand new print. They got the cinematographer [Sergio Salvati] to go down there and colour-time it. Then they screened for me the actual full-scope, gorgeous colour, stereo print of *The Beyond*, and I was like, "Whoa, this is fantastic!" Horror fans

are gonna go nuts just seeing this thing on the big screen in all its glory. You know, no cuts, no nothing. I screened it for Bob Weinstein and a bunch of the guys at Dimension. I told him, "This is going to get an NC-17." I had no plans to cut it or screw around with it. It didn't go out as a Dimension film, but rather a Rolling Thunder film. I wanted to show it to him, and if he liked it and said, "OK, we won't cut it," then we would go ahead with it. And he liked it. He thought it was gory and crazy and everything, but he actually got a kick out of it.

And then we gave it our own little market research screening in Austin. I have a bunch of film prints, and I work [my own screenings] through Rich Linklater's Austin Film Society. I have this thing called the QTAFF – Quentin Tarantino Austin Film Fest. I take a bunch of prints out and just screen them for the fans in Austin. We have all-night horror marathons and things like that. Then, the last night of the festival, we screened *The Beyond*. So this was a jam-packed audience filled with people. The response was fantastic. They just loved it. They caught it with just the right spirit. So we picked it up. Our whole idea was to actually release it as a midnight movie. And theatre owners were really cool with the fact that we came to them with a midnight movie.

What is the most distinctive element of Fulci's work, and also The Beyond?
TARANTINO: I think the most distinctive element of *The Beyond* is that it has an extremely nightmarish quality. It's funny, because there is all sorts of weird stuff in it, and with Italian films you have to kind of know what you're getting into, because some of it is going to seem crazy and outrageous to you if you don't know. Having said that, there's a genuine eeriness and creepiness to the whole mood of *The Beyond*. It is a very unsettling movie. It has this feeling like it is taking place inside a nightmare and has the logic of a nightmare. It has a very frightening, disturbing tone that wears on you as the movie goes on. And that's really cool; that kind of atmosphere is very hard to create, and Fulci pretty much maintains it for the length of the movie.

Some critics felt that The Beyond's **FX scenes are a little excessive. For example, close-ups of tarantulas biting the guy's lips off. How do you feel about that?**
TARANTINO: That's what you get when you see a Lucio Fulci film. I mean, it's an Italian gore film. It's clearly labelled on the box. That's how they do their gore films.

Has the time for these kinds of movies come and gone?
TARANTINO: Yeah. They're hardly making them anymore in Italy. And unfortunately, the days of them getting theatrical releases are pretty much over. That's why it's cool to release this. They're not making them anymore, and even if they are, they're going straight to video. They might not even be released here on video. That's why it's so exciting to actually go to a theatre and see *The Beyond*

Would you direct a film like The Beyond?
TARANTINO: I don't know if I would. I tend to be more story-oriented than Fulci was. But I'd like to make a horror film someday.

What is your involvement with the* Dusk Till Dawn *sequels?
TARANTINO: They're not really *Dusk Till Dawn 2* and *3*. They're just two movies which are kind of in the series. The one that Robert Rodriguez is doing, or rather the one he has developed with his cousin Alvaro, is *From Dusk Till Dawn*: *Hangman's Daughter*. Sonia Braga and Michael Parks star in it. It takes place 100 years prior to *Dusk Till Dawn* in the Old West. It deals with the origin of Santanica Pandemonium, how she first got involved with the Titty Twister and how she became the queen of the vampires.

The other movie is one which Scott Spiegel is directing; he wrote it with Duane Whitaker, who played Maynard in *Pulp Fiction*. Me, Scott and Boaz Yakin came up with the story for it, and it's called *From Dusk Till Dawn*: *Texas Blood Money*. This one takes place two weeks after the first movie. It's about a bunch of Texas bank robbers. One of them, on the way to the rendezvous to rob this bank, goes into what's left of the Titty Twister and gets bitten by one of the vampires. He then goes to the rendezvous and proceeds to little by little bite the other robbers. So as these guys are robbing this bank, they're being turned into vampires.

So your character does not appear in the new films?
TARANTINO: No, no, Richard was killed. They were gonna try to work it in . . .

. . . as kind of a flashback with your character?
TARANTINO: It would've ruined the integrity of it. If Richard was supposed to be alive, I wouldn't have killed him.

Did the first Dusk Till Dawn *achieve what you wanted it to?*
TARANTINO: I love the first movie. I'm very happy with it. It's second only to *Pulp Fiction* as the movie that people come up to me about on the street. It did pretty good in the theatres, but it has found a really big audience on video and cable television.

Has it been fun scaring audiences live in Wait Until Dark*?*
TARANTINO: Yeah. It's a whole different thing. It's really cool, because the play's really scary. And it gets to them. It's a different thing when you're there live in the theatre and you hear the audience react. There's a point in the show where I'm trying to kill the blind girl [Marisa Tomei] and she turns off all the lights, and then you're just sitting there with all these strangers in this big theatre and you can't see your hand in front of your face. Audiences just aren't used to being put in total darkness.

Any chance you'd do a film version?
TARANTINO: There's been talk of that for Showtime or something. But we're not sure yet.

After Broadway, what are your future plans?
TARANTINO: I'm not sure right now. I'm doing the show, but at some point I'll write whatever I plan to do next.

Have you seen any good horror films in the last year?
TARANTINO: I saw *Scream 2* the night it opened.

What do you think of the whole Scream *phenomenon?*
TARANTINO: Oh, I think Kevin Williamson is probably the most talented writer to come out since I've been a professional. The first *Scream* was just a perfect script. It was terrific, and he did a great job with *Scream 2*. I liked the script for *I Know What You Did Last Summer* also.

Where do you see the future of horror going at this point?
TARANTINO: I don't know. But Williamson did with *Scream* what I did with gangster films. Horror was pretty much fucking dead when he did that. Not only did he revitalise it and give some respect to the slasher genre, but he even commented on why all these other horror films have been so crappy. Countless sequel after sequel after sequel. That's why Bob Weinstein said, "*Dusk Till Dawn* did pretty good for us. If we have one that does well, we do six of them." [Laughs]

So beyond the two they just did, there are more coming?
TARANTINO: No, no, no. I was just joking, you know. Like *Children of the Corn 9* or whatever.

quentin tarantino: the film geek files

I'm surprised they didn't decide to go theatrical with the **Dusk** *sequels/prequels.*
TARANTINO: Well, the whole idea is . . . like when they came out with the *Darkman* sequel, straight to video. Now, I didn't see it, but apparently they did a pretty good job with that movie. And it did pretty well, and the idea was to design it to go straight to video but make it really good. Not like, "Oh, we got this piece of crap, let's throw it on video" – no, let's make the decision now to make it really good and come out with it. You don't have to worry about the reviews and everything, it's just what it is for the fans. We're talking about maybe having some very special releases where we show all three of them together. We had a meeting about it with Bob, and he said, "If the movies turn out really good, we can release them theatrically." Robert Rodriguez kicked in and said, "Well if they're really, *really* good, we should make it a point to only go out on video with them. Let's make a really good movie for the horror fans on video. And fuck dealing with the critics." It will get played theatrically like crazy overseas.

Lately there has been much controversy regarding the marketing of monster and horror movies, whether or not to show the monster (i.e. **Godzilla***) until the movie opens. Even the first* **Dusk Till Dawn** *didn't show any vampires in the print ads. How do you feel about that strategy, where they keep the monster under wraps and hide the fact that it's a horror movie?*
TARANTINO: *Scream* kind of made it invalid that horror has a [box-office] ceiling and science fiction doesn't. Look at *Species*: It wasn't sold as a horror film, it was sold as a sci-fi film. Well, it could be that, I guess, and that's what they did with *Mimic*. They don't show the monster in the ads, but they showed the monster in the trailers. I mean, they showed the best shot in *Mimic*, not only in all the trailers but every time someone from the movie made a talk show appearance. They showed the creature sweeping Mira [Sorvino] up off the subway platform, which is like the money shot from the movie. And it's never going to be as effective as the first time I saw it, because I didn't know that shit was going to happen. That blew me away. I remember when we were doing *Jackie Brown*, I was like, "I don't want no damn *Scream* poster that's just everybody lined up looking like a damn *Vanity Fair* photo shoot."

That's kind of what they did, though, wasn't it?
TARANTINO: No, no, ours was like a Seventies action poster. It was everybody with attitude; it didn't look like a *Phantoms/Scream* photo shoot.

What's next after **The Beyond** *for Rolling Thunder?*
TARANTINO: I want to go further with this. They're not releasing Italian horror films anymore in theatres. This is a big, widescreen thing. This may be one of the last times, unless *The Beyond* does well.

We're looking for other stuff. Another one that I bought that we'd like to go out on a midnight-movie basis is a Seventies Hong Kong film called *Mighty Peking Man*, [previously] released in America as *Goliathon*. It's a wild movie. It's basically Hong Kong's answer to *King Kong*. It was their attempt to duplicate the success the Japanese had with their monster movies. It's fantastic. The Shaw brothers did it in ShawScope and stereophonic sound, and it will be a wild night at the movies if we put it out the same way.

blaxploitation: what it is... what it was!

by Quentin Tarantino

When I was growing up, exploitation movies in general really rang my bell. I really liked them. I saw everything from foreign art films to all the mainstream stuff too. But there was a sense of rawness, outrageousness and naughtiness to exploitation films. Whether it be black exploitation films, or redneck movies, the good ol' boy movies, or pom-pom girl movies. The exploitation movies went a little further because that's what they had to offer. They didn't have Paul Newman, right? They had to offer something that the mainstream films couldn't offer. I think if you look at my work, it's not really taking that much from the mainstream cinema. What I've taken from exploitation films in general is that anything can happen. You don't see that very much in movies anymore, that's the thing that kills movies, you've seen it all before.

I've actually looked at black exploitation films in terms of fiction – as black exploitation spaghetti Western.

People who grew up in the Seventies are now looking back to what they grew up with. The Seventies were looked down upon for so long. You never got any respect growing up in the Seventies, you were always told how you missed the Sixties. How the music was happening and you just missed it. In the Seventies you had Elton John and that kind of thing. White pop music, after breaking new ground in the Sixties, became very bland in the Seventies. There were no new Bob Dylans or *Blonde On Blonde* albums.

But for black music, the Seventies was the true explosion as a major provoking artform. It went from Chuck Berry and the Five Satins and that whole type of music in the Fifties to the Sixties with the explosion of Motown and R&B to the Seventies where it became soul music. That was, for my money, the greatest time in black music history – the Seventies. I never felt like I missed the Sixties because I got the black Seventies, and I'd choose that over the hippie Sixties any day of the week.

In soul music, there was Marvin Gaye's *What's Going On*, which was the *Blonde On Blonde* album for soul music. It was one of the very first concept albums that came out.

I grew up in the South Bay area of Los Angeles listening to the KDAY radio station. I grew up in a house where every Saturday, *Soul Train* was on. I lived with my mom and her two roommates. My mom was about 25 and very beautiful and had a lot of friends. We lived with Jackie, a black woman who was also beautiful, and a Mexican gal named

She's the
"GODMOTHER"
of them all

...The
baddest
One-Chick
Hit-Squad
that ever
hit town!

"Coffy"

R RESTRICTED Under 17 Requires Accompanying Parent or Adult Guardian

Samuel Z. Arkoff presents
an American International Picture
"COFFY"

starring
PAM
GRIER · BOOKER
BRADSHAW · ROBERT
DOQUI · WILLIAM ALLAN
ELLIOTT · ARBUS · and
SID
HAIG

as Vitroni   as Omar

Produced by Robert A. Papazian · Written and Directed by Jack Hill · COLOR by Movielab

COPYRIGHT : 1973 AMERICAN INTERNATIONAL PICTURES, INC.

73/157

"COFFY"

Lillian. They were in their twenties and were three young foxy ladies talking about their dates and getting ready while they watched *Soul Train*. As a little kid watching *Soul Train*, I always thought it was really cool. Nearly every commercial was an Afro Sheen commercial with black actors in it. It was a black world. You saw nothing but black faces. Growing up watching the show, I always thought it would be the coolest thing to be the white person on *Soul Train*, that would be the highest honour. I thought maybe some day, I'll be the first white member of the *Soul Train* gang. I'll be out there locking up. Time went on, and I hadn't seen *Soul Train* again for about ten to fifteen years, who knows how long. But when I flipped it on, I just couldn't believe how short Don Cornelius's Afro was. I thought, what did he do? He's not Don Cornelius anymore. They had white people dancing on the show, and they sucked.

You look at black exploitation films today and you see all the big Afros and the one-piece outfits with the zipper going down the middle, and the big platform shoes, and the big coats, with the big endangered species animal fur collar going down. I'm not saying everyone looked like that but it's about an embracing of a culture and an identity.

The film that just knocked my socks off the most was Jack Hill's *Coffy*, from the moment she shot the guy in the head with the sawed off shotgun and his head exploded like a watermelon. I had never seen that before and then it just got better from there. Pam Grier was just like an incredible badass, she was just so great. *Coffy* is one of the greatest revenge movies ever made. Revenge movies were very big in the Seventies. They worked. You watched revenge movies and you got caught up in them. It's almost impossible to watch *Coffy* with an audience and not have them get caught up in the movie. When the film opened, people were standing on their seats screaming at the top of their lungs for her to blow away those guys. Revenge movies were the first movies I got completely caught up in in that kind of way. *Coffy* just works. It's really nice when you have a visceral response to a film at an early age. And, actually, I think I appreciate *Coffy* even more now. It still holds up. I remember when I was younger, people derided the movies and said they were cheap. I never looked at them that way. I always knew kung fu movies were kind of slapped together and I knew Godzilla movies were kind of stupid. But the black exploitation movies were great. They didn't look cheap to me at all. I didn't know what an exploitation movie was. I just knew they had more sex and violence than the other movies, which was a good thing for me.

In terms of what 'exploitation' cinema is, it simply means there's an element in a film that you can exploit. That's what low budget movies had to offer. The way Hollywood movies have run and always will run is that they exist on a star system and that's why people all over the world like to see Hollywood movies. That keeps the machine running. When you make a Harrison Ford movie, you are exploiting the hell out of Harrison Ford's image. You see *Air Force One* posters all over town, *big* giant pictures of a plane in Harrison Ford's face. In big studio films, they are exploiting the presence of a star, that's how they do it. Exploitation films don't have stars they could exploit like that and the things they have to exploit are sex and violence and nudity and car chases or action in motorcycle movies, in kung fu movies it's people fighting, that's what they have to exploit. That's why exploitation movie posters are far more interesting and fun to look at than mainstream movie posters, because a poster of a Paul Newman movie is going to have a picture of Paul Newman and that's the deal. A motorcycle movie is going to have all kinds of action and motorcycles and chicks in short pants and choppers and all that Hell's Angels memorabilia in your face. The term means we may not have the big budget and the stars but we do have action and we do have sex, and we do have a big gory monster. It's what they're selling.

When you talk about Jim Kelly, Pam Grier, Jim Brown, and Fred Williamson, you're actually talking about the same; they were major stars in that world. So they were exploiting the hell out of their images. Burt Reynolds was a redneck Fred Williamson for the Southern drive-in market. When he did his moonshining fast car movies, they were made just the way a Pam Grier movie was made for the black market.

I like the term black exploitation just like I like the term kung fu films even if the movie's about karate or it's a spaghetti Western. It doesn't fit everything. *Cornbread, Earl And Me* is not exploitative in any way. It might be manipulative toward the audience, but it's not exploitative. The staple of black exploitation movies is basically that they were black crime films and they focused on detectives or gangsters, or crooks and criminals. The thing is that a lot of black films were basically just the same as white gangster films, redone James Cagney or Humphrey Bogart movies but set in Harlem. The basic plot is Howard Hawks' *Scarface*. It's *Black Caesar* and it's *The Mack*, it's the same thing down to the good mother who won't take the dirty money that her son brings her and she's played by, of all people, Juanita Moore. She played the god-fearing soul-suffering mother in *Imitation Of Life*.

The sad thing about the genre was when it left, nothing ever replaced it again. The films were made for a black audience. After *Shaft* there really wasn't that much of a thought toward crossover. It was very interesting, because I'm always interested in characters who can be who they are; that's something novels have always been able to do. It's one of the good fights that I've been fighting; characters don't always have to be perfect. In novels you can write about a person who is a fucking bastard, and he can be a fucking bastard – that's OK. Movies lost that pretty much in the Eighties in a big way; we're getting it back in the Nineties. People can be flawed and wrong and they can be scumbags and you can still watch the movie if it's interesting. What I find fascinating is there's still things that they did in black exploitation movies that would be rather rough to do today. It would be tough.

If you look at *The Mack* and *Superfly* it's clear that these films are about nonconformity. The Mack, a pimp, and Superfly, a cocaine pusher, are involved in criminal endeavours that were never looked upon really as criminal endeavours. They are looked at as a fight against 'whitey' . . . as empowerment. They never once say in *Superfly* that what he's doing is wrong, he's just not taking what 'The Man' is dishing out. He's not going to play the game. Listen to the lyrics of the song:

"The aim of his load is to move a lot of blow/ask him of his dream, what does it mean/he wouldn't know. It can't be like the rest/ it's the most he'll confess/but the time's running out/and there's no happiness. Oh Superfly, you're gonna make your fortune by and by . . . "

For that time in the Seventies, there was a very legitimate black cinema going on. It got mired in all the talk about pimps and all that. Major studios jumped on the bandwagon as well as AIP [American International Pictures] in producing the films.

Warner Brothers and MGM were right up there. MGM did *Hit Man*, United Artists did *Cool Breeze* and a ton of stuff. AIP were exploitation filmmakers who set up shop and were consistently cranking them out. The big studios had their own exploitation rings, because the B-movie market, the exploitation movie market, the grind house movie market, was very big in the Seventies; a lot could be made.

The cinema hit all the genres. There were Westerns and horror films made specifically for a black audience and it was fun! *The Legend of Nigger Charley* was a black action film in a Western setting. A lot of the black crime films literally were the old Warner Brothers movies redone with black casts. *Cool Breeze* is a black remake of *The Maltese Falcon*. *Hit Man* is a remake of the Michael Caine British crime film *Get Carter*. There was *Buck And The Preacher* which had a very black exploitation feel to it and also had a big budget and starred Sidney Poitier and Harry Belafonte. There was the crazy Italian production, *Take A Hard Ride* with Jim Brown, Fred Williamson, Jim Kelly and Lee Van Cleef, with a little spaghetti Western thrown in there.

Then consider *Mandingo*, which is a black exploitation movie in every way, shape, and form if ever a description deserved to be applied to a film. *Mandingo* was produced by a big studio and was very successful with black audiences. *Mandingo* is a big studio exploitation masterpiece. It has the same aesthetic as a women-in-prison movie, except far more horrible. It's probably one of the most violent and disgusting films you'll ever see. It's based on a very famous book that showed the real truth about the old South. There is so much wimpiness in major studios' films. To think that *Mandingo* was made by a major studio and they spent so much money on it, and it looks like they did, I'm still flabbergasted, which is one of the reasons why I love that movie so much. I'll never forget it. It exists so much on its own in 1975.

It's very interesting because for so many years people have been putting these films down. It was the rise of hip-hop and rap artists talking about how much they loved black exploitation films and how much they loved *The Mack* and *Superfly* and *Willie Dynamite*, and using Rudy Ray Moore and soundbites from both black exploitation films and kung fu movies in their records. On the song by Public Enemy ['Burn Hollywood Burn'] the guys start talking and going, "*What's playing?* Driving Miss Daisy, *ah man, fuck that shit, man, let's go home and watch* Black Caesar!" A lot of the black stars of the time were embarrassed about being in the Seventies movies, and a standard thing that was said was, "Well at least it's giving good black actors a chance to work, Rosalind Cash got a chance to work . . . " It's just so submissive and degrading to the genre. Rap artists 20 years later were the first people, the first black 'celebrities' to embrace the films. I grew up with the films and I loved them. I didn't need anyone else to tell me. I talked about them with anyone who would listen even before I became known.

A lot of these films are just fun. Of course, there's some really ridiculous ones. There are some that you end up laughing at quite a bit because you know they just didn't date that well. But that's the same for a lot of the hippie movies of the Sixties. They don't date that well. That doesn't mean that they're bad movies, it just means that they look dated; it looks like the times have changed. But there are so many that just stand as wonderful documents of their time.

When I put Pam Grier as the lead of *Jackie Brown*, people said, "Oh, you're doing for Pam Grier what you did for John Travolta." Well, I don't think like that. I cast a good actress in a role that's perfect for her. I'm not thinking about launching or rediscovering, it's not about that. That's a nice thing to write about but it really has nothing to do with the actual work or process involved. It was going to be brought up so much that I thought I had to bring it up to Pam very early on. That's all media machine press work bullshit that really has nothing to do with the work. When I talked to Pam about it she said, "Oh Quentin, don't even think about that, I'm not thinking about that, because I'm not a white male!"

Pam Grier as Foxy Brown *(1974), another 'bad-ass chick' out for revenge. Tarantino was in thrall to the raw power of blaxploitation as a young kid.*

I brought a lot of the feeling of black exploitation films that I like to *Jackie Brown*. It's like the debt that *Pulp Fiction* owes to spaghetti Westerns, *Jackie Brown* owes to black exploitation films. And the relationship that surf music had to *Pulp Fiction*, old school Seventies soul music has to *Jackie Brown*: that's the rhythm and the pulse of the movie.

**8.
jackie
brown**

return of a foxy mama

by Peter Travers

Sorry to disappoint those who longed to see Quentin Tarantino fall on his famously flashy ass, but the overlong, overindulgent *Jackie Brown* – the Q man's first feature as a writer and director since *Pulp Fiction*, in 1994 – scores a knockout just the same. Loaded with action, laughs, smart dialogue and potent performances, *Jackie Brown* is most memorable for its unexpected feeling. Tarantino adapts Elmore Leonard's 1992 crime novel, *Rum Punch*, without losing the author's compassion for compromised characters who defy the reduced options that come with age.

What's this – the greying of *Reservoir Dogs*, raunch tinged with rue? A little bit. But before you get medieval on Tarantino's ass, consider the insinuating premise: Jackie Burke, the book's white stewardess, is now Jackie Brown and played by that icon of Seventies blaxploitation films, Pam Grier (*Coffy*, *Foxy Brown*, *Sheba Baby*). Tarantino was just ten years old back in 1973 when Grier, now 48, played Coffy, a nurse at war with the drug lords who hooked her eleven-year-old sister on smack. Coffy seduces one drooling pusher by letting her breasts slip alluringly from her blouse; she then blows his head off with a shotgun.

Moments like these clearly had a profound effect on young Quentin. His affection for Grier, and the maverick spirit she brought to films most critics wrote off as gory junk, fill every frame. Jackie is still a looker, but a low-paying job flying shuttles between Los Angeles and Mexico has removed some of her sparkle. Things turn for the worse when the LAPD and ATF agent Ray Nicolet (a twitchy Michael Keaton) arrest Jackie for smuggling in money and a bag of cocaine for gunrunner Ordell Robbie (Samuel L. Jackson).

And where is Ordell when his courier is facing prison? He's in the apartment of stoner Melanie Ralston (Bridget Fonda), a past-her-prime surfer girl who gives Ordell attitude for showing chicks-with-guns videos to ex-con Louis Gara (Robert De Niro). Of the virtues of the AK-47, Ordell tells dim-bulb Louis, "When you absolutely, positively gotta kill every muthafucker in the room, accept no substitute." Ordell won't accept Jackie sitting in jail, so he arranges for bail bondsman Max Cherry (Robert Forster) to spring her. That way Ordell can kill Jackie before she rats on him to the feds to save her ass.

Tarantino lets these characters play out their destinies against an atmosphere of seductive B-movie sleaze that is deftly evoked in the cinematography of Guillermo Navarro. Jackson is perfection, combining charm and menace with uncanny brilliance. And Fonda keeps springing surprises. Playing bad liberates her. Tarantino, the screen's leading foot fetishist since the death of Luis Bunuel, has Melanie wiggle her toes to entice Louis. "Wanna fuck?" she asks. "Sure," he says. THREE MINUTES LATER, a title card announces, and they're done. De Niro's performance is one finely calibrated slow burn as Louis withers under Melanie's sarcasm. "How'd you ever rob a bank, Lou-*is*?" she says, putting a hiss in that final syllable each time she says his name, which causes Louis to blow.

The glory of the film resides in the unlikely romance between Jackie and Max. He hears music when he first sees her – it's Seventies soul, of course. And she introduces him to the Delfonics. "How do you feel about getting old?" Jackie asks Max, who admits he bought a wig when his hair started to fall out. "My ass ain't the same," Jackie grudgingly confesses. "Bigger?" asks Max, smiling. "Nothin' wrong with that."

As a 'grown-up' crime film, Jackie Brown *deals with a black, middle-aged, working woman (Pam Grier) trying to keep her life from being flushed down the pan.*

Forster (*Medium Cool*, TV's *Banyon*) broke into movies in 1967 as an object of lust for both Elizabeth Taylor and Marlon Brando in *Reflections In A Golden Eye*. Now, at 56, he brings off a personal triumph as a hard case stirring long-buried emotions. Is Jackie using Max in an elaborate scheme to steal $500,000 from Ordell – Tarantino stages the sting in a shopping mall and milks the money exchange for maximum suspense – or is it true love? Max is afraid to look too closely, which gives Forster's scenes with Grier a heartbreaking intensity.

And Grier, a babe for the ages, is a sensation. Jackie can press a gun to Ordell's dick and stare down a cop with the same icy cool. "Are you afraid of me?" Jackie asks Max. "A little bit," he answers. Jackie is scared, too. Driving toward a new life she can't define, Jackie sings along with Bobby Womack's 'Across 110th Street' on the car radio. It's a Seventies song about busting out of ghettos. Tarantino knows that drill. In this transitional film, he acknowledges his debt to the elegant crime fiction of Elmore Leonard and the crude vitality of blaxploitation. For Tarantino and his protagonist, *Jackie Brown* crackles with the fear and exhilaration of moving on.

killing me softly

by Philip French

Coming out of *Jackie Brown*, I found myself thinking that I had spent two and a half hours in the happy state I have associated all my life with a really good western. A satisfying plot logically worked through and brought to a morally and intellectually satisfying conclusion, acted out in an exciting, exotic landscape by people speaking the right language and marching to a drummer beating out the rhythm of their particular ethos.

Nearly 70 years ago Edmund Wilson identified southern California as the last frontier, the place where "you see the last futile effervescence of the burst of the American adventure. Here our people, so long told to 'go West' to escape from ill-health and poverty, maladjustment and industrial oppression, are discovering that having come West, their problems and diseases remain and that the ocean bars further flight."

Elmore Leonard is the last of the great pulp novelists, though unlike most of them he has lived long enough to be respected, rewarded and to feel comfortable between hard covers. Born in 1925 in the Deep South, he lived in Detroit from the age of ten and, except for a wartime hitch in the navy, he has remained there, working as a copywriter for a local advertising agency until becoming a full-time writer in the Sixties.

His first stories, published in pulp magazines or original paperbacks, were westerns, and it wasn't until 1968 that he turned away from the stylised rural past to listen to the rhythms of the urban present and write the thrillers on which his reputation rests. They are about ordinary people on both sides of the law, many only marginally involved in crime. Their dreams are relatively small-scale, which doesn't mean they are within their grasp, and in seeking to attain them their lives become hopelessly complicated. The tone is wry, tragi-comic, non-judgemental, realistic without being cynical. And the setting is the axis reaching from the Canadian border workplace to the Caribbean playground, from violent, decaying industrial Detroit in the north to violent, thriving, glitzy Florida in the south. They are, with their casual demotic dialogue and unpretentious prose (usually a sort of subjective third person narrative), stylistically and geographically somewhere between the excessive garrulity of George V. Higgins's Irish-American Boston and Raymond Chandler's wise-cracking, metaphor-laden southern California.

Like Chandler, Leonard is very observant of social change. However, he registers it as neither decline nor progress, merely as something that provides opportunities for, or challenges to, his characters. You could call him a humanist, but never a pessimist or an optimist.

Three of Leonard's westerns became classic films as Delmer Daves's *3.10 To Yuma* (which reworked the Grail legend in Arizona), Budd Boetticher's *The Tall T* and Martin Ritt's *Hombre*, all adapted by others in the years before westerns became fashionable. But he has had less success with films of the crime books. He collaborated on the scripts of John Frankenheimer's *52 Pick-Up*, Burt Reynolds's *Stick* and Abel Ferrara's *Cat Chaser*, but they turned out pretty ordinary and the first two went straight to video in Britain. Barry Sonnenfeld's adaptation of *Get Shorty* was a major advance, catching a lot of Leonard's quirky humour, though it ended up as a slick Hollywood-on-Hollywood comedy. Now he has found his most sympathetic interpreter to date and Quentin Tarantino's *Jackie Brown*, based on the 1992 novel *Rum Punch*, is echt-Leonard.

Unless you count *From Dusk Till Dawn* as an unacknowledged version of Jim Thompson's *The Getaway*, this is the first time Tarantino has adapted someone else's material and his changes are not major – principally switching the setting from Palm Beach to Los Angeles, altering the colour of the white heroine's skin, slightly simplifying the plot, introducing additional profanities, and (surprisingly) reducing the violence. The central character, Jackie Brown (Pam Grier), is first seen in profile, a confident figure in her air-hostess's uniform, seemingly floating through space, but in fact on a travelator at Los Angeles airport. Her poise is shattered by an arrest and a night in the slammer. A federal agent (Michael Keaton) and an LAPD cop (Michael Bowen) pick her up in the car park with $50,000 in her flight bag along with a couple of ounces of cocaine.

They're after the man for whom she's smuggling the money from Mexico, the black arms dealer Ordell Robbie (Samuel L. Jackson), and the cocaine (of which Jackie is unaware) gives them the opportunity to set bail at $10,000. A prior conviction for possession (protecting a former husband) lost Jackie her position with Delta and now, aged 44, she risks being fired from her rotten $16,000-a-year job with a crummy Mexican airline. On the other hand, if she collaborates with the police the ruthless Ordell might rub her out, which indeed he intends to when he arranges to pay her bail.

But Jackie discovers a new ally in Max Cherry (Robert Forster), a 56-year-old ex-cop earning a decent, if unsatisfying living as a professional bail-bondsman, working in a no man's land between criminals and the law. Like the alcoholic process-server in the masterly *Unknown Man No. 89*, Max is one of those recurrent figures in the Leonard *oeuvre*, a troubled, inherently decent man with an old-fashioned sense of gallantry where women are concerned. So in a cleverly organised plot, Jackie is the live bait in a deadly cat-and-mouse game between cops and crooks, with Max helping her to play one side against the other.

The movie's action takes place beneath dull, white skies in the anonymous, unglamorous South Bay area of Los Angeles, townships south of Los Angeles airport such as Carson, Hawthorne, Torrance and Compton that foreigners only fly over or drive through by accident. Torrance, however, boasts the largest shopping mall in America, a shimmering shrine to consumerism in which the film's climactic scene is staged. In this inert milieu the characters spend much of their time sitting around eating, drinking and talking. The self-aggrandising criminal Ordell has a passive sidekick in Louis Gara (Robert De Niro), an incompetent bank robber whose friendship with Ordell was forged in Detroit. Leonard's 1978 novel *The Switch* recounts their involvement in a bungled kidnapping scheme. Ordell also has three women, one white, two black, who sit at home in three *menages* ready to provide the sexual and professional services he needs – the idle, coke-sniffing Melanie (Bridget Fonda), who despises him; the middle-aged Simone (Hattie Winston) who dresses up to mime to Motown records; and Sherdona (Lisa Gay Hamilton), a simple-minded, teenage runaway from Georgia who thinks she's a few steps from Hollywood. Ordell is a despicable, misogynistic psychopath, but he's given a sad humanity, as is his fellow psycho Louis, though the removal of a key sub-plot makes Louis's role in the movie less significant than in the novel.

Jackie Brown, like *Reservoir Dogs* and *Pulp Fiction*, is an ensemble piece. But the ultimate focus is on the relationship of Jackie and Max, the bruised and desperate middle-aged pair, and Tarantino exhibits his gifts for reviving careers by casting two familiar faces from the past that we have seen little of recently. The 49-year-old Grier, handsome star of blaxploitation pictures of the Seventies, is wonderfully assured as Jackie, and the 56-year-old Forster, whose only memorable major lead was in Haskell Wexler's *Medium Cool* (1969), exudes a tested probity as Max, a man with a life story written in the lines on his face.

A deliberately leisurely pace enables Tarantino to develop character. Much of the dialogue comes straight from Leonard and there are no obtrusive lines. Max's comment on the work of his assistant, "That's what he does, he finds people who don't want to be found", and Ordell's comment "You shot Melanie? Twice?" produce appreciative laughter in the cinema, but are meaningless out of context.

The action is never tarted up by flashy cutting. One of the few bravura effects is a long take of Jackie becoming increasingly panicky as she walks through the shopping mall, but this turns out to be justified because we later discover that she has been performing for the benefit of police surveillance. There is also comparatively little violence – a mere four killings, each handled obliquely. In one case, the camera is a hundred yards away as two flashes of a pistol in the dark signal the death of a potential informer; in another, the victim is out-of-frame to the right of the camera. Tarantino goes easy too on the movie references. There's a glimpse of Bridget Fonda's father, Peter, on television in *Dirty Mary, Crazy Larry* (a long-forgotten film about two mad young men and a louche broad robbing supermarkets), and a borrowing from Kubrick's *The Killing* of the device of halting at a moment of high suspense to backtrack and present a crucial scene from two other points of view. But that's about all.

If one has a stylistic criticism it is of a redundant map put in to show that Jackie's plane is flying north from Baja California to L.A.

Jackie Brown is the best thing Tarantino has made so far, a first-class job of work that does for Elmore Leonard what Curtis Hanson's *L.A. Confidential* does for another formidable contemporary crime writer, James Ellroy. At 35, Tarantino is the same age John Huston was when he adapted and directed Dashiell Hammett's *The Maltese Falcon*. Huston had nearly 50 years of work ahead of him then.

the 'n' word

by Pascoe Sawyer

Spike Lee's recent outburst against Quentin Tarantino, for using the 'n' word, has opened up a long overdue debate about the increasingly liberal use of the word. Lee claims Tarantino is 'infatuated' with it. That's why it is used 28 times in his highly successful *Pulp Fiction* and 38 times in his new movie *Jackie Brown*.

Lee points out that if he had used a word like "kike" 38 times in one of his films the sheer weight of the public outcry against him would have ended his career as a filmmaker. This is probably true, but Lee's attempt at championing the black cause looks less well considered when we remember that the word "nigger" features prominently in practically every film he has been involved in making.

"Nigger" is also used in critically-acclaimed (in the black community anyway) black-directed films like *Boyz N The Hood* (John Singleton) and *Menace II Society* (Albert and Allen Hughes), apparently with Spike's approval. That's because Lee's problem with Tarantino has less to do with the use of the word "nigger" in his films and more to do with the fact that it's a white director using it. Tarantino, who claims to have been raised on black culture, is unrepentant. Staunchly defending his position in a recent interview, he said: "I'm a white guy who is not afraid of that word. I just don't feel the whole white guilt and pussy footing around the whole racial issue."

Samuel L. Jackson, an actor whose elevation to 'big star' status owes much to his appearances in Tarantino movies, has also been quick to defend the director's right to realistically portray black lifestyles, and states he has no problem being called a 'nigger' or calling other black people 'nigger' on screen, as long as it's in context.

Diran Adebayo, author of the Sega prize winning novel *Some Kind Of Black*, agrees with Jackson. Commenting on *Jackie Brown*, he said: "I don't think the film will in any way affect black people's state of mind. It's Tarantino's homage to one of the cultures he has experienced as he grew up and the film comes from his perspective and there's nothing wrong with that. The only issue for debate is, is it a good film or not? And I think it is."

It's one of the many ironies of this situation that black Americans actually initiated the use of "nigger" as a popular slang word. My first experience of hearing it was through the comedian Richard Pryor. I remember seeing videos of his stand-up routines in the early Eighties and, I must admit, at the time I thought he was side-splittingly brilliant. Pryor wasn't the first black American icon from that era to publicly call himself a "nigger" with pride. The word also features strongly in the blaxploitation films of the Seventies.

It all started going wrong in 1989 when a young L.A.-based gangsta rap group stepped on the scene, with a name that must have brought a sparkle to the eyes of the PR executive given the task of marketing them. No doubt about it, Niggaz Wit' Attitude (NWA) were an extremely talented and innovative group, but the lyrical content of their best selling records helped to make a 'nigga' a hip thing to be, and young black men were particularly attracted to the tag.

Ordell Robbie (Samuel L. Jackson) and Louis Gara (Robert DeNiro) – unequal partners in crime, the black man being the dominant partner.

Other rappers, however, have attempted to accentuate the positive meaning of the word. The infamous Tupac Shakur, in a track from his first album *2Pacalpyse Now*, defines "nigger" as standing for 'Never Ignorant Getting Goals Accomplished'. But does changing the spelling and even the meaning of such a loaded word necessarily change the mental images which subconsciously come to mind when it is used?

While black artists continue to promote the use of the word in popular culture, studies in America show that the word "nigger" is still the most commonly used insult in racially motivated attacks on black people, which takes us to the heart of the issue. For most people black and white, "nigger" still means what it has always meant: the lowest of the low.

This point is beautifully illustrated in a scene from the film *True Romance*. A group of Sicilian gangsters are torturing and about to kill an old man, Clifford Worley (Dennis Hopper). Once the character realises his fate he decides to retaliate:

WORLEY

"Did you know Sicilians were spawned by niggers? It's a fact. Sicilians have black blood pumping through their hearts. If you don't believe me look it up. . . hundreds of years ago the Moors conquered Sicily. . . the Moors are niggers. Back then the Sicilians were like wops from northern Italy, with blonde hair and blue eyes. Then the Moors moved in there. . . they did so much fucking with Sicilian women that they changed the whole blood line forever. That's how blonde hair and blue eyes became black hair and dark skin. And it's always amazing to me that hundreds of years later you Sicilians still carry that nigger gene."

The Mafia boss, who does not usually dirty his hands by carrying out the executions himself, is so enraged by the insult that he repeatedly shoots Worley in the head. The screenplay for *True Romance* was written by Quentin Tarantino.

Today, black street culture and its vocabulary are at the heart of the mainstream, so if black people insist on using the word in public, then there is no justifiable or logical reason why people from other races should not be able to do the same. Black Americans have opened a Pandora's box that only they can close.

fun lovin'
criminals

by Tom Charity

"I was the third brother of five, doing whatever I had to do to survive. I'm not saying what I did was all right, trying to break out of the ghetto was a day-to-day fight . . . You don't know what you'd do till you're put under pressure. Across 110th Street is a hell of a tester . . . Across 110th Street. You can find it all in the street . . . Look around you, look around you, look around you . . . " **Bobby Womack**

The Big Kahuna is back! It's three years, nine months since *Pulp Fiction* wowed the film world at Cannes . . . a leave of absence which has seen Quentin Tarantino's personal and professional reputation slump. There was the well publicised falling out with co-writer Roger Avary; allegations of plagiarism concerning *Reservoir Dogs*; reviled on-screen turns in *Destiny Turns On The Radio*, *Desperado* and others; the *Four Rooms* fiasco; and the arrested adolescence evinced by the belatedly produced script *From Dusk Till Dawn*. As Tarantino himself observed, he'd already become an adjective by the age of 30. What he neglected to mention was that 'Tarantino-esque' had become critical shorthand for hackneyed, would-be-hip, low-budget crime thrillers. If he'd energised American movies, he also bore some responsibility for the trend that turned cinema into assault. His imitators weren't picking up on his virtuoso story structures, insightful casting choices or the restraint which gave his shock effects their impact, they were just peppering gimmicky ideas with has-been actors, gratuitous pop banter and fashionably ironic violence. Tarantino had become the most influential film-maker of the generation, but for mostly the wrong reasons. To top it all, late last year Jane Hamsher's best-selling hatchet job on the making of *Natural Born Killers*, *Killer Instinct*, portrayed him as an illiterate, back-stabbing, egotistical chauvinist . . . a portrait Tarantino himself did nothing to soften by physically attacking Hamsher's business partner, Don Murphy. ("I just bitch-slapped him," Tarantino claimed, charmingly.)

Had the pressure got to him? Was Hollywood's hottest talent already burned out? After all the speculation, a National Film Theatre preview of *Jackie Brown* in January proved that at least Tarantino had lost none of his pulling power. Among the throng were such diverse talents as Terry Gilliam, Sally Potter, Andrew Macdonald, David Thewlis and Jonny Lee Miller, as well as Sharleen from Texas and the odd Gallagher brother. As significantly, perhaps, there were more young black faces than the NFT has seen in a long time. "To me this is a black film made for a black audience," a relaxed, convivial Tarantino told them. "Don't let the pigmentation fool ya. It's a state of mind . . . "

Jackie Brown is based on Elmore Leonard's novel *Rum Punch*. While it's plotted with Leonard's typical offhand intricacy, the set-up is simple enough. Take half a dozen characters who know they're in a fix, and give them half a million dollars to fight over. On the wrong side of the law we have a ruthless arms dealer, Ordell (Samuel L. Jackson), his prison-happy buddy Louis (Robert De Niro), and the reliably duplicitous Melanie (Bridget Fonda). "I don't have to trust Melanie, I know her," Ordell tells a blankly uncomprehending Louis. On the other side, there's a slick, eager cop, Ray Nicolet (Michael Keaton), and the world-weary bail bondsman, Max Cherry (Robert Forster). Meanwhile, Jackie Brown (Pam Grier) is stuck in the middle with the money, wondering if she can't play both ends against each other and get away scot-free.

In Elmore Leonard's world, it always comes down to the survival of the smartest. That's what makes the books so seductive: vivid and deft, they confer street smarts on readers who wouldn't know the difference between an M-16 and a traffic jam. ("This TEC-9? They advertise it as being 'as tough as your toughest customer'. Say it's 'the most popular gun in American crime'. No lie, they actually say that.') If Hemingway had retired to Florida, taken up golf and found true love, instead of blowing his brains out, he might have written these books. It's literary slumming of a peculiarly cool and elegant kind, but the books also have wit, ingenuity and an incomparably sharp ear for the cadence of marginalised Americana. Leonard makes a natural ally for a film-maker who has always stressed his street credentials, suppressing what amounts to a middle-class background. According to Tarantino, he first encountered the novelist's work when he was busted for shoplifting a copy of *The Switch* when he was fifteen – a story which lends some faint outlaw credibility to the relationship, and which actually seems to be true. (By happy coincidence, *The Switch* introduces the characters of Ordell, Louis and Melanie.) Two decades on, he was in a position to press John Travolta to take the lead in *Get Shorty* and take out his own option on four more Leonard titles.

"His westerns adapt like 'Bang!' No worries," Tarantino observes, holding court in a Dorchester suite. He's dressed in black, of course: black jeans, black leather jacket, casual sneakers. It's a step up the style ladder from the tracksuit he sported at the NFT a couple of nights before. "The problem with the crime films, a lot of them just try to turn the book into a standard movie, whereas what's unique about Elmore's thrillers is the rich emphasis on characterisation. They have these wonderful stories, then life gets in the way and screws them up."

Although it's overwhelmingly faithful to the novel, *Jackie Brown* is set in the director's native L.A. in place of Miami, and transforms Leonard's 44-year-old Caucasian airline stewardess Jackie Burke into the ostentatiously black, middle-aged Pam Grier title role (Grier is 48). It's a brilliant casting switch, flying in the face of Hollywood convention – anyone else would have got Julia Roberts, if they could – investing the material with weight and depth, plus the kind of return-of-the-underdog aura which paid off so handsomely for John Travolta. If *Get Shorty* brought out Leonard's comic side, this is certainly the most substantial film adaptation of his work, more serious even than the novel itself. "There's a weight to the characters, I agree with you," Tarantino nods, lighting up a cigarillo. "That's not a better or worse situation, but I do feel the novel is a touch lighter than the movie. I think the casting of Robert and Pam has a lot to do with that. There's this famous thing that you end up dropping scenes in the editing because the script needed them but the movie doesn't. You're further along with visual information than when you read. Seeing Robert behind that desk and knowing he's been there nineteen years tells you everything you need to know."

It's easy to caricature Tarantino as a film geek cocooned in cineliteracy – but hard to think of another art form in which knowledge of the medium would be disparaged like this. There's no denying that the screenplays for *True Romance*, *Natural Born Killers* and *From Dusk Till Dawn* function primarily as vicarious escapades for the rampant adolescent male imagination (not an invalid function, but limited), and it's arguably true that the flamboyance of *Pulp Fiction* camouflages an emotional vacuum at its core – certainly there was something ludicrous about Tarantino talking up the personal angle because he'd been to Amsterdam once. But by the same token, that film's sophisticated ethical play has largely been overlooked, and the pain of betrayal in *Reservoir Dogs* is every bit as emotional as it is physical.

I tell him how I feel the term 'Tarantino-esque' has become degraded, and again he concurs readily enough. (Though he's not encumbered with false modesty, Tarantino has a habit of agreeing with your point before taking off on his own tack. It makes him seem more affable and intelligent than you expected.) "Yeah, I felt that. I never really understood what 'Tarantino-esque' meant. When I hear it applied, it never sounds like a flattering thing because it's so broken down to black suits, hipper-than-thou dialogue and people talking about TV shows. That's not me. I feel there's a lot more to my work than that. The big thing in Hollywood is you can make a whole lot of money on script polishes and I've only done this once, and I'll never do this again, but I did it on *Crimson Tide* as a favour to Tony Scott. I was very proud of what I did, because except for a couple of scenes, the first 45 minutes of the movie is my dialogue, every time anyone opens their mouth, it's my dialogue. And everybody assumes all I did was put in the *Silver Surfer* references, the *Star Trek* jokes, which bothered me at the time . . . "

In this sense, *Jackie Brown* would seem to be consciously anti-'Tarantino-esque'. Don't expect the spectacular fireworks of *Pulp Fiction*. He isn't shooting from the hip this time. In fact, he's playing it relatively straight. He has reined in his knack for dazzling post-modern chronological conundrums (save for one bravura climactic coup), cashed in the pop-cultural name-checks and thought through his over-easy ironic sensibility. While you can point to any number of cinematic influences (the generic abstraction of Jean-Pierre Melville, Brian De Palma's split-screen, Howard Hawks' camaraderie, Takeshi Kitano's detachment, the music and muscle of the entire blaxploitation era), Tarantino wears them gracefully enough. "Quentin is a consummate thief," as Samuel L Jackson puts it. "He steals the best."

The first hour-and-a-half is largely shot in tight close-ups and quite conventional two-shots with long dialogue scenes hinging on familiar Tarantino themes: obligation, negotiation and responsibility. In the final hour, the camera becomes more proactive, the Steadicam pushing forward as the plot picks up pace and things fall apart. "For the first hour, it's not really about plot at all, it's about characterisation. In the backseat, a plot is being nailed into place, but by the time it takes over, you've gotten to know these people. All of Elmore's novels work like that," the director points out. "I could have dropped half an hour out of this movie, and I could have had a much more peppy, *Get Shorty* kind of fun ride, but that wasn't what I wanted."

Tellingly, when Max Cherry goes to the movies, he opts for "something that looks good and starts soon", an unthinkable pronouncement for any earlier Tarantino hero. Similarly, while Mia Wallace (Uma Thurman) felt the need to comment on uncomfortable silences in *Pulp Fiction*, here, Tarantino lets the silence play – how rare it is for a film-maker to trust the moment like that, and allow us to watch a character think. *Jackie Brown* has not exactly set America alight ($38,000,000 in seven weeks and just one Oscar nomination), but then, it's that rare thing in movies, a slow burner. Damn, if the boy wonder hasn't grown up.

"Quentin's got rid of all that star stuff he was so fond of," Sam Jackson tells me later. "When he started writing scripts it was because he wanted to be a movie star, like a lot of people do. Then when he became Quentin Tarantino the star movie-maker, he rode that. People vilified him because he was enjoying it, but so what? He should have. You people told him he was *all that*, and he bought into it for a while, had some fun with it, and now he's been burned. He's learned from it. He's grown."

"I think the film has a sense of maturity about it that doesn't even have anything to do with me personally necessarily, but everybody in the movie is getting old," Tarantino says. "Pam is, like, 45 in the film, Max is in his fifties, Robert De Niro is in his fifties, Sam Jackson is in his fifties. Bridget is 33 but she's very old for what she does. She's over the hill for living off a guy, a professional girlfriend. They're all at the end of their rope. I love the idea of doing a movie with an older sensibility, the desperation of you didn't do what you wanted with the last 25 years, and now you have a very small window to be doing something about it."

"If *Jackie Brown* has a structure," Tarantino told the audience at the NFT, "then it's the structure of a pencil. You go along for the duration of the film, and when you get to the lead, that's the final close-up of Robert. Then the nib, the point, is the final close-up of Pam." So, in the end, it comes down to this: the resonance, promise and melancholy of those two faces . . . People will say the movie's too long, but it's long on human behaviour, short on fraudulence. There isn't a false note in any of the performances. In the big set-piece, the switch, Tarantino shows the same event three times, from three different points of view – with three distinct theme songs. More than just a stunt, it crystallises an impression you also get from reading Leonard, that each of the characters is starring in his or her own movie, no one is privy to the information that they're just supporting characters in the larger scheme of things. This is where Tarantino's respect for actors really pays off to the point where it almost becomes a philosophical principle. He is, after all, the great redeemer, the saviour of lost careers; casting about for his Max Cherry, Tarantino says he considered Gene Hackman, Paul Newman, John Saxon and Robert Forster. Who else would have dreamed up such an egalitarian wish-list? Forster is superb in the role, incidentally, stoic, lovelorn, lost . . . it almost transcends performance.

"There's a wonderful aspect," Tarantino smiles. "I know who Robert Forster is, but a lot of the audience don't. He has no baggage whatsoever. Gene Hackman is one of my favourite actors, but I remember at the time of the casting for *Crimson Tide*, I thought: Oh man, I've seen Gene Hackman do this before. Then I saw the movie and he was so excellent it made me feel like a punk for even thinking that. But having said that, there is something special about introducing an actor of Robert's age to a whole lot of audience members. It's very cool when people say to me: 'Oh, I really like

De Niro and I really like Pam, oh, and Max Cherry!' Or 'that guy that played Max Cherry'. That's who he is to them. He earns that, with the kind of man who he is. There doesn't seem to be an actor-ness about him. If you walk into a bail bond office in Los Angeles, you'll see somebody who looks like Max. Same with Pam. She looks like a stewardess who's been in the business too long. She's one of the most beautiful women in the movies, ever, but when she gets out of that jail, she looks like she's been in jail for two days. A director friend of mine said something so wonderful, she said the film looked 'lived-in.' That's what I wanted. I didn't want 'movie characters'."

Jackie rides off into an L.A. sunset, to the sound of New York ghetto song 'Across 110th Street'.

Pam Grier rap sheet

Alias: Jackie Brown (flight attendant).

Age: 48.

Distinguishing features: A formidable body, big hair, great gangster snarl. She looks ten years younger. "I've been around. This isn't a hobby for me. Just because I'm 48, people expect me to roll up in a wheelchair and put my teeth in a jar. Some people don't believe it, they think it's all a marketing ploy. I've had to show my driving licence! But it's about your energy, how you feel. I meet 20-year old Quentin fans and I tell them, 'Hey, you're going to be 40, if you live. You're gonna lose your hair, lose your erection, lose your job, then you're going to know what Quentin is talking about.'"

Signature tune: 'Across 110th Street' (Bobby Womack), 'Street Life' (Randy Crawford), 'Long Time Woman' (Pam Grier).

Priors: Beyond the Valley of the Dolls (1970), *Coffy* (1973), *Foxy Brown* (1974), *Sheba Baby* (1975), *Escape from L.A.* (1996), *Mars Attacks!* (1997).

Tarantino connection: Grier gets a name-check in *Reservoir Dogs*. She also screen tested for the Rosanna Arquette role in *Pulp Fiction*: "I went in to meet Quentin and there were these posters for my movies from the Seventies on the wall. I asked him if he put them up 'specially 'cos I was coming, and he said no, he was going to take them down because I was coming . . . "

Let's get into character: "We were doing nine-minute scenes, uncut sometimes, and we'd do it five lenses, five times. We'd do one scene a day. Sometimes I was so tired, at night I'd just sit in the tub and cry. But I had a schematic worked out on the wall of my hotel room, about twelve feet long, of all the scenes, with me and each character. We'd shoot out of sequence, so I needed to know where I was on the arc – Where have I been? What am I doing? How do I relate to Robert or Michael or Sam at this point? That's how I work . . . it's mapped out in different colours on my wall. Challenges like this don't come very often, maybe once in a career. It's a proving ground."

Colour: "The casting had nothing to do with colour blindness. A black woman has more political obstacles. She can walk into a store and the guards will wonder if she's a shoplifter. A white woman wouldn't get that attention. So it's social and political consciousness. We shouldn't think that way, but it lingers in the back of people's heads. Jackie doesn't have entitlement. She has more obstacles. With the ATF, the LAPD. She's not a senior flight attendant living in a beautiful townhouse on the beach, she's living on $16,000 and benefits. She should be on another economic level."

The Jackie Brown *effect*: "I started telling people I was doing this project with Quentin Tarantino, Samuel L Jackson, Robert De Niro, Michael Keaton . . . we got *Pulp Fiction*, *Raging Bull*, *Batman*, all in one movie. They thought I was on acid. Now the movie's out, they send me clothes, and cars – cars I've never heard of, like Munchkin cars. I say, 'No thank you, I'll just drive my truck.' I have dogs. Oh, they're sending incredible scripts, too."

Robert Forster rap sheet

Alias: Max Cherry (bail bondsman).

Age: 56.

Distinguishing features: A bit touch and go on top. "In *Alligator* I did a few jokes about losing my hair, which I stuck in 'cos I was in that position at the time. Right afterwards I was in Schwabs drugs store, and a guy in there took me aside. He said: 'Robert, you know I'm your friend, but I got to tell I you, you haven't made it yet, you look better with hair, and you better do something about it.' So that's what I did."

Signature tune: 'Didn't I (Blow Your Mind This Time)' (The Delfonics).

Priors: *Medium Cool* (1969), *Banyon* (TV, 1972), *Stunts* (1977), *Alligator* (1980), *The Delta Force* (1986). "Where have I been? You know, my ex-wives wanna know the same thing. I had a five-year first act and a 25-year second act. I've been sliding quite a long time."

Tarantino connection: QT recommended him for the Christopher Walken role when he first sold *True Romance*, before Tony Scott took over the project. Later, Forster auditioned for the Lawrence Tierney role in *Reservoir Dogs*. "I was hopeful, because this guy obviously liked me, and I needed a job badly then, I was going down fast. After the reading he took me aside and said: 'Listen, this may not work out, but don't worry, one of these days I'm going to use you.' The guy is a straight-shooter, but you never really know. Then, eighteen months ago, I ran into him in a restaurant where I usually go for breakfast, and he said he was adapting *Rum Punch* and I should read it, which I did. Four or five months later, there he is, in my usual spot, and he hands me a script . . . "

Let's get into character: "Quentin said: 'Don't put any pressure on yourself, just prepare the way you usually prepare, and don't forget, I've got a lot of film, so if I only need to go from here to next door, I can go all the way around the world to do it.' Knowing I hadn't had a start like this for 25 years, he made it easy for me. But I identified with Max. He is just a guy like all of us, looking for love, hoping that in this face or that face he's going to find the one th at's for him. Acting isn't hard, getting a job is hard. I can act. Kids can act. After so long, you know what you're doing, it's not a mystery any more. Who you make yourself into as a human being is what you bring to the set. If the part calls for something else, then show a different part of yourself, but if it really calls for who you are, then that's the one you look at in the morning when you shave, it's not a mystery. I told Quentin I appreciate being the good guy again, because I did a bad guy in *Delta Force* in 1985 and I haven't done a good guy since. My kids were getting tired of seeing me kill people. As I left, he said: 'Don't worry, you're going to be a good guy again.'"

The *Jackie Brown* *effect:* "This movie surpasses anything I've ever done. I don't know the dimensions of it yet, but hopefully it gives you opportunities to work – that people are sufficiently aware of you to offer you roles. That's what the actor hopes for, that he doesn't just flash, but that he continues to build and make a decent life out of it. I'd like that. My kids and my ex-wives are pulling for it too. Now that the movie is out in the States, the steam is building, if that's the right metaphor. The water is heating and the whistle is blowing and the tea will be ready in just a minute."

Robert Forster has been nominated for the Best Supporting Actor Academy Award.

Samuel L. Jackson rap sheet

Alias: Ordell Robbie (arms dealer).

Age: 47.

Distinguishing features: Dubious wig. Killer stare. Plaited oriental chin beard. "I'm a big fan of Hong Kong movies, so I came up with the wig and the little beard. Quentin thought it was awesome. It fits right in with the *homage* that he's paying to the blaxploitation films, it's a real *Superfly*-cloned Hong Kong gangster look, which is a totally cool thing to me. The beard is something to tinker with. Like rosary beads."

Signature tune: 'The Lions And The Cucumber' (The Vampire Sound Inc).

Priors: *Jungle Fever* (1991), *Fresh* (1994), *Pulp Fiction* (1994), *Die Hard With A Vengeance* (1995), *The Long Kiss Goodnight* (1996), *Hard Eight* (1997).

Tarantino connection: Jackson was Oscar-nominated for his performance as Jules in *Pulp Fiction*.

Let's get into character: "You start by reading the two novels that Elmore wrote about Ordell, Louis and Melanie, then you have all the information about who these guys are.

Then you figure out the physical characteristics. Ordell is a guy with goals. He wants to make a million dollars and retire, and he's willing to do anything to do that. He has his own set of rules and lives by them – vehemently. I'm not afraid to tap into my dark side. I'm not self-conscious. It's not my life, it's someone else's. I can always stop and be me. I haven't killed anyone in a while."

Ordell makes a point to Louis. Samuel Jackson expressed support for Tarantino's vernacular use of the word "nigga".

Colour: Spike Lee has publicly rebuked Tarantino for the use of the word "nigger" in the film – Ordell uses it every other word. "Spike has an axe to grind for some reason. In my own personal opinion, it's more or less about the fact that Quentin was able to do this good and interesting black movie and Spike hasn't been able to do that for a while. Spike's not the spokesman for the race and nor am I, but he's the last person who should be dealing with censorship in terms of people being artists. Ordell talks the way Ordell talks. That's who he is. I talk that way on certain days when I'm with specific people, and Spike admitted he does too, which is so bizarre – so what's your point? Quentin has no right to allow his characters to speak that way? That's total bullshit. Film-makers are storytellers, and if that's the story you have in you, and you tell it from the heart, then you have every right to do it. I respect him for it."

i, quentin

by Simon Hattenstone

Quentin Tarantino jives on to the stage of the National Film Theatre. His head nods like a hyperactive chicken. He's walking the walk, waggling that famously big bottom, preparing to talk the talk. He glances up and waves at the crowd, shy, self-conscious, almost cool. He could be flapping at a fly.

Tarantino first packed out the NFT just after *Pulp Fiction*. The tickets disappeared in record time. This time round, for the preview of *Jackie Brown*, they say they went even quicker. Back in 1994, Tarantino was the nipper, the boy wonder. And Tarantino-esque was an incipient adjective embracing hip music like Dick Dale and Stealer's Wheel (that had been unhip till rediscovered by Tarantino), hip actors like John Travolta (who had been unhip till rediscovered by Tarantino), talk, talk, talk, and just as much blood. The high priests of pop culture declared him a postmodernist because he chopped up time and his bloody shootouts were mixed with a thirst for the demotic – lots of gabbing about Madonna followed by a hail of bullets, even more gabbing about burgers called Royales followed by another hail of bullets.

"I became an adjective sooner than I thought I was going to be . . . every third script out there is described as Tarantino-esque," he said then. Today, Tarantino's arrogance is undiminished.

He is asked what Elmore Leonard made of the movie. And he tells us that Leonard didn't just think it was fine, not even mighty fine, not even the best adaptation of his work he's had the pleasure to see. No, says Tarantino, now lapping up the audience, "he said it was the best script I've ever read". He talks quickly, punctuating his sentences with an aetiolated variant of "all right"– "ahhrite".

The questions invite him to restate his genius – yes, it was inspired to cast the heroine of blaxploitation movies Pam Grier; he agrees that if you're a good enough film-maker a two-hour movie just flies past; sure he knew there was more to him than two movies and it's great to silence the sceptics. Thank you everyone.

But Tarantino is a controversial film-maker, and he must expect difficult questions. His films have been called amoral splatterfests. *Reservoir Dogs* was not allowed a video certificate for eighteen months. His story of two serial killers, which became Oliver Stone's film *Natural Born Killers*, was accused of prompting copycat killings. Spike Lee raged against his exploitation of the blaxploitation genre and for colonising the word nigger. Even the Tarantinis in the audience must be looking forward to challenging questions.

A black man tells Tarantino that *Jackie Brown* is a terrific film but, he says, you just can't get away with all those offensive "nigger" references. We prepare for the heat and dust of debate. Well says Tarantino, pausing for effect, "well, I *do*". His elastic thin lips stretch into the cheesiest of smiles. The audience cheer and join his laughter. A few of us are burning for Tarantino's hubris and the young man's public humiliation. When Tarantino is asked a difficult question he turns into the playground bully, rounding up his gang before delivering the killer put-down.

After the talk, there is a little party. His publicists are worried because Tarantino has a bad cold. They want him in bed with a hot water bottle. There are plenty of names at the party, but Tarantino is yacking away to the kids. He can't stop. He seems to be talking movies and dreams and did you see that one and wasn't it just great, and I notice the black guy who was short-changed in the audience.

Next day I turn up for the interview. The publicists are exhausted. You know, they say, we didn't get away till half two in the morning. "He just wouldn't leave." I ask them what he was doing – getting drunk, being loud, doing movie star things? "Not at all, a lot of the time he was talking to this guy about the word nigger."

Today's Tarantino is still a scruffbag but somehow he looks different, more expensive – a chunky gold bracelet, waxed leather coat, top-of-the-range trainers, even the blob of beard looks as if it set him back a bit. He sounds different, too – quieter, less laddish, as if he's been to a Barbara Follett self-improvement class. He drinks water, smokes an elegant cigarillo, tells me he's an artist.

Have I seen the film? Yes, twice. "Great. Plays even better the second time doesn't it?", and he says it so gently I'm not sure if I've heard right.

In its purest sense, *Jackie Brown* is about two middle-aged people – a bail bondsman and an air stewardess – facing up to their under-achievement and loneliness. Many Tarantino addicts are disappointed. They say it is too slow, the dialogue is not snappy enough, the blood not bloody enough. Others, me included, say it is his best film because its story is human, you can weep as the characters' hopes and loves sail past, just out of reach. *Pulp Fiction* and *Reservoir Dogs* had a flashy brilliance. Technically superb, beautifully acted and great fun to watch, they had iron bullets in their soul. Does *he* feel *Jackie Brown* is a more human film? "I don't think you can get much more human than *Reservoir Dogs*." Tarantino is astonishingly defensive. If you paid him myriad compliments but threw in a single criticism he would gnaw away at the one bone of contention. "My characters have a *tremendous* amount of depth. I think I write very human individuals and that's why people respond to them, ahhrite, and you know they are all people with wit and pain and decisions to make."

If the films are so human, why have his detractors suggested they are amoral? He rattles his glass and takes a slurp of water. "I get a kick out of that because actually I think my movies have an *extremely* strong moral centre. It's there in the screenplay, it's not even that you have to read between the lines." I think he means that the irredeemable villains get blown away really nastily. Despite appearances, there is something very conservative about Quentin Tarantino.

But, I suggest, perhaps art doesn't have to be moral anyway. If a movie or book doesn't offer easy platitudes, if it disturbs us and forces us into fresh thought, isn't that enough? "No, I don't think art needs a moral focus or a moral conscience. Actually I take that back, art does need a moral focus, but the moral focus is the truth of itself, that's the only morality that counts, the truth of the art, the truth of the creator, the truth of the maker, you just can't lie." *The Creator! The Maker!* He is getting more Old Testament by the minute.

Having poo-poohed the notion that his two previous films are anything less than a hymn to humanity, he does concede that he enjoys the fact *Jackie Brown* is dealing with older people and quieter themes. Does his mother like it? "She loves it. It's her favourite movie of mine. It's very obviously the product of a single mother." What does he mean? "Well, Jackie Brown is a strong woman and a strong, older woman. I got my view of women from my mother, by example of her being both my father and my mother and being a working woman and proving herself to be a success and pulling herself up from her own bootstraps. At the end of the day, yes a father would have been great, but I didn't really *miss* it."

Tarantino's mother, Connie Zastoupil, gave birth to him in Tennessee when she was just sixteen. She had already married and been dumped by his father, an Italian-American actor called Tony Tarantino. She moved to California and worked as a nurse in his early years and gradually made her way out of the underclass, becoming an executive in the medical insurance business.

Pam Grier as Jackie, "not walking down the street to burn Harlem to the ground",
but bargaining her way out of a tight spot with Agent Nicolet (Michael Keaton).

His mother moved around a lot, so he often changed schools before he'd made friends. Once Connie bought him a puppy and a few days later found him banging its head against a brick wall – young Quentin said he was just trying to be affectionate. At the NFT, he said he'd gone to an all-black school, which made a few audience members titter. Surely not *all-black*? "It was a very small percentage of whites and a large percentage of blacks. I naturally hung with the black kids." Did he feel an outsider? "No, not at all because I completely identified with black culture. My house was raised as a kind of United Nations assembly, my Mom went out with a lot of black guys, my Mom's best friend is a woman named Jackie and she was like my second mother and her daughter is like my sister."

quentin tarantino: the film geek files

Talking to Tarantino I'm reminded of Gary Oldman's absurd character in the Tarantino-penned movie *True Romance* – a white man in dreadlocks talking in patois, the archetypal "white nigger". So is he a wigger?

"I don't really buy that," he says, wincing. But even his friends, like the actor Samuel L Jackson, say he'd rather be black? "No, that expression doesn't sound authentic to me. It sounds like a movie line to me, so I don't really buy it. It's not so much I want to be black . . . we all have different parts of us and one part of me is black, ahhrite, as far as my upbringing and affinities go. That's my heart, just a shade of me, it's not all of me."

The past few years must have been both wonderful and unnerving for Tarantino. I can think of no other film-maker who has been simultaneously lauded and vilified on such a scale. For every Adrian Noble thanking him "for the revival of Shakespearean cinema" there has been a voice railing against him as a one-trick pony with a lust for cartoon violence. For every actor saying he "inspires loyalty . . . everyone laughs, not just the big guys, the crew love him" (Oscar-nominated Robert Forster), a former collaborator has crawled out of-the woodwork to suggest Tarantino owes his success to ripping off former friends. And when he took bit-part roles in bit-part films like *Desperado* and *Destiny Turns On The Radio*, the critics said he'd obviously lost it as a director, and as as for his acting, well he could *never* act.

Tarantino says it's crazy that people make such assumptions. "When I've done six movies, you can start drawing some conclusions. I've made three movies and all those movies have been massively different from each other." He says the adjective Tarantino-esque is used to mean "people in black suits, violence, cursing or a certain kind of language" and that is an unflattering, demeaning interpretation of what he does. It diminishes his art.

"You can definitely tell I made all three movies, but they're trying to do three different things. They're not Woody Allen movies or Spike Lee movies or Robert Altman movies where there's a certain sameness to them. That's not putting those guys down . . . " But, of course, he is. He says if you must compare, try Scorsese because his movies are, likewise, both individual and recognisably his own.

Not only have the media got his movies wrong, says Tarantino, they have also got *him* wrong. For example, the nerd who came out of nowhere – just not true. When he said he "became an adjective sooner than I expected" he meant it – he did always expect to become one, just as he always figured "I'd have my place in film history." He explains what he meant by an adjective, saying you talk of Allen or Scorsese or Coppola, but you're never talking about the actual person. I say it's slightly different, an advance to talk of "Tarantino-esque" just like "Wellesian". " . . . Well, I don't know if it's one step ahead of Wellesian . . . " Which is not quite what I meant.

What gave him his confidence? "I always thought I could do anything I wanted because my Mom came from hillbilly roots and achieved a lot of success in her chosen field. You don't really have a class system in America, people can rise. You don't have a station. It just takes ambition, desire, courage to get out of it." And then there is the perception of Tarantino, the geek, the man who lives, breathes and shouts movies. Wrong, he says, quite, quite, wrong. "I once described myself as a film geek in an interview: and I had no idea how seriously journalists would take that, a little bit of self-deprecating humour. And all of a sudden they create a Cinderella story. True, I had been four years earlier working in a video store, but a lot of emphasis has been placed on that that has nothing to do with me as an artist. I was working at a video store because it was better than working in a burger bar, ahhrite."

The "ahhrites" become a tick when he's excited. "I was already knowledgeable about films before I worked in the video store, ahhrite, that's how I got the job. So I didn't like learn my aesthetic from working behind that counter. This whole thing of a guy who doesn't live, who just loves movies and that's all he does, that has no correlation with my real life. The film lover is one of the facets of my personality, one of the heads of my dragon, and that's a good guy, that's *a good guy*, but that is not who I am," he says, like the most pretentious nerd in the video store.

What about the other common line on Tarantino? The unmitigated shit who would put his granny through a mangle if there was a decent tracking shot in it? His former friend and collaborator Roger Avary has accused him of stealing his stories. The producer of *Natural Born Killers*, Jane Hamsher, wrote the fabulously bitchy book *Killer Instinct*, in which, by the by, Tarantino was accused of being a double-dealing, illiterate lech – a letter was printed as evidence in which the *wunderkind* complimented Jane on her gorgeous "leggs".

Now this is not an easy question to ask anyone, let alone the hypersensitive Tarantino. I'm trying to think of ways to soften the blow, but it comes out wrong. So is it true, Quentin, that you systematically fucked over all your friends to get to the top? The room seems very quiet, like a western bar before the baddie with the shooters bursts through the swing-doors. "Just think about what you've just asked me, you've just asked me am I a bad person." But I'm only giving you the opportunity to set things straight, I whimper.

"You've just asked me . . . *who has to fucking deal with a question like that in their life*, somebody posing to them are you a bad person, did you screw over your friends? I try to be the exact best person I can possibly be. And I have done a lot to help a lot of people and the people I haven't been able to help, well it isn't actually my *jo-aaarb*, ahhrite, to live other people's lives for them, ahhrite. You know it's like when I hear Roger Avary talking, the only thing I can do is sing Bob Dylan's 'Positively Fourth Street' ['You got a lot of nerve to say you are my friend'] and then I feel a lot better."

Last year, it was reported that Tarantino gave a good kicking to Hamsher's partner and fellow producer Don Murphy, who is now suing him for five million dollars. Did he feel better afterwards? "Uh-huh, well that *always* feels good." Does he often do it? "Well, I haven't been provoked to such a degree often." What provoked him, the book *Killer Instinct*? "No, I haven't even read the book, I can't go into too much detail because there is a law suit going on." He claims that Murphy stalked him for three years. "I had three ways that I could have responded. I could have been a gangster and go out and book it for him, ahhrite, fuck him up, ahhrite, well I didn't want to do that, ahhrite, I didn't care enough about him. Or two, I could talk bad about him in the press, well that's what he wants, I'm not going to push him that kind of power, or three, I could just wait. Hollywood's a small town, one day I could walk into a place and he'll be there, and I'll deal with it then." Did he win? "It wasn't even a fight, uhuh-uhuh, two people have to be fighting for it to be a fight, uhuhuh, it was an ass kick not a fight," and he laughs like Mutley, the cartoon dog.

We talk about life outside the movies, but invariably roll back to the cinema.

Is he still living with the actress Mira Sorvino? "Oh yes I sure am, *I sure am*," and his face lights up as if he still can't quite believe his luck. Is he political? Well, he says, years ago, he was a militant. "A good majority of my twenties I had a lot of rage in me. I have a lot of rage now, but in my twenties, I acted on that rage. It was two-fold. I felt I was an artist whose voice wasn't getting expressed. Second, he says, as an impoverished aspirant film-maker he sank back into the white underclass, "and you know the white underclass is no different from the black underclass."

He says he voted for Clinton, but he no longer considers himself a political agitator. "Unless something is a ridiculous injustice that personally affects me I'd rather not be an outraged citizen all my life." It reminds me of his famous quote when he sacked his long-term manager. "My career is launched and your job is done. I don't need you any more."

Robert Forster lost the role of Joe Cabot in Reservoir Dogs *to Lawrence Tierney. Eventually, his role as Max Cherry brought him a Best Supporting Actor nomination.*

Quentin Tarantino is the most arrogant, precious, pretentious, unquestioning, solipsistic, self-deluded man I've ever met. So I can't work out why I almost like him. Maybe, it's because I don't believe he did shaft his friends. Maybe it's because, however shallow he is, he is also a bit of a genius. Maybe it's because he just says what he thinks and he happens to think he's the greatest. When I re-listen to my tape and hear him saying "*Jackie Brown* plays even better second time," and that he's not so sure if Tarantino-esque is one better than Wellesian, and how profound his characters are, and how painful it was when he wasn't recognised as an artist, I want to go back and say, Quentin you just can't get away with these things, you really can't. I know what he'd say, though. "But I do . . . I *do*." And he'd be right.

9.
kill bill

quentin bloody quentin

by Henry Cabot Beck

At the beginning of *Kill Bill Volume 1*, the Bride – as Uma Thurman's character is known in Quentin Tarantino's new movie – lies on the floor of a ramshackle wedding chapel, paralysed with pain. A man speaks to her from off-screen in a gentle, apologetic fashion before he shoots her in the head.

When the Bride wakes from her coma four years later, determined to find the man, Bill (David Carradine), and the venomous female assassins who helped take her out, she is neither gentle nor apologetic. She embarks on a bloody killing spree unlike any seen before in a Hollywood movie.

"It's what I think of as the badass chick genre," says Tarantino, "which is a staple of Asian cinema, one I really love. I'm kind of secretly hoping that *Kill Bill* inspires some thirteen-year-old girl to put up a poster of Uma Thurman in her Day-Glo track suit, or maybe causes some Asian teenager who doesn't have any role models to look up at Lucy Liu on the screen and feel empowered."

Liu, Daryl Hannah and Vivica A. Fox play the other targets of the Bride's revenge, each as deadly as the snake she's named after. As for Bill, audiences will have to wait until the February release of *Kill Bill Volume 2* – not a sequel, but the second half of the film - to find out what happens to him.

"It's really a love story between me and Uma," says Carradine, "like *Duel in the Sun*. But Bill is not really a villain, contrary to the impression people might have from the first half. Like most of Tarantino's main characters, nobody is all bad or all good."

"What *Kill Bill* is," says Tarantino, "is me taking the [films] I love – kung fu movies, samurai films, Italian spaghetti Westerns and some Japanese animé – and doing them my way, doing what I always wanted to see done with the material.

"I see the picture as very similar to the *Star Wars* and *Indiana Jones* movies that [Steven] Spielberg and [George] Lucas made, when they reached back into the past to all those old serials and adventure and science-fiction movies, the movies they had so much affection for."

Despite having directed only three previous full-length features – *Reservoir Dogs* (1992), *Pulp Fiction* (1994) and *Jackie Brown* (1997) – Tarantino is the brand-name object of one of the most remarkable cults in recent movie history. He is the cinematic equivalent of the elephant in the famous Indian parable, the one the blind men find impossible to define, since he's more than the sum of their assumptions. In other ways, he's the 800-pound gorilla who sits wherever he wants to.

"He is arguably the most influential filmmaker of the Nineties," says Emanuel Levy, author of *Cinema of Outsiders: The Rise of American Independent Film*. "He popularised independent film more than any other director. As a result, all the critics got tired of having to say, 'This is yet another Tarantino-esque movie.'"

For example, Levy adds, "Bryan Singer's *The Usual Suspects* owes its entire existence to Quentin Tarantino. It would not have been made, or had as much success, if it hadn't been for him. I think that influence reaches all the way to more recent films like *Memento* [2000]."

"I have to say, the egotistical artist part of me loves that I got into that position so soon in life. I didn't expect it, but I love it," Tarantino admits.

Tarantino's story – raised by his mother in Los Angeles and Tennessee, he became obsessed with low-budget potboilers and exploitation films in his teens and worked in a California video store – has become the stuff of legend. A generation of fans can recite the events of Tarantino's life as though they were Davy Crockett yarning about his backwoods encounters with grizzly bears.

What made Tarantino significant as a filmmaker was that he had the audacity to create an unusual new kind of modern movie from the dismembered pieces of old genres. As he did so, he hit filmgoers squarely between the eyes at a moment when they were hungry for something unique – yet oddly familiar.

"With *Reservoir Dogs*, he brought back *film noir* and the crime genre," says Levy. "Although other filmmakers, like the Coen brothers, were also in the same field, Tarantino emphasised characterization as well as plot through a very unique sensibility that also stressed dark humour. Even if you take the violence out of *Reservoir Dogs* and *Pulp Fiction*, you still have very strong narratives. He's a good writer."

When *Pulp Fiction* became the first of a new generation of independent films to gross more than $100 million at the box office, it changed all the rules.

"It's indisputable that there was a real magic to the money that *Pulp Fiction* made, and that it changed forever the world of independent film," says John Pierson, author of *Spike, Mike, Slackers & Dykes: A Guided Tour Across a Decade of American Independent Cinema*. "For better or worse, Miramax Films is really The House That Quentin Built, and the result is that all the other major studios started their own [new] businesses in order to compete for independent films that might do the same kind of business."

As the tectonic plates were shifting in the film world, Tarantino made a movie that didn't – indeed, couldn't – climb out from under the shadow that he himself cast. *Jackie Brown*, based on a book by crime writer Elmore Leonard, was treated with indifference and scorn by many of the same people who had hailed Tarantino as a genius.

"It's funny," says Tarantino, "but people kept suggesting that I try to make something less genre-specific, a little more serious and relationship-driven, which I feel I did with *Jackie Brown*. It had some of the trappings of blaxploitation movies, but it played more real life than anything. I think it abandoned genre and aimed at being all about character, rather than plot twists and so forth.

"I have to say that it's amusing that critics are now bringing up *Jackie Brown* with a kind of revisionist perspective," he adds. "I think it might have to do with the fact that most critics saw the earlier two movies three, sometimes four times at festivals before they reviewed them."

The critical backlash sent Tarantino into semi-reclusion. Always hungry to act as well as direct, he ventured out to play the villain in *Wait Until Dark* on Broadway, opposite Marisa Tomei. But the critics were waiting for him, and their nearly

The Bride (Uma Thurman) locked in deadly combat with Gogo Yubari (Chiaki Kuriyama). Ms. Kuriyama's schoolgirl garb refers to her role in Kinji Fukasaku's Battle Royale.

unanimous attacks added insult to injury, and only served to bury him deeper.

But Tarantino quietly went about re-examining the film genres he loved growing up – and compacting his findings into a single explosive package: *Kill Bill*. It is something of a comedy, though it remains to be seen whether audiences will get the humour, especially as it is generating controversy about its extreme violence and goriness.

"Quentin is constantly telling jokes throughout the movie," says Liu. "There's a scene where I cut a guy's head off and there's an incredible spray of blood followed by a few final spurts, and some people don't realise that's the comedy of it."

Says Tarantino without remorse, "I had to say to Harvey Weinstein [co-chairman of Miramax], 'Harvey, understand – when somebody gets their arm cut off and they have garden hoses for veins and there's this absurd fountain spray of blood, that's just them having a good time.'"

"Someday I'm going to get the rights to do *Casino Royale*, the first James Bond novel, and do it the right way. I really wanted it to be my followup to *Pulp Fiction* and do it with Pierce Brosnan, but have it take place after the events of *On Her Majesty's Secret Service* – after Bond's wife, Tracy, has been killed. "I want Bond to be in mourning when he falls in love with Vesper Lynd, the woman in the novel. From what I know of Brosnan and read in interviews, I think he'd want to go in the direction I'd want to take Bond, though I'm not certain producers of the series would agree."

"When I eventually make my World War II movie, *Inglorious Bastards*, it will use Robert Adlrich's *The Dirty Dozen* and a lot of those late-'60's/early-'70's epic war movies as a starting-off point – pictures like *Where Eagles Dare*.

"More so even than *Kill Bill* – it will be my true spaghetti Western-influenced film, but set in Nazi-occupied France instead of the Old West. I see it as a time when you had these no-man's lands in Europe that really did resemble the Western landscapes of Sergio Leone (director of the Clint Eastwood *Dollars* trilogy)."

kill bill
volume one

reviewed by Wesley Morris

The worst thing about the first Quentin Tarantino picture in five years is that after 93 minutes of some of the most luscious violence and spellbinding storytelling you're likely to see this year, *Kill Bill* ends.

Anyone breathless to learn how the Bride (Uma Thurman) does, indeed, kill Bill, her wicked groom, has to wait until February. So, dear Miramax and Quentin Tarantino: *hiss*. *Kill Bill*, which opens nationwide today, is actually *Kill Bill Volume 1* and Tarantino, who wrote and directed this pulse-quickening martial-arts magnum opus, decided somewhere during the production to split the film comic-book-style into a two-part serial – thus leaving 'em wanting more.

Volume 1 is broken into five chapters and told out of sequence. The effect is less surprising than it was in *Pulp Fiction*,' where Tarantino messed with temporality to create a karmic cosmos coloured by sin and redemption. *Kill Bill* uses time as an instrument to ratchet up the suspense.

The story is simple and sad enough. A woman whom Tarantino calls the Bride is shot by her husband (David Carradine, heard but never fully seen) and bludgeoned by his four assassins – Vivica A. Fox, Lucy Liu, Daryl Hannah, and Michael Madsen. Quite pregnant and on her wedding day, too! Bill puts a bullet in her head, leaving her as carrion, but somehow she wakes up hospitalised from a coma four years later, her baby dead, a metal plate in her skull, and night after night of a nurse letting strangers molest her in bed. This movie is a country song expanded into a bellicose adventure in retribution – Bobbie Gentry righteously dropped into *Enter the Dragon*. Thurman, for her part, is game to be dragged through the bowels of hell. Her gritty, physical performance is balanced with a comedienne's wit. The only conventional thing about her character is Tarantino's dopey decision to keep track of her kills via a to-do list – as if she'd forgotten what the movie is called. It was silly 35 years ago when wronged and murderous Jeanne Moreau was crossing names off her list in Francois Truffaut's *The Bride Wore Black*, a lark whose revenge plot seems polite by Tarantino's standards. Two electric brawls bookend the film. *Kill Bill* more or less opens with the first, a knock-down, drag-out waltz between the Bride and the wonderfully named Vernita Green (Fox), one-fourth of Bill's Deadly Viper Assassination Squad (or DiVAS). Choreographed with precise brutality by Yuen Wo-Ping and edited with breakneck glee by Sally Menke, it's a street fight set in Vernita's suburban Los Angeles living room: coffee tables and good china demolished; family portraits smashed out of their frames. In a classic Tarantino moment, Vernita and the Bride viciously eye each other on opposite sides of a window, through which we see a school bus pull up and a little girl get out, walk up to the door, and enter the house. It's Vernita's daughter, and the ladies, coated in blood, sweat, and broken glass, stash their cutlery behind their backs and pretend for the kid's sake to be old girlfriends. It's hard to think of another sequence that combines irony, suspense, dread, comedy, surrealism, violence, and swollen faces with as much stupefying zest as the one Tarantino has concocted. Hong Kong action pictures are renowned for these sorts of absurdist scenarios, but *Kill Bill* pushes the absurd to the brink of horror by having it operate according to recognisable moral boundaries: *no stabbing in front of the kids*. Yet, in spite of those guidelines, children play a consciously disturbing role in the picture, subjected to adult violence, always without warning. The person most defined by a destructive childhood legacy is O-Ren Ishii, the DiVAS member the Bride has flown to Japan to kill. Her back story is told partly as a deadly-serious interlude of subtitled Japanese animation that explains how a little girl became the unlikely queen of the Tokyo underworld: by avenging her father's murder. The passage communicates the grisly soul of great animé and Japanese comic books. It's not a superfluous touch, either. It's the most graphic sequence in the film, cleverly taking what, as live action, would be essentially unfilmable (killer eleven-year-olds and whatnot) and still finding ways to make the conflict both harder to watch and more resoundingly human than the flesh-and-bone material that surrounds it. The sword fight showdown between the adult O-Ren, played by a fantastic Liu, and the Bride occupies the last third of *Kill Bill*. And to divulge much about it would just be rude. Just know that the Bride first has to extinguish O-Ren's sizable retinue and that the ever-imaginative cinematographer Robert Richardson has outdone himself here. The sequence is a sort of ballet that unfolds in four distinct movements – one of which is a disco bolero with the fighters silhouetted against panels of indigo light. It might be the most entertainingly ludicrous fight sequence ever filmed. Better than nearly any American director, Tarantino deploys the history of screen violence – from slapstick foolery to utter doom – to enthrall. In the film's opening line, Bill asks his blood-spattered bride, ''Do you find me sadistic?'' and Tarantino must be wondering if we think the same thing about him. The answer is yes. But he's also the movies' sadist laureate. His brand of violence has the uncanny ability to seduce without desensitising you to pain. (Enough can't be made of how much of Thurman's performance is spent wincing and groaning.)

With these first 90 minutes of *Kill Bill*, Tarantino reinvents the American action flick, using his usual arsenal of allusions and verve to make pop art of cult schlock. The movie lifts Japanese-Hong Kong grind-house violence to a rare operatic territory, without putting the martial-arts genre and the samurai flick out of business. He's fused them into a single cinematic species. It has nothing mind-blowing to say about the human condition – although his movies suggest that it's grim. For now, he's content to continue pouring his heart and soul into trash, making, with *Kill Bill*, the year's most important unimportant movie.

The resulting mongrel isn't just a blood bath, it's blood bathhouse, with sake-soaked references to carnage kings as diverse as Sonny Chiba, Sergio Leone, and Kinji Fukasaku. *Kill Bill* has more samples than 800 Costcos – lord knows how many aisles you'd have to walk down to taste them all. You'll have plenty of time to try, though. February seems a light year away. Apparently, the Bride's revenge can wait. But can you?

quentin tarantino reveals almost everything that inspired kill bill

by Tomohiro Machiyama

PREVIEWS OF COMING ATTRACTIONS

Hi, I'm Tomohiro Machiyama. I usually write only for Japanese Magazines, but I would like you people who cannot read Japanese to read my interview because Mr. Tarantino told me a lot of information that American critics and viewers might never know. The night before this interview, I first spoke with Tarantino at a party after the screening of *Kill Bill*. Unfortunately, I didn't bring my tape recorder. We were both totally smashed, but I remember these things he told me.

The bloody killing spree at the climax of *Kill Bill* is a kind of re-enactment of *Shogun Assassin* (Kenji Misumi, 1972, Japan). And he also admitted to adding a dash of *Ichi the Killer* (Takashi Miike, 2001, Japan) in it as well. For the orange sunset sky behind the airplane, he wanted to evoke the look of the opening scenes from *Goke, Body Snatcher from Hell* (Hajime Sato, 1968, Japan). He ordered the staff to shoot a miniature set of Tokyo like a landscape from the giant monster movie *War of the Gargantuas* (Ishiro Honda, 1966, Japan). He even screened a video of *Gargantuas* to Daryl Hannah because in his mind, *Kill Bill* is a kind of *War of the Blonde Gargantuas*. So, I didn't ask about these things in the next day interview. Are you ready? Here we go.

AND NOW. . . OUR FEATURE ATTRACTION

Tomohiro Machiyama: Can you give me some comments about some of the films referenced in *Kill Bill*?

Quentin Taranatino: Ok. Cool, cool.

TM: The scene where Go Go Yubari (Chiaki Kuriyama) stabs a guy who approaches her for sex. . . was this from *Battle Royale* (Kinji Fukasaku, 2000, Japan)?

QT: I went out to dinner with Kinji Fuaksaku and Kenta (Kinji's son) and I was going, "Man, I love this movie! It is just so fantastic!" And I said, "I love the scene where the girls are shooting are shooting each other." And then Kenta starts laughing. So I ask, "Why are you laughing?" He goes, "The author of the original *Battle Royale* novel would be very happy to hear that you liked that scene." And I go "why?" And he says, "Well, because it's from *Reservoir Dogs*!" Even when I was watching it I was thinking "God, these fourteen-year-old girls are shooting each other just like in *Reservoir Dogs*!" And Kenta said, "He took that from *Reservoir Dogs*, so he'll be very proud that you like that!"

TM: I'm wondering why you changed the name of the girl force from Fox Force Five, in *Pulp Fiction*, to DiVAS in *Kill Bill*?

QT: Well, the thing is, as similar as they are to each other, they are different. Fox Force Five were crime fighters. They were secret agents. The Deadly Vipers are NOT secret agents! They are killers! But the idea is very, very similar. It's like the flipside.

TM: The DiVAS look like *The Doll Squad* (Ted V. Mikels, 1973, USA), right?

QT: Oh yeah, very similar. They definitely have that *Doll Squad* or *Modesty Blaise* look to them. Those girls just look cool in their turtle necks. *Honey West* was an American TV show, and that's in there as well.

TM: How about *The Bride Wore Black* (1968, Francois Truffaut, France)?

QT: Here's the thing. I've never actually seen *The Bride Wore Black*.

TM: Really?

QT: I know of it, but I've never seen it. Everyone is like, "Oh, this is really similar to *The Bride Wore Black*." I've heard of the movie. Its based on a Cornell Woolrich novel too, but it's a movie I've never seen. The reason I've never seen it is because. . . I've just never been a huge Truffaut, fan. So that's why I never got around to see it. I'm not rejecting it, I just never saw it. I'm a Godard fan, not a Truffaut fan. So I know of it, I know all that stuff, but it's a movie I've never seen.

TM: I thought of it because the Bride has that list of names she checks off.

QT: Oh, is that in there too?

TM: How about *Hannie Caulder* (Burt Kennedy, 1971, USA) ?

QT: Oh yeah. Hannie Caulder is definitely in there. That was definitely one of the revenge movies I was thinking about. I had a whole list of revenge movies, especially female ones like *Lady Snowblood* (Toshiya Fujita, 1973, Japan). But one of them definitely was *Hannie Caulder*. You know who I love in *Hannie Caulder* so much is Robert Culp. He is so magnificent in that movie and I actually kind of think there's a bit of similarity between Sonny Chiba and Uma and Raquel Welch and Robert Culp in *Hannie*.

TM: How about *Dead and Buried* (Gary Sherman, 1981, USA)?

QT: Ok, yeah. I've seen *Dead and Buried*. So what's the connection?

TM: Daryl Hannah disguises herself as a nurse and tries to kill the Bride in a coma with a syringe.

QT: Oh! Yes! Lisa Blount! The girl from *An Officer and a Gentleman!* Yeah, exactly. Actually, to tell you the truth, there's another movie that I kind of got that idea a little bit more from. And that's John Frankenheimer's *Black Sunday* (1977, US). There's a scene where Marthe Keller goes into the hospital and disguises herself as a nurse and she's going to kill Robert Shaw with a poisoned syringe.

TM: The character of Daryl Hannah is based on *They Call Her One Eye* (aka *Thriller*, Bo Arne Vibenius, 1974, Sweden)?

QT: Oh, definitely! I love Christina Lindberg. And that's definitely who Daryl Hannah's character is based on. In the next movie, she's wearing mostly black. Just like *They Call Her One Eye*, she's got some colour co-coordinated eye patches. And that is, of all the revenge movies I've ever seen, that is definitely the roughest. The roughest revenge movie ever made! There's never been anything as tough as that movie.

TM: It was supposed to be a porno.

QT: Well, it has those insert shots in there. I remember showing Uma the trailer to *They Call Her One Eye*, and she said, "Quentin, I love that trailer. . . but I don't know if I can watch that movie! I'm actually scared to watch it. It looks too tough." I showed Daryl the movie. I gave her the video tape. She watched it without subtitles, just in Swedish. And she said, "Quentin! You had me watch a porno!" I said, "Yeah, but a good porno!" She'd never had a director give her a porno movie to watch as homework!

TM: How about *Master Killer* (aka *The 36 Chambers of Shaolin*, Chia-Liang Liu, 1978, Hong Kong)?

QT: I'm a huge fan of *Master Killer* and of Gordon Liu in particular. He's fantastic. He doesn't look any goddamn different today then he did back then. And it's just so cool to see both him and Sonny Chiba in the same film together. They are every bit the superstars. Living legends. As I am framing shots, I'm thinking, "I can't believe Gordon Liu is in my movie! I can't believe it." And to have been so influenced by seventies kung fu films and to have, as far as I'm concerned, my three favourite stars of kung fu from three different countries. . . Gordon Liu representing Hong Kong. Sonny Chiba representing Japan. And David Carradine representing America. That's a triple header. A triple crown. If Bruce Lee was still alive, he'd be in it. If Fu Sheng was still alive, he could be in it too.

TM: So will David Carradine play a flute in the sequel?

QT: Oh yeah! He does! You saw that in the trailer, right? And it's actually "The Silent Flute". It's a flute he made, he carved it out of bamboo. And that is the silent flute from the movie *Silent Flute* (aka *Circle of Iron*, Richard Moore, 1979, US). You've got a great thing with David because Bill really is a mix of Asiatic influences and genuine American Western influences.

TM: Not only was he on *Kung Fu*, but he was also one of *The Long Riders* (Walter Hill, 1980, USA).

QT: Yeah, and who else are you going to get to do that?

TM: How did you get the rights to use the music cue from *Masters of the Flying Guillotine* (Jimmy Wang Yu, 1975, Hong Kong)?

QT: We bought the rights to it. First, we had to find out what it was ('Super 16' by German group Neu!). Once we tracked it down, we went to them and just commissioned it and they gave it to us. That little bit of music is even on the *Kill Bill* soundtrack album. (imitating music) "Doing! Doing! Doing!"

TM: I can't remember the title, but there is a Hong Kong movie where Jimmy Wang Yu fights with 100 enemies. The fight in the House of Blue Leaves reminds me of it.

QT: That's from *Chinese Boxer* (Jimmy Wang Yu, 1969, Hong Kong). It's where he's created the iron fist. He's turned his fists into iron and they're burned black. He's got a surgical mask over his face and he's got these mittens on his hands and Lo Lieh is the bad guy and he goes into the casino. Well, did you know that this is a very historically important movie? That was the first full-on open handed contact movie in Hong Kong. *Chinese Boxer* is the first movie where the hero didn't fight with swords. He just fought with his hands. That was the first time that was done. I mean, there are kung fu movies before that. But this kind of like, what we know today as a real kung fu movie. Before that, they were doing wushu, swordplay; and even though they were doing it in a Chinese style, they still had one foot in the Japanese samurai movies. But with *Chinese Boxer*, they took that foot away. And that fight scene is so fantastic. That's become one of the staples of the genre: one against a hundred. Well, that was the first one. Wang Yu directed it too. It was so cool because I remember showing Yuen Woo-Ping that scene to show him something I wanted to capture and Woo-Ping goes, "Hey! That's my dad!"

His father was one of the guys in the movie. You know, when all the guys are circling Wang Yu, he's the one with the chain. His dad was Simon Yuen, the old guy from *Snake in the Eagle's Shadow* and *Drunken Master*. That's Woo-Ping's father.

TM: How about Takashi Miike's *Fudoh* (1996, Japan)?

QT: I haven't seen *Fudoh*. I know of *Fudoh*. I've seen the trailer for it. I couldn't be a bigger fan of Miike, but I've never seen *Fudoh*. I've been meaning to see it, but that's one I haven't seen yet.

TM: I thought the idea of the Crazy 88s was inspired by the teenage gangs from *Fudoh*.

QT: I just thought that once O-Ren became the queen of crime in Tokyo, which is kind of a reference to *Black Lizard* (Kinji Fukasaku, 1968, Japan) because O-Ren runs the city the way Black Lizard did. . . she wouldn't have a bunch of bruisers. No! She'd have a bunch of moptops. This isn't in the movie, because I'd have to stop and tell the audience this but the Crazy 88s are. . . because O-Ren is half-Chinese and half-Japanese, so is her army. So there's 44 Chinese people and 44 Japanese people! But that's part of the mythology I would only go into if I wrote a book. The black suits are from *Reservoir Dogs*. And the masks are from Kato. I just thought that it looked really cool. Now, while I'm saying that I haven't seen *Fudoh*, I'm not saying I haven't been influenced by Takashi Miike. Personally, my favourite cinema right now is this violent pop cinema coming out of Japan. As far as a group of directors that are my favourites. . . and there's a lot of American directors that I really like. . . my favourite as far as a group is all the directors doing those kinds of movies in Japan. Obviously, I'm talking about Takashi Miike, Takashi Ishii, Sogo Ishii.

TM: How about Teruo Ishii?

QT: Oh, Teruo Ishii is a fantastic director, a great director! I love Teruo Ishii. Also, Kiyoshi Kurosawa. And the other guy. . . I know him, I'm friends with him, but I keep forgetting his name. . . the guy who did *Shark Skin Man* and *Peach Hip Girl* and *Party 7* (Katsuhito Ishii). He actually did some work on *Kill Bill*. He did the character drawing that starts the animé when you see O-Ren when she was eight and then you see Boss Matsumoto, you know, just those two drawings? He did those drawings for me just as a present. He didn't do any of the animé. That was Production IG. But he did those character drawings and I ended up using them in the movie. And, not only that, he did a drawing of Elle Driver (Daryl Hannah) in her nurse's outfit and she had a red cross on her eye patch. And I thought it was such a good idea that I put it in the movie. His name is in the credits, but he didn't get paid for it or anything. It was a gift. I met him in Hawaii and we became friends and I see him whenever I'm in Japan.

TM: How did you come up with the name O-Ren Ishii?

QT: It wasn't like, "I'm going to honour this movie or this thing," but finding the right name for your character is one of the most important things about writing them. You almost can't really go forward until you get the right name. And what is the right name? Well, who the fuck knows that? You'll know it when you hear it. So as I'm just formulating the movie, I'm also watching a bunch of stuff to get myself going again on it. They used to show the Sonny Chiba TV show *Kage no Gundan* (*Shadow Warriors*) on a Japanese TV station out here in Los Angeles during the eighties. Me and a bunch of my friends used to get together and watch it. And we'd tape it. So I'm going through my tapes from the eighties to look at the show. And one of the female ninja (played by Etsuko Shihomi, aka Sister Streetfighter) on *Kage no Gundan 4* was named O-Ren. I thought, "Well, that a pretty name. And it's unusual too." Also the combination of O-Ren with the name Ishii I thought worked really good together. I wasn't necessarily trying to do an overt homage to *Kage no Gundan*, even though I love that show, but once I saw that name, I went with it. Then, that became her name. Lucy Liu fell in love with it. Everyone responded to it. Even Japanese people were like, "well. . . that's a Japanese name, a very unusual one, but it's a good name." About *Kage no Gundan* for a bit. There's like multiple sequel shows. You know, *Kage no Gundan 1, 2, 3, 4*. Every time they did a new series it was always a different Hattori Hanzo. It was set a little further in history. Hattori Hanzo number three, Hattori Hanzo number four. It just kept on going down. So now Sonny Chiba is playing Hattori Hanzo 100 and still continuing that character. Now the thing about this is that, the audience doesn't need to know any of this. I'm very much a believer that if you're creating your own universe and your own mythology, you can have no question unanswered. But here's the thing: I don't have to answer the questions to you the audience. You just need to know I know the answer. I can tell you the whole story of how Hattori Hanzo ended up in Okinawa and why he didn't make a sword for 30 years, and who the bald guy is. I can tell you that. I don't have to tell you this during the watching of the movie, but you need to know how large this world is. This is how much I'm going to tell you now, and what I don't tell you, you can figure out. You can make up your own things. I know what's going to happen with Nikki (Vivica A. Fox's daughter). She will grow up and she will seek her revenge. I could go backwards. Once we get all done with this, we're talking about the concept of doing a couple of prequels with maybe Production IG just doing full-on animation. You know, the origin of Bill for instance. But I could do it with any of the characters. As far as actually continuing the story. . . again, I don't know about shooting this in live-action or animation or writing it as a paperback, who knows? But it would be every ten years. Right now, the Bride is 30. The next one would be at 40. The last one would be ten years later when she's 50.

TM: How about the quotation which went something like, "If you want revenge, you have to be willing to kill God and even the Buddha"?

QT: That was actually paraphrased – I rewrote it, just like I did with the Bible in *Pulp Fiction* – from the speech of the Yagyu ninja that Sonny Chiba would repeat at the beginning of every episode of the *Yagyu Family Conspiracy* TV show. And at the end of the movie, when Uma is in her helmet giving that speech, that's the theme from *Yagyu Family Conspiracy* playing in the background.

TM: Did you get any inspiration from Seijun Suzuki?

QT: It's funny. . . I'm not inspired by his movies as a whole, but by certain shots and just his willingness to just completely experiment to try and get images that are really cool or psychedelic. I'm very inspired by that. To me, his films. . . well, he's a little bit like Russ Meyer for me. It's easier to like sections of his films than the whole movie. I'm not putting him down, it's just that I think he works better in sequences and scenes. And some movies work better than other movies. As for Russ Meyer, *Faster, Pussycat! Kill! Kill!* (1966, USA) is a complete masterpiece. That was one where everything worked. Suzuki did that with *Branded to Kill* (1967, Japan) even though I do like the first half better than the second. When you bring up Suzuki, are you more or less thinking about the Kabuki fight in the House of Blue Leaves with the silhouettes?

TM: Yes.

QT: To me that was more something in my brain from Japanese cinema in general than Suzuki stuff in particular, but I do know what you are talking about. You'll see it again in *Volume 2* when the Bride is in her training session with Pai Mei (Gordon Liu), there a big silhouette sequence against a big giant red background. Every fifteenth movie in Hong Kong had an opening sequence where the characters were doing martial arts in front of a background. Sometimes you saw them, sometimes you didn't. And usually Isaac Hayes' theme music from *Shaft* was playing!

TM: Here's a very general question. Should I laugh at this movie, or not?

QT: I don't think you should laugh AT it, I think you should laugh WITH it.

TM: Because I heard you laughing through the screening.

QT: I don't hold a Japanese audience to the same rule that I would hold a black audience to. A black audience is like, "Ha ha ha ha!" You Japanese are a little more subdued when you watch a movie. Just because they're not going, "Ha ha ha ha!" when they're watching it doesn't mean they're not enjoying it. I was having a good time because I was able to watch the audience without being intrusive. So I was smiling all the way. All my movies are funny, but I also wanted to go up and down, up and down. I want you to laugh, laugh, laugh, and then stop you laughing and show you something else. Maybe start you crying, and then get you laughing again. I want to just constantly keep moving. For me, if I'm watching a movie and I'm going from laughing to crying, that's me having a good time. That's when I know I'm seeing a movie. I'm being jerked around emotionally and it's great.

TM: I guess I'm thinking specifically about the scene at the end of the duel with Lucy Liu.

QT: It's supposed to be kind of amusing and poetic at the same time. And also just a teeny-tiny bit solemn. When you see her head, it's funny. And then her line, "That really was a Hattori Hanzo sword," that's funny. But then, the next shot is not funny, when she tips over and Meiko Kaji is singing about revenge on the soundtrack. So, it's all together. Funny. Solemn. Beautiful. Gross. All at the same time.

TM: Do you think American audiences have this kind of taste?

QT: The thing is, for some people they'll be seeing things they've never seen before. In Hong Kong, in China, in Japan, in Korea, they are going to have a context for where some of this stuff is coming from. Even when it comes to stuff like macaroni Westerns (the Japanese name for spaghetti Westerns). Most young people in America have never seen a macaroni Western. That actually can be an extremely good thing! You know where these things are coming from, but it's still kind of a new experience to see *Kill Bill*, right? Well, for them, imagine how new it is going to be.

TM: About the *Ironside* musical theme. That music is very popular in Japan. That theme was used on an *Inside Edition*-style tabloid show.

QT: Here's the thing. They use that theme in *Five Fingers of Death* (Chang Ho Cheng, 1973, Hong Kong) and every time, the screen glows red. You know it from this tabloid show, but when I was a kid, I knew it from *Ironside*. So every time the screen would glow, people in the audience would bust up laughing because it was the *Ironside* theme. But at a certain point, they actually begin to like it better in the movie. By the third time they hear it, the audience is going, "YEAH! KICK ASS LO LIEH!" I think it works great. And in *Bill* the third time you hear it, you know she's going to kick ass! Uh, hey, can I ask you a question? Did you have a favourite scene in the film? Can I ask you what was it?

TM: I think the fight with Go Go Yubari (Chiaki Kuriyama).

QT: That's mine too. I'd never shot action before, and this was my chance to really do it, and that was my first action scene. That was how I learned to do it, on that one. And I think that may be, so far, my favourite thing I've ever shot. Just cinematically, director-wise, I think that might be the best thing I've done so far.

TM: During the fight, Go Go is kind of a Master of the Flying Guillotine.

QT: She definitely is. That was Chiaki doing most of that stuff. She spent three months learning how to mess with that ball. People ask me, "Where did you get that ball from?" Actually, I didn't really take it from any movie. I mean, I've seen Hong Kong movies where they swing things, but this one I kind of created. So people say, "What's it called?" And I say, "The Go Go Ball!"

TM: Do you think Japanese audiences will understand the line, "Silly rabbit, Trix are for kids?"

QT: Oh yeah, the Trix commercial. There's all of these Japanese and Chinese things in the movie that I have no expectations that Americans will get at all and that's one of the things that I don't expect anyone outside the US to get. In my thought, that was something O-Ren and the Bride used to say to each other when they were Deadly Vipers on a job. It was a private joke between the two of them.

TM: How about the samurai swords on the airplane?

QT: Well, this whole movie takes place in this special universe. This isn't the real world. It's funny that you bring it up because in the original script, Bill was going to have a different introduction. This is back when I was writing the part for Warren Beatty. The idea was that Bill would show up at this casino carrying a samurai sword, and the bodyguards, who also have samurai swords, ask him to leave it at the front desk. Warren goes, "Wait a minute, hold it Quentin. Everybody has a samurai sword?" I go, "Yeah." He says, "How does that happen?" I say, "That's the world that this movie takes place in. Everybody has a samurai sword." And he goes, "Oh! So this isn't real life?" I go, "No! this is a movie, movie universe and in this universe, people carry samurai swords." Not only do they carry samurai swords, not only can you bring a samurai sword on an airplane, there's a place on the airplane seat to put your samurai sword! Now, I'm not saying you can do this on every flight, but on Japanese airlines you better believe there's a place for you to put your samurai sword!

TM: I think maybe you should have directed *Road to Perdition* because it was inspired by *Lone Wolf and Cub*.

QT: I haven't actually seen that. I remember me and Samuel Jackson saying, "Oh shit! This is just *Lone Wolf and Cub*! What the fuck is this?" I wouldn't mind seeing it, but it just looked so arty. You know, drowning in art. That was one of the things I wanted to be really strong about when it came to *Kill Bill*. This isn't an art film mediation on these movies. This is the genuine article. The real deal. And that was one of the ideas behind splitting it in half. There just seems something pretentious about a three-hour exploitation film. But two! Two exploitation movies! That's ambitious.

kill bill volume two

reviewed by Peter Travers

Uma Thurman doesn't get nailed to a cross in *Kill Bill Volume 2*, but writer-director Quentin Tarantino runs her battered character, called the Bride, through a gauntlet that is gory enough to make Mel Gibson flinch. No matter. You'll thrill to the action, savour the tasty dialogue and laugh like bloody hell. Tarantino has done more than continue the revenge tale he started in *Volume 1* – the Bride wants payback after being left for dead in her wedding dress by Bill (David Carradine) and four other killers in his Deadly Viper Assassination Squad, of which she was once queen bee. *Volume 2* ties the events of *Volume 1* together, just like *The Return of the King* did for the *Lord of the Rings* trilogy. You watch and think, "I get it now." Tarantino has made the hottest mix tape in the history of cinema. Like a master DJ, he samples every lowdown, B-movie genre that formed him, from kung fu and samurai flicks to animé and spaghetti westerns, then filters it through his imagination to create something totally Tarantino: a blast of pure movie oxygen.

Volume 2 dives into emotional waters merely skimmed in the brilliant exercise that was the first film. For those who think dividing *Bill* in half was a sucker punch to make us pay for the same film twice, I can only say that the sum of both films is what makes *Kill Bill* a triumph. I'd prefer four hours of untamed Tarantino to one film edited into a multiplex-friendly two hours.

OK, so where did *Volume 1* leave off? The Bride travelled to Tokyo to battle O-Ren Ishii (the sublime Lucy Liu) and to Pasadena, California, to slaughter Vernita (Vivica A. Fox), two of the five assassins who wiped out her wedding-rehearsal party in a chapel in El Paso, Texas. The Bride was pregnant with Bill's baby when he shot her in the head and put her in a coma for four years. The last words of *Volume 1* came in a question posed by Bill: "Is she aware her daughter is still alive?"

That's the bait. *Volume 2* begins with the Bride looking glam in a top-down convertible, addressing the audience like an avenging angel out of a 1940s Hollywood melodrama: "When I arrive at my destination, I am gonna kill Bill."

That's the hook. But first, Tarantino takes us back to that wedding chapel to show us the events before the massacre. The Bride is marrying an outsider, running from her old life. Then Bill shows up at the rehearsal, playing a flute and turning on the charm. "How did you find me?" asks the Bride with a grin. "I'm the man," says Bill, grinning back. And so he is. Carradine – reduced to a disembodied voice in *Volume 1* – owns the screen this time and is flat-out sensational in a role once intended for Warren Beatty. Bill is a pimp of death with a long line of protegees. Carradine, the hero of the 1970s TV series *Kung Fu*, invests this villain with a purring, seductive danger. He and the sizzling Thurman make the sexual tension between Bill and the Bride palpable. This is a love story lit by flashes of vivid violence. Tarantino, stingy with dialogue in the action-mad *Volume 1*, gives the actors words they can feast on, full of sassy wit, as in the way the Bride introduces Bill to her groom. No fair telling how.

Volume 2 keeps popping us with surprises, including the Bride's fight training under the cruel tutelage of Pei Mei, the white-bearded monk played by Chinese legend Gordon Liu. You might want to remember the five-point exploding-heart trick. Tarantino, working in tandem with martial-arts adviser Yuen Woo-Ping, keeps the action coming like gangbusters as the must-own soundtrack booms with his favourite musical influences, including Ennio Morricone's haunting theme from *The Good, the Bad and the Ugly* and Charlie Feathers going all rockabilly on 'Can't Hardly Stand It.'

The Bride under the cruel tutelage of Pai Mei (Gordon Liu). Martial arts star Liu also fought against his own character, Taoist warrior monk Pai Mei, in his earlier films.

The bonus this time is that the actors hold their own against the flying swords and fists of fury. Michael Madsen is killer good as Budd, Bill's beloved kid brother, who mistakenly thinks he can keep the Bride down by burying her alive. And Daryl Hannah mesmerises as the eye-patch-wearing Elle Driver, the Bride's replacement in Bill's heart, not to mention a tough opponent in a showstopping catfight. Of course, all roads in *Kill Bill* lead to the Bride's face-off with Bill and the daughter she didn't know she had. Bill puts their kid to sleep with videos of *Shogun Assassin*. In a lovely touch, the Bride looks pleased. But there is hell to pay. Thurman gives an electrifying performance that busts your chops and breaks your heart with no mercy. Tarantino wouldn't have it any other way. With *Kill Bill*, both volumes, he wants to take us on a wild ride into the dirty fun of movies and do it so artfully that we want to return to the film to shake out its secrets. It's a bold swing, and Tarantino knocks it out of the park.

tarantino talks kill bill vol. 2

by Fred Topel

Quentin Tarantino is a handful during an interview. Transcribing him is even more so. If you've ever seen or heard an interview with him, you know how fast he talks, how many thoughts fit into a single sentence without pause, and how he says "alright" and "okay" in between every clause. In presenting this interview, we've tried to maintain his colloquialisms as much as possible, while editing for readability's sake.

When *Kill Bill: Volume 1* hit theatres in October, it was highly anticipated because we had not seen a Tarantino movie since 1997's *Jackie Brown*. It was also controversial, because many questioned why it should be split into two movies, when it could be just one long epic. Fans and critics still debate that point, but as *Volume 2* hits theatres, everyone wants to know how the story ends.

Uma Thurman plays the Bride, assassinated by her own hit squad on her wedding day. We've seen her kill Vernita Green and Oren Ishii, but we still need to see her get Elle Driver, Budd and of course, Bill. The end of *Volume 1* also gave us a vital piece of information that may change her entire quest. We'll preserve that secret in case you have yet to see the first part.

Did cutting the film in half change the dramatic structure?
Yeah, I guess that it did, actually, as opposed to a movie where the whole first half is just complete viscera and eye popping action and just meant to blow you away, alright, and then, the resonance comes in the second half. And the second half, with more of the depth and resonance coming in, I guess that it did because [*Volume 1*] is just about the good time, fun movie, movie aspect of the movie and the second one will be the deeper exploration of it. So, I guess that it did, yeah.

And you would have had to cut a lot to make it one movie, right?
Right, and the thing about it is, if I truly thought it would be better or there would be too much of the emotional aspect in the movie lost by splitting it in half, then I would've done that. If it would've been a better movie at a smaller thing, I didn't think so. The way that I wrote the script, the things that I would've lost in *Volume 1* would've been the Texas Rangers, the animé sequence would've been cut way down and to me, that's what makes it special. It wasn't some long, uncontrolled epic, uncontrolled film. I'm telling a very simple story, but it had a very big canvas, and it needed all of those little moments in the canvas to make it work.

Is *Volume 2* less violent then?
Well, I mean, it's still pretty fucking violent, but there's not a fourteen-minute

sequence there. One of the big differences between *Volume 1* and *Volume 2* is that if you remember Sonny Chiba's little speech that he gives at the very, very end where he goes, "Revenge is never a straight line, it's a forest. It's easy to get lost and forget where you came in." Well, *Volume 1* is the straight line. *Volume 1*, it was hard for her to do what she had to do, but it's like, "Kill old man, take on the army, burn Tokyo to the ground, did that, done that. Kill Vernita, did that, done that." Now is the forest. Now, human stuff starts getting in. Now, it's not just killing them all the way down the list. It gets more complicated, it gets complex now. It's not quite as easy. The best way to describe it is that *Volume 1* is, for lack of a better term, my Eastern with a Western influence, a spaghetti Western influence. *Volume 2* is my spaghetti Western with an Eastern influence.

The dialogue in *Volume 1* was very different from your usual style.

Well, like I said, *Volume 2* has much more of the dialogue that you've known me for, but there was not a decision like, "Okay, I'm going to really blow people's mind. I'm going to cut down on the dialogue." It was just indicative of this kind of movie.

Are there more pop culture references then?

No, it's not about pop culture. If you think that all my dialogue is pop culture, then you probably are going to be disappointed, but no, it's just more dialogue. In my other movies, characters get to a place and hang out there for a while as they talk, and there are a few more monologues and stuff, but the thing that I actually love about my dialogue in this movie is like, that is my dialogue. It's just in Japanese this time.

Where would the story pick up if you hadn't split it up?

Where it would've ended more or less if I hadn't had broken it up, okay, if I was just going to have an intermission, the intermission would've happened right before where you saw my credit happen. Uma [Thurman] giving that speech, Sofie in the trunk of the car, "And soon, they will all be as dead as the rest." That would've been at intermission. So, I added the tag just to give you a little something extra, a little idea of what we were going to have for you. I didn't want to show you a little trailer even though I always liked that like in *The Three Musketeers* because I didn't even know that there was going to be a *Four Musketeers* when I saw it. And you watch *The Three Musketeers* and all of a sudden, "Coming soon, *The Four Musketeers*," and you see scenes and go, "Wow, that was cool." I tried to do that with this, but it just didn't seem right emotion-wise. I didn't want to break the emotion that I'd already set up. I wanted to deepen it. So, yeah, that little tag was added in there for this, but I think that it works very good. I'm very happy with it.

How did *Kill Bill* originate?

It's coming from, in its basic form, all of these different revenge genre movies that I was jumping off from. The Bride could easily be this cowboy character from this spaghetti western. She could easily be Angela Mao character in *Deep Thrust* or *Broken Oath*. There's two characters that Japanese actress Meiko Kaji played. One was a character named Scorpion. She did about four movies with that, and she did a great revenge samurai movie called *Lady Snowblood*. She could be that character. You could keep going down the whole list, but she falls in that whole long line of hellbent for revenge characters.

How much did you revisit these movies when you were writing?

Another Tarantino pop-culture resurrection: the director coaches former Kung Ku/B-movie star David Carradine, as the seductively amoral title character, Bill.

Well, they had a tremendous amount of influence because I own all of those movies. Not these beautiful, Technicolor restoration prints, but like, my seventh generation bootlegs from New York's 42nd Chamber of Shao Lin in Times Square. That's where I had them all, and when I was writing this movie, I had the fortunate fun of being able to watch at least one Shaw Brothers movie a day, if not three, and the reason I was doing it is that I wanted to immerse myself so much in that style of filmmaking so that the things that they did would be second nature to me. It would be my style of filmmaking as far as this movie was concerned. I wouldn't have to think about it. I wouldn't have to be self conscious about it. I would've just known exactly how they would've done it and I would decide do I want to do that too? Get that comfortable with the zoom because no one does zooms anymore, not like that. I wanted to get that comfortable with it and it worked so well that, to me, during that entire year, the movies that were coming out of Hollywood were like these weird artistic, fringe movies. I was like someone who lived in Hong Kong in the Seventies. When you thought of movies, you thought of Kung Fu movies. The Shaw Brothers, the Shaw Scope Logo and then, the Feature Presentation thing which I grew up watching, I always hear that tune before a movie starts. That just lets you know right away where I'm coming from and just sit back and have a good time and know from whence this came.

Does that make this a compendium of all the movies you've watched in your life?
You know, pretty much. The expression that I've used, and I'm not trying to over use it, but it just worked really good because it's pretty precise in describing it, is it's like taking 30 years of my favourite grind-house movies and genres and sticking them

into a press and that's this movie. The thing is, if you're a film geek and you like this stuff, then you're going to see it on one level and you're going to appreciate it and enjoy some of these touchstones and references and allusions. And hopefully, you'll enjoy what I've added new to it, and the way that I've taken all of these things, and the way that I use it is what makes it original or different. The spaghetti Western music and the animé and the thing is, if it only worked that way, it would be a rather limiting experience. You need to see this movie and if you see this movie and you've never seen any of those movies, maybe you were too young to see them or maybe they just weren't ever your cup of tea and you watch it, conceivably, those people could like it even more. They don't have any reference for this. So, it's all new to them. They're taking it all in. Where, if you understand where I'm coming from, your feet can be more firmly planted on the ground when my fastballs come at you, but if you don't know at all where it comes from, then you can really be taken off of your feet and you can also reject it and that's fine as well.

Why did it take so long to write this?

I wrote the first 30 pages and the basic idea on the set of *Pulp Fiction*, but then it was put away, and I don't really consider that a ten-year process because I mean, that's part of being a writer. You write something, and it's not ready yet, and so, you just put it in the incubator and wait until it's done. So, when I actually take it out of the incubator and really start, that's when it starts.

Did you need six years since *Jackie Brown* to develop the story?

There might actually be something to that to tell you the truth, but not that I was ever thinking about that at the time. I mean, what I was doing during those six years is that I was writing. It's like, I mean, people are like, "You were in seclusion?" I just wasn't on talk shows and when I was on them, everyone was complaining that I was on them. I didn't think that I would be missed, but the thing is that I was writing and writing is a more solitary experience. Acting is out there, directing is out there. Writers go into cabins in the woods and they write.

Were you writing other scripts simultaneously?

Oh, yes I did, yeah. I got lost in a beautiful way, but I got lost writing this big World War II, a bunch of guys on a mission thing that was turning into a gargantuan novel, not a movie and probably into three movies, not like this, but three separate things. I was trying to juggle them all for a little too long, but also, I was loving just going back to complete writing where it's just me and a pen and a blank piece of paper. That was wonderful, but one thing to remember though is that when I came out with *Reservoir Dogs*, I already had *True Romance* written, I already had *Natural Born Killers* written, I already had *From Dusk Till Dawn* written. Within about seven or eight months after *Reservoir Dogs* coming out, I had *Pulp Fiction* written and lo and behold, it all came to pass. Everything got produced. The thing about it is, I don't like *Natural Born Killers*, but the point being is part of the reason that you're sitting here talking to me. Maybe my body of work feels like more than [just what I've directed] because you've gotten a good sense of my voice, my writing talent or the lack thereof depending on who you are. All of that stuff, you got from that and that's because I was able to do a whole big body of work. The reality though is that once you become a writer-director, after you finish your next movie, if you're a writer-director, it's always start from scratch all over again. And you start the whole process all over again and you're going to get a little bit more precious about it each time, so much so that if you think about it – I'm obviously not talking about John Sayles or Woody Allen – but a lot of writer-directors, what will happen is at a certain point, they stop being writers. They just become directors. It's just easier to buy a script that you like or you like something in it and then you kind of rewrite it which is not as hard and sometimes, they don't even rewrite anymore, they just hire people to do it, and then, they guide it. Oliver Stone was a writer-director. He's not really a writer-director anymore. There's like nine people on all of his scripts. Robert Zemeckis used to be a writer-director, he's not anymore. I like their films better when they were writer-directors. So, coming back to all of this is the fact that now I have a lot of stuff to do. I now have close to the same stock-pile of stuff to do that I had before when I came with *Reservoir Dogs* and that was a good six years, and that was a good six years of living life too. I was in the best part of my thirties. I didn't want to spend all of that time on a movie set, all of that time in a mixing stage. I mean, it's fun, but if it ever gets to be too much, it can never be a job for me. It's got to be a calling. It's got to be the most important thing in my life.

What's the biggest misconception about you do you think?

I guess the biggest misconception about me is that I never live life. All I do is watch movies and that's all that I know from life, what I've watched, from watching movies and that's all I have to offer, you know, having seen this, that and the other.

How do you deal with the critics?

Well I mean, there are few directors who have been treated as well in their time by the critics as I have. I can't really complain about my perception as far as that stuff is concerned because I mean, I always thought that I'd be the director like all the directors that I admired that, yeah, some people might like my stuff, but people would catch up with it. It would be rejected out of hand because it's too lurid, but then, five years later or ten years or twenty years, "Oh, this guy is fantastic." Sergio Leone didn't get these great, glowing reviews in America when his stuff came out and now, he's considered to be the man.

filmography

reservoir dogs

MR WHITE (Larry)	Harvey Keitel
MR ORANGE (Freddy)	Tim Roth
MR BLONDE (Vic)	Michael Madsen
NICE GUY EDDIE	Chris Penn
MR PINK	Steve Buscemi
JOE CABOT	Lawrence Tierney
HOLDAWAY	Randy Brooks
MARVIN NASH	Kirk Baltz
MR BLUE	Eddie Bunker
MR BROWN	Quentin Tarantino
TEDDY	Michael Sottile
SHOT COP	Robert Ruth
YOUNG COP	Lawrence Bender
SHOCKED WOMAN	Linda Kaye
SHOT WOMAN	Suzanne Celeste
THE VOICE OF K-BILL	DJ Steven Wright

Crew:

Casting	Ronnie Yeskel
Music Supervisor	Karyn Rachtman
Radio Dialogue	Quentin Tarantino/Roger Avary
Costume Designer	Betsy Heimann
Special Make-up Effects	KNB EFX Group
Production Designer	David Wasco
Editor	Sally Menks
Director of Photography	Andrzej Sekula
Executive Producers	Richard N. Gladstein/ Ronna B. Wallace/Monte Hellman
Co-Producer	Harvey Keitel
Producer	Lawrence Bender
Written and Directed by	Quentin Tarantino

1992, 102 mins (Live America)

true romance

CLARENCE WORLEY	Christian Slater
ALABAMA WHITMAN	Patricia Arquette
CLIFFORD WORLEY	Dennis Hopper
MENTOR (Elvis)	Val Kilmer
DREXL SPIVEY	Gary Oldman
FLOYD	Brad Pitt
VINCENZO COCCOTTI	Christopher Walken
ELLIOT BLITZER	Bronson Pinchot
BIG DON	Samuel L. Jackson
DICK RITCHIE	Michael Rappaport
LEE DONOWITZ	Saul Rubinek
MARY LOUISE RAVENCROFT	Conchata Ferrell
VIRGIL	James Gandolfini
LUCY	Anna Thomson
NICKY DIMES	Chris Penn
CODY NICHOLSON	Tom Sizemore

Crew:

Casting	Risa Bramon Garcia/Billy Hopkins
Music Supervisor	Maureen Crowe
Costume Designer	Susan Becker
Special Effects	Robert Henderson/ Larry Shorts
Prosthetic Make-Up Effects	Frank Carrisosa
Editors	Michael Tronick/Christian Wagner
Director of Photography	Jeffrey L. Kimball
Executive Producers	James G. Robinson/Gary Barber/ Bob Weinstein/Harvey Weinstein/Stanley Margolis
Co-Producers	Don Edmonds/James W. Skotchdopole
Producers	Bill Unger/Steve Perry/Samuel Hadida
Written by	Quentin Tarantino
Directed by	Tony Scott
Music by	Hans Zimmer
Additional Music by	Mark Mancina/John Van Tongeren

1993, 116 mins (Morgan Creek/Warner)

pulp fiction

PUMPKIN	Tim Roth
HONEY BUNNY	Amanda Plummer
VINCENT VEGA	John Travolta
JULES WINNFIELD	Samuel L. Jackson
MIA WALLACE	Uma Thurman
BUTCH COOLIDGE	Bruce Willis
THE WOLF	Harvey Keitel
MARSELLUS WALLACE	Ving Rhames
LANCE	Eric Stoltz
JODY	Rosanna Arquette
FABIENNE	Maria de Madeiros
CAPTAIN KOONS	Christopher Walken
WAITRESS	Laura Lovelace
COFFEE SHOP	Robert Ruth
MARVIN	Phil LaMarr
ROGER	Burt Steers
BRETT	Frank Whaley
FOURTH MAN	Alexis Arquette
PAUL	Paul Calderon
TRUDI	Bronagh Gallagher
BUDDY HOLLY	Steve Buscemi
BUTCH'S MOTHER	Brenda Hillhouse
KLONDIKE	Sy Sher

ESMARELDA VILLALOBOS	Angela Jones
DEAD FLOYD WILSON	Carl Allen
WILSON'S TRAINER	Don Blakely
PEDESTRIAN/BONNIE	Venessia Valentino
GAWKER	Karen Maruyama
HERSELF	Kathy Griffin
MAYNARD	Duane Whittaker
ZED	Peter Greene
THE GIMP	Stephen Hibbert
JIMMIE	Quentin Tarantino
MONSTER JOE	Dick Miller
RAQUEL	Julia Sweeney
YOUNG BUTCH	Chandler Lindauer
MARILYN MONROE	Susan Griffiths
MAMIE VAN DOREN	Lorelei Leslie
JERRY LEWIS	Brad Parker
DEAN MARTIN	Josef Pilate
JAMES DEAN	Eric Clark
ED SULLIVAN	Jerome Patrick Hoban
RICKY NELSON	Gary Shorelle
PHILLIP MORRIS PAGE	Michael Gilden
SHOT WOMAN	Linda Kaye
LONG HAIR YUPPIE SCUM	Lawrence Bender
'HOLD HANDS YOU LOVE BIRDS'	Emil Sitka
SPORTSCASTERS	Robert Ruth Rich Turner

Crew:

Casting	Ronnie Yeskel/Gary M. Zuckerbrod
Music Supervisors	Karyn Rachtman/Kathy Nelson
Costume Designer	Betsy Heimann
Special Effects	Wesley Mattox/Stephen DeLollis/ Pat Domenico
Special Make-Up Effects	Kurtzman, Nicotero and Berger EFX Group
Editor	Sally Menke
Director of Photography	Andrzej Sekula
Executive Producers	Danny DeVito/Michael Shamberg/ Stacey Sher/Bob Weinstein/ Harvey Weinstein/Richard N. Gladstein
Producer	Lawrence Bender
Stories	Quentin Tarantino/Roger Avary
Written and Directed by	Quentin Tarantino

1994, 154 mins. (Morgan Creek/Warner)

four rooms

interlinking sequences:

TED THE BELLHOP	Tim Roth
BETTY	Kathy Griffin
SAM THE BELLHOP	Marc Lawrence
MARGARET	Marisa Tomei
LONG HAIR YUPPIE SCUM	Lawrence Bender

Crew:

Written and Directed by	Allison Anders/ Alexandre Rockwell/ Robert Rodriguez/Quentin Tarantino

the missing ingredient:

JEZEBEL	Sammi Davis
DIANA	Amanda De Cadanet
ATHENA	Valeria Golino
ELSPETH	Madonna
EVA	Ione Skye
RAVEN	Lili Taylor
KIVA	Alicia Witt

Crew:

Editor	Margaret Goodspeed
Director of Photography	Rodrigo Garcia
Written and Directed by	Allison Anders

the wrong man:

ANGELA	Jennifer Beals
SIEGFRIED	David Proval

Crew:

Editor	Elena Magnani
Director of Photography	Phil Parmet
Written and Directed by	Alexandre Rockwell

the misbehavers:

HUSBAND	Antonio Banderas
WIFE	Tamlyn Tomita
SARAH	Lana McKissack
JUANCHO	Danny Verduzco
CORPSE	Patricia Vonne Rodriguez
TV DANCER	Salma Hayek

Crew:

Director of Photography	Guillermo Navarr
Written, Directed and Edited by	Robert Rodriguez

the man from hollywood:

CHESTER	Quentin Tarantino
NORMAN	Paul Calderon
LEO	Bruce Willis (uncredited)

Crew:

Editor	Sally Menke
Director of Photography	Andrzej Sekula
Written and Directed by	Quentin Tarantino

General credits:

Special Effects	Hunter Gratzner Industries
Costume Designer	Mary Claire Hannan
Production Designer	Gary Frutkoff
Music Composed/Performed	Mark Mothersbaugh/ Esquivel
Executive Producers	Alexandre Rockwell/ Quentin Tarantino
Co-Producers	Paul Hellerman/Scott Lambert/ Heidi Vogel
Producer	Lawrence Bender

1995, 97 mins (A Band Apart/Miramax).

from dusk till dawn

JACOB FULLER	Harvey Keitel
SETH GECKO	George Clooney
RICHARD GECKO	Quentin Tarantino
KATE FULLER	Juliette Lewis
SCOTT FULLER	Ernest Liu
BORDER GUARD/CHET PUSSY/CARLOS	
	Cheech Marin
FROST	Fred Williamson
SEX MACHINE	Tom Savini
SANTANICO PANDEMONIUM	Salma Hayek
OLD TIMER	Marc Lawrence
TEXAS RANGER EARL McGRAW	Michael Parks
NEWSCASTER KELLY HOGUE	Kelly Preston
FBI AGENT STANLEY CHASE	John Saxon
RAZOR CHARLIE	Danny Trejo
BIG EMILIO	Ernest Garcia
PETE	John Hawkes
RED-HEADED HOSTAGE	Heidi McNeal
BLONDE HOSTAGE	Aimee Graham
HOSTAGE GLORIA	Brenda Hillhouse
TITTY TWISTER GUITARIST/VOCALIST	
	Tito Larriva
TITTY TWISTER SAXOPHONIST	Pete Atasanoff
TITTY TWISTER DRUMMER	
	Johnny Vatos Hernandez
DANNY	Cristos
MANNY	Mike Moroff
DANNY THE WONDER PONY	Himself
MONSTERS	Jon Fidele/Michael McKay/
	Walter Phelan/Henrik Von Ryzin/
	Jake McKinnon/Josh Patton/Wayne Toth

Crew:

Casting	Johanna Ray Elaine J. Huzzar
Costume Designer	Graciela Mazon
Original Songs	Tito Larriva
Special Make-up Effects	KNB EFX Group
Production Designer	Cecilia Montiel
Editor	Robert Rodriguez
Director of Photography	Guillermo Navarro
Executive Producers	Lawrence Bender/
	Robert Rodriguez/Quentin Tarantino
Co-Producers	Elizabeth Avellan/Paul Hellerman/
	Robert Kurtzman/John Esposito
Producers	Gianni Nunnari/Meir Teper
Story	Robert Kurtzman
Written by	Quentin Tarantino
Directed by	Robert Rodriguez

1996, 108 mins (A Band Apart, in association with Los Hooligans Productions/Miramax).

jackie brown

JACKIE BROWN	Pam Grier
ORDELL ROBBIE	Samuel L. Jackson
MAX CHERRY	Robert Forster
LOUIS GARA	Robert De Niro
MELANIE	Bridget Fonda
RAY NICOLET	Michael Keaton
MARK DARGUS	Michael Bowen
SHERONDA	Lisa Gay Hamilton
WINSTON	Tom 'Tiny' Lister, Jr.
SIMONE	Hattie Winston
BEAUMONT LIVINGSTON	Chris Tucker
PUBLIC DEFENDER	Denise Crosby
JUDGE	Sid Haig
AMY BILLINGSLEY SALES GIRL	Aimee Graham
BARTENDER	Ellis E. Williams
RAYNELLE	T'Keyah 'Crystal' Keymah
ANSWERING MACHINE VOICE	Quentin Tarantino
	(uncredited)

Crew:

Casting	Jaki Brown/Robyn M. Mitchell
Costume Designer	Mary Claire Hannan
Production Designer	David Wasco
Editor	Sally Menke
Director of Photography	Guillermo Navarro
Executive Producers	Richard N. Gladstein/
	Elmore Leonard/Bob Weinstein/Harvey Weinstein
Co-Producer	Paul Hellerman
Producer	Lawrence Bender
Written by	Quentin Tarantino
Adapted from the novel *Rum Punch* by	Elmore Leonard
Directed by	Quentin Tarantino

1997, 154 mins (Lawrence Bender Productions/ Mighty Mighty Afrodite Productions/A Band Apart/ Miramax).

kill bill vol. one

THE BRIDE	Uma Thurman
O-REN ISHII	Lucy Liu
VERNITA GREEN	Vivica A. Fox
ELLE DRIVER	Daryl Hannah
BILL	David Carradine
BUDD	Michael Madsen
SOFIE FATALE	Julie Dreyfus
GOGO YUBARI	Chiaki Kuriyama
HATTORI HANZO	Sonny Chiba
JOHNNY MO	Gordon Liu
EARL McGRAW	Michael Parks

BUCK	Michael Bowen
Crew:	
Casting	Koko Maeda,
	Johanna Ray
Original Music	The RZA,
	D. A. Young
Costume Design	Kumiko Ogawa/Catherine Marie Thomas
Set Decoration	Yoshihito Akatsuka,
	Sandy Reynolds-Wasco
Art Director	Daniel Bradford
Production Design	Yohei Taneda/David Wasco
Fight Choreographer/ Samurai Sword Adviser	Sonny Chiba
Martial Arts Adviser	Woo-Ping Yuen
Martial Arts Coordinator	Ku Huen Chiu
Special Makeup Effects Artists	Jake Garber,
	Chris Nelson
Special Makeup Effects Supervisors	Howard Berger,
	Gregory Nicotero
Visual Effects Supervisor	Jack Ho (uncredited)
Special Effects Supervisor	Jason Gustafson
Editor	Sally Menke
Director of Photography	Robert Richardson
Associate Producers	Koko Maeda,
	Dede Nickerson
Executive Producers	Erica Steinberg/E. Bennett Walsh/
	Bob Weinstein/Harvey Weinstein
Producer	Lawrence Bender
Written by	Quentin Tarantino
(Dialogue for the Bride	Q & U)
Directed by	Quentin Tarantino

112 mins, 2003 (Miramax Films/A Band Apart/Super Cool ManChu)

kill bill vol. two

THE BRIDE (aka BEATRIX KIDDO aka BLACK MAMBA aka MOMMY)	Uma Thurman
BILL ('SNAKE CHARMER')	David Carradine
O-REN ISHII ('COTTONMOUTH')	Lucy Liu
VERNITA GREEN ('COPPERHEAD')	Vivica A. Fox
PAI MEI	Gordon Liu
BUDD ('SIDEWINDER')	Michael Madsen
ELLE DRIVER ('CALIFORNIA MOUNTAIN SNAKE')	Daryl Hannah
ESTEBAN VIHAIO	Michael Parks
REVEREND HARMONY	Bo Svenson
MRS. HARMONY	Jeannie Epper
JOLEEN	Stephanie L. Moore
ERICA	Shana Stein
JANEEN	Caitlin Keats
TOMMY PLYMPTON	Chris Nelson
RUFUS	Samuel L. Jackson
LUCKY	Reda Beebe
JAY	Sid Haig
Crew:	
Casting	Koko Maeda, Johanna Ray
Original Music	The RZA, Robert Rodriguez
Costume Design	Kumiko Ogawa/Catherine Marie Thomas
Set Decoration	Sandy Reynolds-Wasco
Art Director	Daniel Bradford
Production Design	Cao Jui Ping/David Wasco
Fight Choreographer	Yuen Wo-Ping
Martial Arts Coordinator	Ku Huen Chiu
Special Makeup Effects Artists	Jake Garber,
	Chris Nelson
Special Makeup Effects Supervisors	Howard Berger,
	Gregory Nicotero
Visual Effects Production Manager	Jaime Norman
Special Effects Supervisor	Jason Gustafson
Editor	Sally Menke
Director of Photography	Robert Richardson
Associate Producer	Koko Maeda
Executive Producers	Erica Steinberg/E. Bennett Walsh/
	Bob Weinstein/Harvey Weinstein
Producer	Lawrence Bender
Written by	Quentin Tarantino
(Dialogue for the Bride	Q & U)
Directed by	Quentin Tarantino

136 mins, 2004 (Miramax Films/A Band Apart/Super Cool ManChu)

sin city

HARTIGAN	Bruce Willis
MARV	Mickey Rourke
NANCY CALLAHAN	Jessica Alba
DWIGHT	Clive Owen
ROARK JR./YELLOW BASTARD	Nick Stahl
SENATOR ROARK	Powers Boothe
CARDINAL ROARK	Rutger Hauer
KEVIN	Elijah Wood
GAIL	Rosario Dawson
JACKIE BOY	Benicio Del Toro
Producers	Frank Miller/Robert Rodriguez/
	Elizabeth Avollan
Written by	Robert Rodriguez
Special Guest Director	Quentin Tarantino
Directed by	Frank Miller and Robert Rodriguez

124 mins, 2005 (Troublemaker Studios/Dimension Films)

inglorious bastards

BABE BUCHINSKY	Michael Madsen
Producers	Lawrence Bender/Quentin Tarantino
Written and Directed by	Quentin Tarantino

2006 (Miramax Films/A Band Apart)

acknowledgments

The following articles appear by courtesy of their respective copyright holders: 'Introduction' by Paul A. Woods copyright © 2005 Plexus Publishing Ltd. 'Revenge of the Nerd' by Jeff Dawson, reproduced from *Tarantino: Inside Story* by Jeff Dawson by permission of Cassell. 'Reservoir Dogs' by Todd McCarthy from *Variety* 27 January 1992, copyright © 1992 *Variety*. 'Reservoir Dogs' by Leonard Klady from *Screen International* 24 April 1992, copyright © 1992 *Screen International*. 'Mr Blood Red' by Ella Taylor from *LA Weekly* 16 October 1992, copyright © 1992 Ella Taylor. 'The Men's Room' by Amy Taubin from *Sight and Sound* December 1992, copyright © 1992 *Sight and Sound*. 'It's Cool To Be Banned' by Quentin Tarantino reproduced from *Index on Censorship* 6 1995, edited excerpts from *Kaleidoscope* courtesy of BBC Radio Four. 'Eastern Dogs' by Paul A. Woods copyright © 2000 Plexus Publishing Ltd. 'Natural Born Killers' by Jeff Dawson from *Empire Magazine* November 1993, copyright © 1993 Emap Metro. 'Walken v. Hopper in *True Romance*' by Jonathan Miller from *Creative Screenwriting* v.5 n.1, 1998. Reprinted by permission of *Creative Screenwriting* and the author. 'Pulp Action' by Emma Webster reproduced from *The Face*, October 1994. Reprinted by permission of the author. 'Pulp Fiction' by Todd McCarthy from *Variety* 23 May 1994, copyright © 1992 *Variety*. 'Tarantino on the Run' by Jim McLellan from *The Observer* 3 July 1994, copyright © 1994 *The Observer*. 'X Offender' by Sean O'Hagan, reproduced from *The Times Magazine* 15 October 1994. Reprinted by permission of the author. 'Quentin Tarantino on *Pulp Fiction*' as told to Manohla Dargis, from *Sight and Sound* November 1994. Reprinted by permission of *Sight and Sound*. 'Quentin Tarantino's Pulp Fantastic' by Geoffrey O'Brien from *Filmmaker* Summer 1994. Reprinted from *Filmmaker*: the magazine of Independent Film, Summer 1994, vol 2, #4, by permission of the Publisher. 'The Next Best Thing to a Time Machine: Quentin Tarantino's *Pulp Fiction*' by Peter N. Chumo II from *Post Script* Summer 1996, copyright © 1996 *Post Script*. Reprinted by permission of the Publisher and the author. 'True Lies' by Jeff Dawson from *Empire Magazine* March 1997, copyright © 1997 Emap Metro. 'Four X Four' by Peter Biskind from *Premiere* March 1996. Reprinted by permission of the author. 'Four Rooms' by Emanuel Levy from *Variety* 25 September 1995, copyright © 1995 *Variety*. 'Tarantino's Pulp Horror' by Michael Beeler originally published as 'Humble Beginnings' in *Cinefantastique* January 1996. Reprinted by permission of the author. 'Tarantino Rewrites Tarantino' by Cynthia Baughman from *Creative Screenwriting* Winter 1995. Reprinted by permission of *Creative Screenwriting* and the author. 'Tarantino and Juliette' by Mim Udovitch originally published in *Details* February 1996. Reprinted by permission of the author. 'The Price of Fame' by Michael Beeler originallly published in *Cinefantastique* January 1996. Reprinted by permission of the author. 'Tourantino!' by Jayne Jain Kennedy from *Empire Magazine* May 1995, copyright © 1995 Emap Metro. 'Don't Try This at Home' by Ian Penman originally appeared in *Vital Signs* by Ian Penman published by Serpent's Tail. Reprinted by permission of the Publisher. 'A Rare Sorrow' by Quentin Tarantino from *Sight and Sound* February 1993. Reprinted by permission of *Sight and Sound*. 'To the Dawn and Beyond' by Anthony Timpone from *Fangoria* September 1998. Reprinted by permission of the author and the Publisher. 'Blaxploitation: What It Is … What It Was!' by Quentin Tarantino originally appeared in *What It Is … What It Was!* by Gerald and Diana Martinez and Andres Chavez published by Miramax Books, Hyperion. Reprinted by permission of A.M. Heath. 'Return of a Foxy Mama' by Peter Travers from *Rolling Stone* 22 January 1998. All Rights Reserved. Reprinted by Permission of Straight Arrow Publishers Company, L.P. 1998. 'Killing Me Softly' by Philip French from *The Observer* 22 March 1998, copyright © 1998 *The Observer*. 'The "N" Word' by Pascoe Sawyer from *Black Filmmaker* vol I. Issue 2. Reprinted by permission of *Black Filmmaker*. 'Fun Lovin' Criminals' by Tom Charity from *Time Out* 25 March 1998. Reprinted by permission of *Time Out*. 'I, Quentin' by Simon Hattenstone from *The Guardian* 27 February 1998 copyright © 1998 *The Guardian*. 'Quentin Bloody Quentin' by Henry Cabot Beck from the *New York Daily News* 5 October 2003, copyright © 2003 *New York Daily News*. 'Kill Bill: Volume 1' by Wesley Morris from the *Boston Globe* 10 October 2003, copyright © 2003 *Boston Globe*. 'Quentin Tarantino Reveals Almost Everything That Inspired *Kill Bill*' by Tomohiro Machiyama from Japattack.com 2003. Reprinted by permission of Japattack.com 2003. 'Kill Bill: Volume 2' by Peter Travers from *Rolling Stone* 29 April 2004, copyright © 2004 *Rolling Stone*. 'Tarantino Talks *Kill Bill Vol.2*' by Fred Topel from *Screenwriters Monthly* February 2004, copyright © 2004 *Screenwriters Monthly*.

We would like to thank the following photographers and picture agencies for supplying photographs: BFI Stills, Posters and Designs, Channel 4, Ixtlan/New Regency/Warner Bros, Live America Inc, Mainline Pictures, Miramax Films/Buena Vista International/Disney, Morgan Creek Productions Inc/Warner Bros, Ronald Grant Archive, Rysher Entertainment/Savoy Pictures/Jim Sheldon, Miramax International, American International Pictures Inc, Sportsphoto: Graham Whitby, Armando Gallo/Retna Ltd, Peter Smith/Retna pictures.